THE NEW AMERICAN

WORKPLACE

THE NEW AMERICAN WORKPLACE

JAMES O'TOOLE
EDWARD E. LAWLER III

THE NEW AMERICAN WORKPLACE

SOCIETY FOR
HUMAN
RESOURCE
MANAGEMENT

First published in hardcover in 2006 by
PALGRAVE MACMILLAN™
175 Fifth Avenue, New York, N.Y. 10010 and
Houndmills, Basingstoke, Hampshire, England RG21 6XS.
Companies and representatives throughout the world.

PALGRAVE MACMILLAN IS THE GLOBAL ACADEMIC IMPRINT OF THE PALGRAVE
MACMILLAN division of St. Martin's Press, LLC and of Palgrave Macmillan Ltd.
Macmillan® is a registered trademark in the United States, United Kingdom and other
countries. Palgrave is a registered trademark in the European Union and other
countries.

ISBN-13 978-1-4039-8491-3 paperback
ISBN-10 1-4039-8491-3 paperback

Library of Congress Cataloging-in-Publication Data

O'Toole, James.
    The new American workplace / by James O'Toole and Edward E. Lawler III.
        p.   cm.
    Includes bibliographical references and index.
    ISBN 1-4039-6959-0 (alk. paper)
    1. Quality of work life—United States.   2. Labor market—United States.
3. Labor supply—United States.   4. Industrial organization—United States.
5. Industrial sociology—United States.   I. Lawler, Edward E.   II. Title.
    HD6957.U6O86 2006
    331.10973—dc22

A catalogue record for this book is available from the British Library.

Design by Letra Libre, Inc.

First PALGRAVE MACMILLAN paperback edition: August 2007
10 9 8 7 6 5 4 3 2 1

Printed in the United States of America

CONTENTS

Acknowledgments   vii

Foreword   ix
    Susan R. Meisinger

Part I
Introduction

1.   Work in America   3

Part II
Changes in the American Workplace

2.   The Nature of Organizations   25
3.   The Work Itself   39
4.   The Employment Relationship   61

Part III
Consequences for the American Worker

5.   Careers   83
6.   Work/Life Balance   93
7.   Health and Safety   101
8.   Job and Life Satisfaction   107
9.   Performance Pressure   111
10. Compensation   115

11. Employee "Voice"   121

12. Training and Development   127

13. Community and Commitment   133

14. Winners and Losers   139

Part IV
Choices and Future Directions

15. Organizations and Competitiveness   151

16. Public Policy   185

17. Individuals   215

Part V
Conclusions

18. Future of the American Workplace   233

Authors of Papers Commissioned for this Study   245
Notes   247
Additional Information   255
Index   258

ACKNOWLEDGMENTS

We are indebted to a number of individuals and organizations who supported the research and writing of this book. The Society for Human Resource Management provided major financial support for our research. SHRM also conducted surveys and focus groups of its members for the project. Debra Cohen of SHRM provided substantive advice, wisdom, and invaluable aid in managing our relationship with SHRM. We are grateful to the organization's CEO, Susan Meisinger, for allowing us a free hand to pursue our research interests and to state our views in the book, which do not necessarily reflect those of SHRM.

The corporate sponsors of the Center for Effective Organizations also provided financial support as well as research data. Their continuing support makes it possible for CEO's professional staff to do organizational research that influences both theory and practice.

We appreciate the contributions of the members of our *New American Workplace* advisory task force—John Boudreau, Susan Cohen, Debra Cohen, David Finegold, Alec Levenson, Susan Mohrman—for helping us to structure our research and to identify authors of the papers commissioned for the study. The authors of those contributed papers, whose names and affiliations are listed separately, provided us with important material that has allowed us to ground our findings in solid research. We thank them all.

We also owe special thanks to the staff members of the Center who helped us with data gathering and analysis and manuscript preparation: Dan Canning, Arienne McCracken, Alice Yee Mark, Beth Neilson, Nora Osganian, and Anjelica Wright.

We wish to acknowledge the help and support of Jim Levine, our literary agent, and that of the editorial and marketing team of Palgrave Macmillan, under the leadership of Airíe Stuart. Robert Schrank deserves a tip of the hat for his years of pestering us to "take a fresh look at *Work in America.*"

Finally, we wish to recognize the courageous contribution made by the late Elliot L. Richardson when, in 1972, as Secretary of Health, Education and Welfare, he commissioned a task force of scholars to prepare an objective report on the conditions of *Work in America,* which he then released with his commendation. Sadly, he and too many members of that task force will not see the publication of this book, which we dedicate to him and to them—Elizabeth Hansot, William R. Herman, Neal Herrick, Elliot Liebow, Bruce Lusignan, Harold Richman, Harold Sheppard, Ben Stephansky, and James Wright—both the living and those no longer with us.

FOREWORD

SUSAN R. MEISINGER
President and CEO
Society for Human Resource Management

In the 1970s, Louis "Studs" Terkel, the Chicago radio broadcaster, oral historian, journalist, and author interviewed more than 130 working American men and women of different ethnicities and ages and captured their voices for his book *Working*, about the realities of employment in America. Published in 1974, the award-winning work carried the subtitle: "People Talk about What They Do All Day and How They Feel about What They Do."

While immensely popular, Terkel's book was based on a less comprehensive study than another, more formal, examination of the nation's working conditions, *Work in America*, which was conducted in 1972–1973 by a task force formed by U.S. Secretary of Health, Education and Welfare, Elliot L. Richardson. The task force's chairman, James O'Toole, was the principal author of the survey report and, not coincidentally, is also the coauthor, with Edward Lawler, of this publication, *The New American Workplace*. Since the study documented in this book employed the same methodology as the earlier study, the current work can be viewed as a fresh take on that government-sponsored effort.

Some might argue that it's superfluous to point out that working conditions have changed in the three decades since Studs Terkel's *Working* and the *Work in America* report. After all, even a casual look at America's workplaces today reveals that the working environment has been radically transformed, and the very nature of work itself and the character of the social contract between employer and worker have been irrevocably altered. But there is more to the story than these dramatic changes.

Jim O'Toole and Ed Lawler have produced a compelling and comprehensive account that—in addition to chronicling U.S. workplace changes—examines the factors underlying these developments, details their impact on workers, and explores future workplace scenarios for both workers and the organizations that employ them. And in keeping with the spirit of Terkel's book and *Work in America,* considerable ink is devoted to the values, attitudes, needs, and expectations of workers themselves.

Even though American workplaces have evolved in ways unforeseen at the time of the *Work in America* study, readers of *The New American Workplace* will draw at least one conclusion that remains unchanged from the earlier study: Satisfying work is a basic human need that establishes individual identity and self-respect and lends order to life.

While this publication discusses the growing importance of people strategies and argues for progressive HR management practices, this book is fundamentally about business and O'Toole and Lawler have exhaustively covered the business-relevant aspects of workplace issues in present-day America. For that reason alone, this book should be required reading for every business professional.

More and more, we are seeing and hearing references to "human capital" in essays, op-eds, columns, and business seminars. SHRM has been driving this bandwagon for years, and now others are climbing aboard. We believe it's impossible to overstate the importance of human capital in today's global economy—people really are organizations' "most important asset," and effective human resource management is critical to organizational success.

Studies such as *The New American Workplace* can help organizations and their HR professionals effectively manage their human capital by identifying and analyzing the critical workplace issues that impact performance. Given the importance of these findings to the work of the human resource profession, and to overall organizational success, this up-to-date picture of the American workplace is much-needed and extremely practical. I think Studs Terkel would agree.

Congratulations to Jim and Ed for a job well done, and a sincere "thank you" from all of us who toil in the field of human resource management.

SOCIETY FOR
HUMAN
RESOURCE
MANAGEMENT

HR: Leading People,
Leading Organizations

The research for this book was supported by a grant from the Society for Human Resource Management.

The Society for Human Resource Management (SHRM) is the world's largest association devoted to human resource management. Representing more than 200,000 individual members, the Society's mission is to serve the needs of HR professionals by providing the most essential and comprehensive resources available. As an influential voice, the Society's mission is also to advance the human resource profession to ensure that HR is recognized as an essential partner in developing and executing organizational strategy. Founded in 1948, SHRM currently has more than 550 affiliated chapters and members in more than 100 countries. Visit SHRM Online at www.shrm.org.

PART I

INTRODUCTION

1

WORK IN AMERICA

In 1972, the United States Secretary of Health, Education and Welfare, Elliot L. Richardson, formed a task force to evaluate the state of working conditions in the nation. A year later, after reviewing hundreds of scholarly studies and interviewing dozens of experts, the Work in America task force reported to the Secretary that the health and social well-being of many Americans were being adversely affected by the conditions of their employment. The task force cited a growing body of evidence that too many Americans were engaged in narrow, repetitive, and routine jobs—especially in the manufacturing sector—and that was leading to a variety of mental and physical health problems. The task force offered concrete examples of how companies could redesign jobs to reduce the negative consequences for workers, noting that redesigning work also would increase productivity and the international competitiveness of American corporations.

Executives in the 1970s and 1980s heeded the advice of the experts and began to pay attention to the quality of work life in their factories and offices. They redesigned some jobs to make them more challenging and fulfilling, automated other tasks, and exported many of the remaining "bad" jobs to the developing world. The combined effect of these actions led to an improvement in the quality of working conditions in the nation but, in the process, created a new set of issues and challenges. Even a casual look reveals a new world of work in America:

☐ Countless workers—whose "offices" are in their cars, hotel rooms, and Starbucks cafés—are on the phone in the middle of the night to "colleagues" in Indonesia and Thailand whom they may never have met, and may never meet.

☐ To make ends meet, some middle-class couples hold down three weekday jobs between the two of them, with the occasional part-time gig on weekends, besides caring for their kids and elderly parents.

☐ Significant numbers of managers and professionals, a great many of whom are women, work for large corporations on a limited contract (or contingency) basis, having replaced "organization men" who had lifetime security.

☐ Service representatives of American software providers are located in call centers in Bangalore, India.

☐ Chinese engineers design, and seventeen-year-old girls assemble, toys for American companies in the special economic zone in Chenzen, China.

☐ The average CEO in a *Fortune* 500 company takes home over 400 times the pay of the average employee (in 1973 the ratio was 40 to 1).

☐ For the majority of the U.S. population who haven't attended college, their incomes are stagnating, if not declining.

☐ American executives decide against creating new jobs in the United States because of the prohibitive cost of providing health insurance, and workers choose otherwise undesirable jobs simply because they offer health coverage for themselves and their families.

☐ A young software engineer in Silicon Valley is "downsized"; after a year of failing to land a comparable job in a tech industry, she becomes a self-employed entrepreneur, opening an online e-art gallery.

☐ Employees in factories and stores organized in self-managing work teams select their own members, make their own work assignments, and are paid bonuses based on their performance.

☐ A seventy-year-old "retired" American accountant starts a new career as a financial consultant to small, start-up businesses in Asia. He is "greeted" at Wal-Mart by a part-time employee his age who is still working because she doesn't have sufficient savings to retire.

☐ Undocumented alien workers gather outside Home Depot stores hoping for day jobs, while able-bodied U.S. citizens panhandle on the streets of American cities refusing to look for paid employment.

What is going on in this crazy-quilt world of work? What are the causes and consequences of these seemingly unrelated events and trends? While there are no simple answers to these questions, we believe some clearly identifiable developments help to explain what has happened in the recent past, and what is likely to happen in the future, in the American workplace.

RIDING THE WAVE OF THE GLOBAL ECONOMY

It is now widely recognized that a new global economy is emerging. It is characterized by the transnational flow of capital, goods, services, and labor; by greater national specialization and increased competition across borders; and by the use of new technologies that radically disrupt traditional ways of doing business. The United States is positioned at the crest of this competitive wave, having adopted the de facto national strategy of being the leader of this fast-paced, unpredictable, and unsettling global process of economic and industrial transformation. This strategy is not official by any means, nor has it been chosen consciously; instead, it is the result of countless piecemeal actions of American corporations and is buttressed by the nation's free-trade policies.

In seeking competitive advantage, the United States has targeted a niche for itself at the top of the world economy: it has opted to use the highest technology, to have the most capital- and knowledge-intensive industries, and to produce the highest-quality and highest-value-added goods and services. Surfing the crest of this giant wave is not easy: to maintain its prosperity, the U.S. economy must be in a state of constant change, driven by a process of "creative destruction." Inefficient products, companies, and entire industries continually need to be replaced by new ones employing ever-more complex processes. And the nation's industrial knowledge base needs to be enhanced constantly to yield the high profit margins required by the new standards of international finance.

On one hand, if the economy fails to advance fast enough, America will fall off the back of the wave and be overtaken by more effective competitors. On the other hand, if the economy moves too quickly, our industrial practices will be out of sync with our social expectations and institutions, running ahead of the nation's educational and health systems and outpacing the ability of individuals and communities to adjust to constant, major dislocations. If that occurs, the nation could experience a social backlash like those that occurred in France and the Netherlands in 2005, when voters in those countries rejected the proposed European constitution largely on the grounds that it left workers vulnerable to the forces of international trade and low-wage competitors.

Whether the new global economy is a good or a bad thing, and whether America's chosen strategic position is the correct one or not, are issues beyond the scope of this book. Instead of exploring the wisdom of what might have been, or could be, we have taken as givens the new global economy and the nation's competitive strategy. Our objective is to identify the consequences of these momentous changes on the conditions of work in America and on the lives of American workers. We have undertaken this analysis as objectively and rigorously as possible, recognizing the complexity of identifying and evaluating the various costs and benefits the strategy brings to the American society and to its economy, business organizations, and individual consumers and workers. Grounding our observations and conclusions in sound data wherever available, we ask what must be done in private workplaces and public institutions to make the strategy succeed in the long term: *If America wishes to continue to be the world's leading economic power, what workplace practices and public policies are required to ensure that it succeeds?* Our single bias is toward solutions that serve both the well-being of employees *and* the effectiveness of their employing organizations in the belief that doing one without the other is not viable in the long term.

Our general conclusion is that, in far too many instances, the United States is attempting to implement tomorrow's competitive strategies with yesterday's managerial ideas and public policy infrastructure. We see a disturbing disconnect between the rhetoric of competitiveness and the reality of how American corporations are managed. All too many compensation practices, training programs, and job- and organization-designs are poor fits with today's competitive realities. Many global corporations have been quick to change the way they compete globally, but too often these fast-changing businesses are out-of-step with worker aspirations, social expectations, and public policies. Further, the business models and human resources strategies of many slower-moving companies lag far behind global and domestic competitive realities. Harkening back to the 1970s, we believe that attention again must be paid to the nature of work itself. Large American corporations spend billions on recruiting, training, assessing, and rewarding workers, but many have lost sight of the importance of the design and structure of jobs and careers.

In addition, America's health and education institutions, trade unions, and governmental and nonprofit agencies charged with addressing employment matters too often are constituted to meet the challenges of yesterday's economy, not tomorrow's. We conclude that unless major change occurs, America's current managerial practices and public education, labor, and social policies are unlikely to provide the mix, quality, and supply of jobs and trained workers needed for success in the emerging global economy. The good news is that the nation does not yet face a crisis. America's strategy of riding the crest of the global competitive wave can succeed if its business owners, managers, educators, citizens, workers, and political leaders focus on, and clarify, the consequences of the public and private choices they now face and then choose wisely among the available alternatives.

Since it is difficult to gain perspective while riding atop a giant, fast-moving wave, we provide a framework for identifying and evaluating the major workplace and workforce alternatives available to the nation. We explore the new context of global competition and changing technology, and what it means for the nature of work in America and for those who do it. We also examine how these changes affect domestic industries not directly active in the global economy. We identify what these sea changes mean to businesses attempting to recruit and motivate a productive workforce, government agencies looking to provide appropriate support for workers and effective incentives for business, and individual workers trying to manage their careers in this complex new environment.

HOW THE STUDY WAS CONDUCTED

In doing this study, we have used the same basic method employed by the Work in America task force in 1972. We began by commissioning papers from the nation's leading experts on workplace matters. We asked these contributors to review the research literature in their areas of specialization and to interpret for us what the findings say about the state of U.S. workplaces. These papers (a list of which appears at the end of this book) are published in a companion volume, *America at Work: Choices and Challenges*. In addition, an extensive bibliography is available at http://www.newamericanworkplace.com.

We also drew on the results of twenty-five years of research undertaken in American workplaces by our colleagues and ourselves at the University of Southern California's Center for Effective Organizations (CEO), including a 2005 update of our triennial national survey of management practices in *Fortune* 1000 corporations. In addition, we analyzed survey data collected by the University of Michigan's Institute for Social Research in 1977 and again in 2002. Finally, we analyzed a series of structured interviews and electronic surveys of members of the Society for Human Resource Management conducted in 2005 for this study.

As in 1972, we begin our analysis by inquiring about the values and needs of American workers. In a democracy, it is appropriate to begin from the perspective of the aspirations of the citizenry.

WHAT DO WORKERS WANT?

Unfortunately, research provides no simple answers to questions concerning what Americans want from their jobs and employers. Individuals with different interests, resources, personalities, and family requirements want different things, and those things often change at different stages in their lives. Moreover, since it is not possible for employers to satisfy all workers' constantly expanding wants, it is more useful to consider what they *need* and how employers can meet those various needs. Decades of research establish the fact that three major human needs can be satisfied by gainful employment: (1) the need for the basic economic resources and security essential to lead good lives; (2) the need to do meaningful work and the opportunity to grow and develop as a person; and (3) the need for supportive social relationships. Good work, as we define it here, satisfies all three of those fundamental needs.

It is critical to keep in mind the distinctions among these three types of employment needs—the extrinsic tangible rewards, the work itself, and social relationships—and to understand that jobs satisfying the requirements of one, or even two, of these needs may not satisfy them all. For example, a job may pay well but, at the same time, be dull and unfulfilling. A truly fascinating job may pay poorly, and a well-paying, intrinsically interesting job may be overseen by an abusive supervisor.

The relative importance of each of the three types of needs varies dramatically from worker to worker. Some people are willing to do dull—even dirty—work if it pays well, and some will tolerate incompetent supervision if they find the work itself enjoyable. At least, some people are willing to tolerate poor work for limited periods of time, or even for long periods if they have no alternatives. But all three needs must be satisfied before most people will say they have a "good job." Indeed, for most workers, whichever need is unmet on the job becomes the one they are most concerned about fulfilling next. In 1973, the Work in America task force found evidence that many workers were dissatisfied with the nature of their work because it was monotonous, repetitive, and meaningless. Today, most likely because many routine manufacturing jobs have been automated, exported, or redesigned, employees are more likely to voice concern about pay, benefits, security, and the environments in which they work, particularly the nature of their supervision, opportunities for training, and work/family balance.

Before we examine what it takes to meet the needs of workers, we must acknowledge questions that employers might legitimately raise: Why is it important for them to provide jobs that meet *all* the needs of their workers? If workers have enough money to satisfy their basic financial needs—and a few extra dollars to partake in the pleasures of our abundant consumer economy—isn't that enough? Isn't the crucial policy issue finding ways to give employers enough flexibility to respond quickly to competitive challenges? Moreover, isn't it unreasonable to expect employers to attempt to address the full range of employee needs—social relationships and meaningful work, in addition to financial ones?

We believe research evidence shows that satisfying the needs of Americans for good jobs is important, if not essential, for the prosperity, health, and social well-being of the nation. If the economy does not provide a sufficient supply of good jobs, the United States will lose its competitive edge and, with it, the economic resources necessary to provide for the material requirements of a growing population. By all accepted standards, the world's wealthiest nations offer their citizens a preponderance of good jobs, while the economies of the poorest nations are characterized by bad jobs. In wealthy nations the value-added of each worker contributes to a nation's high overall productivity; in poorer nations the economic contribution of a worker is minimal, and the nation's wealth is relatively, and consequentially, meager. Especially in service- and knowledge-based economies like that of the United States, national productivity is determined by the efforts, initiative, and skills of employees. If workers are not committed, motivated, engaged, trained, and appropriately supervised, they will underperform. In economic terms, that results in an inefficient use of human capital, with disastrous consequences for a nation's global competitiveness. Hence, with over 90 percent of Americans employed today in nonmanufacturing jobs, it is absolutely essential for the nation's human capital to be efficiently utilized. While that also was true in 1973, today's global economy is so much more competitive, and the work people do so much more complex, companies today have far less margin for error than they did in the past.

The exigencies of global competitiveness are only a third of the story. Good work also is necessary to provide individuals with the opportunity for social and economic mobility—that is, the opportunity to pursue the American dream of realizing their potential. Finally, because work is a major source of identity, status, fulfillment, and meaning, a sufficient supply of good jobs is necessary for individual psychological and physical health. In sum, the costs of an insufficient supply of good work include a declining standard of living, a lower quality of life, increased social conflict, the loss of America's unique standing in the world as the leading economic power, and an inability to attract human and financial capital from around the world. Ensuring an appropriate mix and sufficient supply of good work is therefore an important issue for all Americans. So, how are we doing?

THE NATURE OF WORKPLACES TODAY

An evaluation of the current state of working conditions in America must begin with recognition of the fact that there are many different kinds of employers and workplaces. In this study we focus on the large and midsize private sector companies that drive the economy, serve as the standard for employment in other sectors, and are the subject of most workplace research. While we do not directly address the unique issues confronting small businesses, government agencies, and the growing not-for-profit sector—

nor the workplace issues of the millions of people overseas who directly and indirectly work for American employers—we nonetheless believe that many, if not most, of our findings are relevant to those workers and to the organizations employing them.

To further sharpen and direct our analysis, we have identified three emerging management models that are becoming dominant in the economy. As the old-line bureaucratic, hierarchical firms that once dominated the *Fortune* 500 lose their relative importance, they are being replaced by three readily recognizable types of organizations: Low-Cost Operators, Global Competitor Corporations, and High-Involvement Companies. The nature and conditions of work, careers, benefits, and forms of compensation vary markedly among and between these three generic organizational types.

Low-Cost Operators

Large grocery, discount, fast-food, and mall-store chains have pushed many small and local retailers, corner cafés, and "mom and pop" stores to the verge of extinction, making the cost-conscious customer "king" in the fast-growing services sector of the U.S. economy. To keep the prices of goods and services as low as possible, managers of these Low-Cost (LC) companies have developed a business model focused on continuously reducing all the costs of their operations. In LC stores and restaurants, front-line employees often are paid close to the minimum wage, receive few if any benefits, have no job security, and are given only the amount of training needed to do jobs that have been designed to be simple and easy to learn. The same conditions exist in many low-value-added, unskilled jobs in the food processing, agriculture, manufacturing, hospitality, and construction industries.

Because there is little opportunity for workers who are at the bottom in LC companies to make a good living or to do interesting work—much less to make a career—these jobs mainly attract employees who cannot find other jobs: retirees, young workers and students (particularly those living with their parents and covered by their health insurance), less-educated workers with few other options, immigrants with limited English-language skills, and those who are unable or unwilling to take jobs requiring more responsibility. They also are a source of "second jobs" for those who can't live on the income from their primary employment. The environments in LC workplaces may be clean and safe, but the work itself is, in many ways, similar to the routine, low-level tasks that were the norm in manufacturing in an earlier era.

Since LC companies are primarily domestic and typically do not face significant foreign competition, at first glance they may not appear to be affected directly by the new global economy. Yet closer examination reveals they are driven by the same dictates of international business and finance as are global companies:

1. They compete with global companies for capital and investors, and thus must offer similarly high returns on investment.
2. They often go offshore in search of ever-cheaper goods to sell domestically, thus linking them to the broader world economy.
3. Many of them are expanding overseas, and thus are becoming global competitors themselves.
4. They increasingly define their mission as making cheap goods available to the growing number of blue-collar and low-wage Americans who have lost purchasing power due to the export of manufacturing jobs and, ironically, to those who work on the front line in LC companies themselves.
5. They compete with global competitor companies for critical categories of human capital: executives, marketing experts, purchasing managers, and information technologists.

Global Competitor Corporations

Characterized by their enormous size and geographic reach, Global Competitor (GC) corporations compete in terms of the financial capital, skills, knowledge, and technology they are able to command. They are the glamour companies of the age: industry leaders in information and telecommunications technology, consumer products, pharmaceuticals and biomedicine, financial and professional services, and media and entertainment. These agile, global wave-riders move products, services, capital, jobs, operations, and people quickly and frequently across borders and continents.

There is little stability in GC corporations, particularly for contingent employees. However, their permanent, full-time employees—especially executives and those with critical skills—enjoy the highest pay found in corporations anywhere in the world. Increasingly, GCs hire people on a contractual basis and, where possible, outsource and offshore their work. These companies offer their "contingent" workers no security beyond the time limits of their contracts and no promise of continuing employment. At

GC companies, decisions regarding whether to "buy or build" talent are based on cost/benefit and return on investment analyses that aim for a quick payback. Consequently, they increasingly look outside to hire even permanent and top-level employees, carefully considering how much to spend on developing managers and professionals and what career paths to create. Frequently they offer "new employment contracts" in which they commit to telling employees what their strategy is, what their plans are related to technology and growth, and where and what they think future jobs in the organization will be. They also provide job information, including a list of openings and the competencies required to perform them. And workers are told that their continued employment depends on their performance and the fit between their skills and the needs of the business.

GC corporations are constantly searching for talent—for individuals with the skills needed for today's challenges—and pay top dollar to get them. Those they hire work long hours and are expected to produce. In exchange, they are given the opportunity to develop their skills—and thereby increase their future employability. The relationship between these companies and their employees is thus transactional, not one based on loyalty. The rewards at GC companies are interesting work and high pay, not being part of a community or a long-term employment relationship.

High-Involvement Companies

The High-Involvement (HI) organizational model had its genesis prior to the publication of the *Work in America* report. HI companies are found in many, if not most, industries (although their numbers are relatively few in comparison to LC and GC companies). HI organizations offer workers challenging and enriched jobs, a say in the management of their own tasks, and a commitment to low turnover and few layoffs. They promote mainly from within, offering clearly defined career paths and extensive training and development opportunities. HI companies are relatively egalitarian workplaces with few class distinctions between managers and workers. Usually there is a strong sense that every employee or "associate" is a member of a supportive community.

Employees in these companies tend to be salaried workers, participate in company stock ownership in one form or another, and share in company profits or from gains in productivity. HI companies use work teams in most operations and offer generous benefits to employees and their families. They value worker loyalty and try to build commitment to the organization, not simply to high job or financial performance.

WHAT WE CONCLUDE FROM OUR ANALYSIS

For the sake of clarity, we present the LC, GC, and HI organizational models as distinct and separate types. They provide useful illustrations of the various alternatives managers have when they make choices with respect to the workplaces they create and the working conditions they offer. In practice, of course, some companies have elements of two, or even all three, of these models. There are identifiable costs and benefits, winners and losers, advantages and shortcomings, and better and worse practices associated with each model. In terms of meeting the employment requirements of American workers, Global Competitor and High-Involvement companies clearly offer the best jobs, although they differ in that they tend to satisfy workers with different needs and interests. In financial terms, it is not clear that any one of the three models is always the right one, or even better than the others: there are examples of each that have been extremely successful and examples of each that have failed. In addition, certain business conditions seem to favor one model over the others. Thus it is as important that each company makes the right choices in adopting a set of workplace practices as it is that each appropriately executes and implements the particular model it chooses.

Indeed, it is in the choices that business executives make relating to working conditions that we find the greatest opportunity for the improvement of work in America. We are concerned especially with the growing number of executives who conclude they have "no choice" but to match the worst employment practices of their competitors. In this regard, we document numerous examples of business leaders who have found productive alternatives to the standard workplace practices in their industries and created significant competitive advantages in the process.

MAJOR THEMES

As we undertook our analysis of how these three types of American corporations are managed, and the consequences for American workers, the nation's economy, and society, we identified several key themes running through the research we examined:

☐ *Insufficient creation of new "good jobs."* Today, fewer than 10 percent of American workers are employed in manufacturing, down from about 25 percent in the early 1970s. There is no inherent problem with this trend; indeed, it is a positive indicator of increased productivity and national wealth, as illustrated by America's last four decades of steadily increasing real output of manufactured goods. This trend should have led to the creation of new, higher-value-added, higher-paying service-sector jobs—as a similar transformation a century earlier from agricultural to industrial employment improved the American standard of living. But it has not yet done so to the extent expected. Instead, it appears that too many of the new jobs that have been created are not as high paying, on average, as the old manufacturing jobs that have been lost.

☐ *Increased choice and risk.* Workers today face a wider array of choices than ever before, choices concerning what career to pursue, how much and what form of education to obtain, where to work, how to mesh work with other aspects of life, when to change jobs and careers, how to make trade-offs among various benefits, and when, or if, to retire. Obviously, better-educated and better-paid workers have more options than others, but what most American workers have in common today is that they are bearing increased risk compared to the workers of previous generations. Increasingly, LC and GC employers have transferred onto their workers the burden of risks related to employment security, healthcare, training, career and lifestyle choices, forms of compensation and benefits, and retirement.

☐ *Increased influence of competitive and economic drivers.* The decisions employers make about the pay, benefits, and working conditions they offer are increasingly driven by competitive and financial considerations. Today, most companies put the needs of shareholders above the needs of workers. Indeed, in LC and GC companies, workers are seen mainly as a cost of doing business, and executives in LC companies explicitly state that their purpose is to serve Americans as consumers, not as workers. In contrast, one of the main distinguishing characteristics of HI companies is their "stakeholder" orientation: the needs

of employees, customers, and owners are all seen as equally legitimate. Moreover, mangers of HI companies act on the belief that they
have a responsibility to meet the needs of Americans in their roles as
workers, in addition to meeting their needs as consumers.

☐ *Increased tension between work and family life.* As women have entered
the paid workforce in increasing numbers, men and women in all categories of employment—front line, technical, managerial, and professional—cite a desire for greater balance between work and other
aspects of life, particularly their family lives. Among lower-paid
workers, the cause of this tension is that two parents increasingly
need to work long hours to make ends meet; among professionals
and executives the tension stems from the fact that work has increasingly become a 24/7 activity; and the growth in the number of single
parents is a contributor across all economic levels.

☐ *Mismatch between skills and business needs.* The primary and secondary educational system in the United States is failing to provide the
skills millions of workers need to escape minimum-wage and dead-
end employment. At the other end of the system, higher education
fails to produce an adequate supply of men and women with sufficiently strong backgrounds in mathematics, science, and engineering.
At the same time, corporations are cutting back, or misallocating,
their expenditures on education and training.

☐ *Increased social stratification based largely on educational attainment.*
Related to the problems in education are signs of increasing workforce stratification, with clear winners and losers and decreasing economic mobility. In terms of real wages, executives and technically
skilled workers have fared spectacularly in recent years, and college
graduates, in general, have fared well relative to the rest of the labor
force, at least until recently. At the same time, the relative wages of
blue-collar workers have lagged significantly behind their better-educated and white-collar peers, and low-skilled workers have fared dis-
astrously relative to other Americans. The income of one's parents has
become an increasingly powerful predictor of whether one will attend
college, and attending college has become an increasingly powerful
predictor of getting a job with a good salary.

☐ *Changing nature of careers.* In the private sector, the once-common
career path for middle-class men—attending college right after high

school, working for one company until age sixty-five, then retiring—
has all but disappeared. For women, the once-common path of working until they have children, and then leaving the paid workforce to
care for them until they go off to college, is also becoming increasingly rare. And almost all young, educated men and women today expect to work for multiple employers, to move back and forth between
work and education and between work and family responsibilities,
and, perhaps, never to retire.

☐ *Reduction in community and commitment.* The new employment contracts found in GC corporations and the high rates of employee
turnover characteristic of LC operators have reduced the opportunity
for workers to satisfy their needs for belonging to supportive workplace communities. The lack of community also may be having a
negative impact on worker motivation and commitment, although
the research is less clear on this score.

☐ *Shortcomings of the healthcare system.* The major public policy issue
related to work in America today is the nation's long-standing and
unaddressed healthcare crisis. The high and growing costs of health
insurance are driving countless business decisions, causing companies and industries to be unprofitable, putting American exporters at
comparative disadvantages in world markets, discouraging the creation of jobs and leading to the export of others. At the same time,
too many American workers and their families have no insurance
and face financial ruin if they or a family member should fall gravely
ill. Finally, concerns about health insurance coverage limit the mobility of workers and create dysfunctional tension between labor and
management.

☐ *The boomer demographic imperative.* The oldest members of the
largest age cohort in history turn sixty in 2006, and the other members of the boomer generation will follow suit over the next two
decades. Depending on public and private choices that must be made
soon, in the near future there may be (a) a shortage of skilled workers, (b) a shortage of jobs for older workers who cannot afford to retire, (c) a rapid decline in the demand for goods and services as
boomers retire with insufficient incomes, (d) steady economic growth
as boomers continue to make economic contributions well into their
seventies and eighties, (e) the end of retirement as we know it, (f) a

demand for increased immigration, or (g) all, some, or none of the above.

☐ *Unrealized opportunities to make more effective use of human capital.* Current workplace practices, such as the use of contingent and part-time workers, preferences for younger over older workers, under-funding of training, growing gaps between the salaries and benefits of executives and average employees, and a 24/7 working environment, appear to be having negative effects on worker turnover, motivation, loyalty, and job satisfaction. Yet, there exist a number of underuti-lized workplace "best practices": flexible working hours, company-sponsored tuition reimbursement, benefits for part-timers, employee participation in decision making and profit sharing, the redesigning of jobs to make them challenging, and the providing of on-the-job developmental opportunities all seem to have positive effects on worker productivity and job satisfaction but are not widely used. Dis-appointingly, those practices were identified, and their benefits doc-umented, more than thirty years ago in the 1973 *Work in America* report.

In the pages that follow, we explore these themes in depth as we analyze and assess the state of the American workplace, offering data and research find-ings to support our conclusions about the impact of the three emerging management models on both the productivity of the nation and the well-being of its workers. We recommend specific actions for employers, the gov-ernment, and workers themselves to take to maintain and improve the nation's economic strength and to meet the legitimate needs of the work-force.

PART II

CHANGES IN THE AMERICAN WORKPLACE

In retrospect, business life was relatively simple in the 1970s. The United States was the world's leading manufacturing country, but that almost didn't matter because international trade accounted for only 15 percent of the nation's manufacturing output. American industry at the time was dominated by a few giant corporations, household names with blue-chip stocks: "the Generals" (General Electric, General Motors, and General Foods), the numerous offspring of Standard Oil (Exxon, Amoco, Chevron), the AT&T monopoly, U.S. Steel, RCA, DuPont, and a small number of upstart technology companies (IBM, Xerox, and Polaroid).

No one in the 1970s anticipated the now-obvious—at least, in hindsight—forces that have led to revolutionary change in the structures and practices of many large U.S. corporations including, most notably, globalization, technology, and the nature of equity ownership. In particular, the emergence of a global economy has had a transformational impact on American corporations, forcing many to reinvent themselves to meet increasing competition from overseas. To continually improve their performance, large American businesses now organize with an eye toward being able to change products and strategies rapidly. In many cases, U.S. companies have established operations around the globe.

Asian and European companies have proven to be effective competitors in industries where, only a few decades ago, Americans were the dominant players. Today, Japanese, Korean, German, Dutch, French, Swiss, and British multinationals not only compete successfully against U.S. firms in world markets, they manufacture goods in this country for sale here. The entry into world markets by countries where labor is relatively cheap, most notably China and India, has placed enormous pressure on American-based companies to cut costs. And the continued high quality of goods manufactured by Japanese and Korean automobile and electronics companies has created the competitive necessity to continually make American products better and faster.

Foreign companies in countless industries—even in aerospace, professional services, and agricultural equipment, where only yesterday America was preeminent—are now challenging U.S. businesses. As a result of these new challenges, when it comes to measuring the performance of American companies, what recently was good enough, big enough, advanced enough, fast enough, and cheap enough is not sufficiently competitive today. This fact has put enormous pressure on corporations to redesign, rethink, and restructure their operations. In particular, the recent increase in technical knowledge has generated pressure on corporations to change their structures and practices. As competitors have become more sophisticated, American corporations have been forced to find new, better, and faster ways to develop products and to bring them to market. New and more-effective management techniques and streamlined organizational structures have been introduced. Today, there simply is no time for bureaucracy. And nothing has added to the imperative of speed as much as the explosive growth in information technology. Instant global communications are now the norm in all large corporations, creating dramatically new forms of virtual relationships, not only within an organization but also among a company and its suppliers, customers, and strategic partners.

The third major factor in the transformation of the American workplace has been the rise of institutional stock ownership. In the 1970s, corporations largely were owned by individual shareholders; today, the dominant stockholders are financial institutions, in particular, private- and public-sector employee pension funds. This change has led to a reconceptualization of corporate capitalism, the most profound consequence of which has been Wall Street's heightened emphasis on short-term performance. Complementing this shift has been a transformation in economic values in which the responsibility of publicly traded corporations to create shareholder wealth now takes precedence over their responsibilities to other stakeholders, in particular, to their employees. In general, corporate executives now believe their personal interests are more aligned with those of their share-holders than with those of their workers. When MIT's Paul Osterman surveyed members of the Society for Human Resource Management for this study, asking these human resources professionals whether their senior management made decisions in the best interest of employees, only 59 percent were somewhat or very confident that was the case; when asked if senior management made decision in the best interest of shareholders or owners, 84 percent were somewhat or very confident on that score.[1]

As the three forces of globalization, changing technology, and demanding ownership have converged, many executives have concluded they have no choice but to equip their corporations for rapid response to whatever changes may occur next in the competitive environment. As the half-life of their products and services—like the half-life of knowledge and technology—keeps getting shorter, corporate executives have come to see the ability to change as key to organizational survival. They are scrambling to adjust to the new environment by demolishing traditional corporate policies and practices and introducing radically new strategies and structures, all with an eye to facilitating perpetual organizational transformation.

The quintessential manifestation of this new global economic order is the emergence of the Global Competitor organization, the corporate model built to change. This new mode of structuring and managing organizations has enormous consequences for the people who work in them. In creating GC organizations, executives are reconfiguring the American workplace, introducing new patterns of work and careers, new forms of rewards and benefits, and an entirely new social contract between employee and employer.[2] In general, GC corporations today employ fewer people and they produce more goods and services than in the past. Those employees are working longer and harder, and expectations about their performance have increased. Those who produce more are paid more, and they move up the organization faster. And employees are moving in and out of GC companies more frequently. As a result, these companies are becoming increasingly competitive in three senses: they are able to compete more efficiently against each other; they compete among themselves for the most highly qualified workers; and employees within them compete more for rewards and for fewer slots at the top of the hierarchy.

Yet it is with some reluctance that we begin our analysis of changes in the American workplace with these Global Competitors. We are not ready to join the chorus of those who offer breathless descriptions of a world suddenly "gone flat" as the result of the practices of these admittedly fascinating organizations, with their "new employment contracts" and "global sourcing." In fact, the practices of GC corporations are far from the norm and are representative of only a minority of U.S. businesses. Nor is it the case that the majority of American companies are becoming like them. Doubtless, the three macroforces we've identified are in the process of altering the American workplace, but economic change is evolutionary, not revolutionary. When it arrives in a complex, pluralistic society, it comes in a variety of forms and sizes, not as a uniform package. Hence we do not argue that America faces a sudden crisis as the result of the undeniable forces of change that we all observe. Instead, to analyze the American workplace accurately and objectively, we believe it is almost as important to acknowledge the internal forces of continuity and stability as it is to address the external forces of change.

The most obvious reason why there is no workplace crisis in America today is that the great majority of jobs in this country are isolated from the prime forces of change outlined above. Although 22 percent of the nation's gross national product is now related to international merchandise trade, the flip side is that 78 percent is domestic. And while everyone talks about working for Microsoft and General Electric, less than 20 percent of Americans actually are employed by *Fortune* 1000 companies (the organizations most likely to be involved in the global economy). Many of those companies are purely domestic (without foreign competitors, and neither exporting nor importing), including most of those in construction, healthcare, transportation, real estate, retailing, and insurance. Only the very largest firms in those industries are likely to be involved directly in the global economy, and, in general, most small businesses in every industry are purely domestic. As officially defined, "small businesses" in the United States account for something like half of all American jobs and the creation of 75 percent of new ones.[3] In addition, some 19 percent of Americans work for government agencies and another 8 percent are employed in the nonprofit sector, which is largely domestic in its operations.[4]

All told, the large number of Americans employed in domestic-oriented jobs buffers the effects of the cheap foreign labor that causes the export of manufacturing jobs. Also, smaller businesses, which are often in a single location, are less likely to experience job loss as the result of information technology. And the managers of those companies are far less likely to be under pressure from Wall Street to produce short-term profits than are executives of large Global Competitor corporations. That said, many small businesses today are subjected to international competition, and that trend is likely to increase in the future.

Given the attention Global Competitor corporations receive in the press, and the degree to which Silicon Valley has come to symbolize American dominance of the world economy, it is sobering to note that the United States is now a net *importer* of high-tech products. The country's share of global high-technology exports fell from 30 percent to 17 percent over the last twenty years, and its trade balance in manufactured tech goods went from a $33 billion surplus in 1990 to a $24 billion deficit in 2004. Because complicated economic and technological trends aren't always what they seem—and seldom are they as simple to understand and respond to effectively as one might wish—we begin our analysis in the chapters that follow by digging deeply into the changes that have occurred over the last three decades in organizations, in work itself, and in the employee-employer relationship.

We examine these changes from the perspective of thirty years of research on the effectiveness of business organizations and the well-being of workers. As we explore current business challenges and managerial premises through the lens of social science data, readers may have some hunches and impressions confirmed, may be surprised by other findings, and may even wish that some of what is true were not. And their conclusions may differ about what, if anything, should be done to influence the nature of working conditions in the future. But, at least, all will have the benefit of starting from the common ground of hard data. We believe that sound and prudent corporate and national policy must be based on thorough analyses of all the relevant facts, open-minded consideration of all the alternatives available, and with regard to the potential consequences for all constituencies affected. Too often the failure of decision makers to consider all of these factors leads to their being satisfied with simplistic assumptions that overly constrain the range of options they consider, and to flawed (and sometimes even panicked) policy making.

2

THE NATURE OF ORGANIZATIONS

The corporate giants of the 1970s were slow-to-change, bureaucratic organizations built on the structures and management principles developed by Alfred Sloan at General Motors in the 1920s. Whether organized on divisional or functional lines, all the employees in these monolithic corporations knew where they stood in the organizational hierarchy. At the bottom were the "workers," most often unionized, whose lifelong job security offset the tedium of their tasks and chafing from overly close supervision. The layers of managers above them had a defined pecking order, each level with a clear reporting relationship to the managers above them. These "organization men" pursued clearly demarcated career paths from the mailroom in the basement up to the executive suite. Finally, the man with the cigar who sat at the apex of the corporation almost invariably had worked his way up from the bottom to the top in a long process of promotion after promotion in the only company he ever had worked for. (No woman would become CEO of a major U.S. company until the 1990s.) Overall, the facts of organizational life in the 1970s were not much different from what they had been ten, twenty, and even fifty years earlier.

One need only compare the 1975 list of *Fortune* 500 industrial companies to today's list to see how much change has occurred in the intervening years: half of the top twenty industrial firms at that time are no longer in business, and many of the survivors are mere shadows of their former selves. For example, General Motors and Ford have less than half the number of employees today that they had in the mid-1970s. The rate of extinction of these giant American corporations is indicative of the fundamental changes they have undergone in terms of what they make, where and how they operate, who owns them, and how the key factors of industrial success have undergone radical transformations.

FROM MANUFACTURING TO SERVICES

Contrary to conventional wisdom, manufacturing is far from dead in the United States. There are over 100,000 manufacturing companies in the country that have twenty or more employees, among which are such diverse, and successful, ones as Dell, Procter & Gamble, Alcoa, and Trek bicycles, companies we discuss in greater depth in pages to come. These companies often are niche players, offering high-tech products, as WL Gore does, or unique products, as Harley-Davidson does. The U.S. manufacturing sector is bigger than the entire Chinese economy, accounting for 23.8 percent of the world's total manufacturing output in 2004, as measured in value-added, down only by about 1 percent since 1982. What has declined is the percentage of American workers employed in manufacturing, down from 25 percent in the 1970s to a little less than 10 percent today.[1] Trends in auto production are illustrative: the number of cars made in North America has risen by 65 percent since 1980, but employment in the industry has shrunk by 34 percent over the same time period.[2] The relative size of U.S. manufacturing firms also has shrunk: companies employing fewer than a thousand people now account for 80 percent of the nation's manufacturing value-added.

Offsetting the shrinkage in manufacturing employment has been marked growth in the number of jobs in services-related industries, which now account for over 80 percent of American jobs. Indeed, today the largest U.S. corporations, and the largest employers, are services companies. Some of these companies, like the largest U.S. employer, Wal-Mart, are pure retailers. But others once categorized as manufacturers—IBM, Xerox, General Electric, Sun, and Cisco, for instance—are becoming or already are predominantly services providers. They may still make some goods (or sell products made abroad by other companies under their brand name), but most of their profits and growth come from services rather than manufacturing. For example, large American information technology (IT) companies no longer simply sell "boxes" to their corporate clients; instead, they sell "information systems and solutions"—basically their expertise is in systems design (what laypeople think of as engineering and consulting work). And these companies often manage the systems they install in other large companies on an ongoing basis as outsourcing contractors.

One manifestation of the shift to services in the United States is the demise of the *Fortune* Industrial 500, which, as recently as the 1980s, constituted the premier list of American corporations. While *Fortune* also published a separate ranking of services organizations, being on that list wasn't nearly as prestigious. The two lists were combined into the *Fortune* 1000 in 1995, largely because the integration of services and manufacturing in so many corporations made it increasingly impossible to assign companies to one or the other sector. There are some complicating factors as in measuring manufacturing employment: some of the decline results from the outsourcing of services, as when a car manufacturer contracts out the janitorial and cafeteria jobs that used to be done by company employees. Does that constitute a loss of manufacturing jobs? A gain of services job? A wash? Only an economist can say for sure!

Today it is difficult to generalize about the nature of the jobs in any company based on its industry classification. Retailer Wal-Mart, for example, offers both low-level *and* skilled-technical jobs. On one hand, most of the million or so people it employs in the United States are low-wage clerks and shelf stockers engaged in simple tasks; on the other hand, because Wal-Mart has highly sophisticated purchasing operations, distribution systems, and inventory and store management, it competes directly with the nation's technically most advanced firms for managerial, technical, and professional talent. In our terminology, the broad base of Wal-Mart is a Low-Cost (LC) organization, but a smaller Global Competitor (GC) company is perched on top.

Among the leaders of yesterday's *Fortune* Industrial 500 that have shifted from a manufacturing to a services orientation are two of the largest U.S. employers, IBM and General Electric. While IBM is farther down this path than GE, both companies now see their futures in services because that is a higher value-added activity than manufacturing. In plain English, today most large American companies can make more money selling knowledge than they can by making and selling things. Since computer hardware increasingly has become a commodity, and profit margins from selling it have dropped accordingly, it is not surprising that IBM now advertises itself as a company offering business "solutions." For example, IBM recently signed a large contract with Procter & Gamble to handle that company's IT and human resource systems, and it has the capability to do the same with the finance, accounting, and marketing information systems at other giant corporations.

As IBM's technical services businesses are growing—and becoming more global—it has been selling off some of its product businesses. In a dramatic move in 2005, IBM exited the personal computer (PC) business it once dominated, selling it to a Chinese company. As the cost of PCs continued to fall for over two decades, and the product had become almost a commodity, IBM found that it could not compete against companies with greater expertise in mass manufacturing. In a clear illustration of the global, technical, and financial challenges of the times, even an American company with the resources, brand name, and technical expertise of IBM could not maintain a sufficiently profitable business manufacturing a product that it practically invented.

The consequences of IBM's numerous strategic changes for its American workforce add up to a good news/bad news story typical of hundreds of similar industrial tales that could be told. Indeed, the transformation of IBM over the last decade is representative of the transformation most of the *Fortune* 500 is undergoing, or will undergo, in coming years: IBM is changing from being an old-line American industrial bureaucracy to becoming a GC organization. In the process, the company has lost American blue-collar jobs, eliminated ranks of managers, and replaced older employees with outdated skills with younger, better-educated (or at least more up-to-date and technically knowledgeable) professionals. As old divisions have been closed or sold and new ones created, the company's workforce has been in a state of flux, with layoffs here and hirings there and, most recently, ten thousand jobs shifted from the United States and Europe to China and India.

The good news for those looking for jobs at IBM is that the higher levels of education and technical knowledge required by its services businesses should give American workers a competitive edge over workers in developing countries. Even as more software development is being offshored, typically the most complex work is still done in the United States, as is the management of the development process. For example, IBM's overall American workforce may be smaller than in the recent past, but, on average, it is better educated, more professional, better compensated, and engaged in more interesting jobs.

Even though the skill base of the Asian workforce is improving rapidly, it will take decades before such countries as China and India can close the enormous educational gap that separates them from America. If the United States continues to make heavy investments in education, training, and research and development, and if more Americans choose to pursue scientific, engineering, and technical educations and professions, there is no reason why this country should lose its commanding lead in knowledge-based industries. Of course, those are enormous ifs, and we return to them many times in the course of this book.

GLOBAL ORGANIZATIONS

More and more American corporations are becoming global players. Iconic U.S. corporations that once sold only products made in America, or only did business in America, now operate on a global basis. Coca-Cola, Procter & Gamble, IBM, and Citibank, for example, have global brands and do much if not most of their business offshore. As a result of globalization, an increasing number of employees of major U.S. corporations work overseas, the percentage growing from 21.2 percent in 1988 to 27.8 percent in 2003.[3] In particular, many manufacturing corporations have adapted to the dictates of the global economy by moving production offshore. Mattel—the southern California birthplace of Barbie, the All-American doll—now does all its manufacturing in Asia, as do all other major U.S. toy manufacturers. Even in high-tech fields, manufacturing is increasingly done in Asia. Many Silicon Valley companies outsource their manufacturing to America's Solectron Corp., which then turns the actual production over to workers in Asia. In both toys and information technology—one a low- and the other a high-tech industry—design, sales, and upper-management are done in the United States, but the labor is done offshore.

There are a number of reasons why more and more corporations have chosen to go global besides searching for cheap—and, in some cases, skilled and cheap—labor. Globalization offers three benefits to companies: (1) the ability to operate twenty-four hours a day and seven days a week and, therefore, speed up their production and design processes; (2) the ability to sell on a global basis provides economies of scale that help offset the tremendous cost of developing and producing new products; and, (3) by sourcing globally, firms can get the best deals on materials, products, and labor. Moreover, there is a domino effect with respect to globalization: Company A feels it must go global once its customer B does so because A fears losing B's U.S. business to global competitor C. That's because B says it wants to deal with only one supplier worldwide. Then, once A goes global, its own suppliers, companies D and E, feel the same pressure to do so. Suddenly, an entire supply chain is global!

There is an additional reason for going global, one that isn't always acknowledged: Much of the work done in Asia for companies like Mattel and Solectron involves the assembly of small parts, repetitive and eye-straining work requiring incredible levels of concentration and manual dexterity for hours on end. Americans simply are no longer willing to do such work, and it cannot be profitably automated.

Increasingly, American service jobs also are being exported. With the growth of the Internet and global telecommunications, some "back-office" and call center jobs now can be done overseas. Although the offshoring of such jobs has generated great attention, if not alarm, in the U.S. press, there appear to be limits to how far the trend can be taken, at least in the near- to mid-term future. For example, the supply of men and women in India who speak fluent English is relatively limited, and the Indian school and university systems are designed to produce a few first-rate graduates, not masses of educated people.[4] Until India reforms its education system—not likely in the near future and, if it does so, the effects will be gradual—the number of high-pay, high-skilled services jobs that can be exported to India will be constrained by the scarce supply of trained talent. In addition, many services must be offered face-to-face and, as some U.S. companies are discovering, the efforts and costs involved in managing offshore services often outweigh the benefits. Indeed, some executives interviewed for this study report that their companies are actually reimporting services jobs to North America. Hence, while American prudence is advisable in this regard, panic seems premature.

The McKinsey Global Institute characterizes jobs eligible for offshoring as "any task that requires no physical or complex interaction between an employee and customers or colleagues and little or no local knowledge."[5] Researchers Ashok Bardhan and Cynthia Kroll identify six specific attributes of jobs that increase their likelihood of being targeted for offshoring:

1. No face-to-face customer service requirement
2. High information content
3. Work processes that are telecommutable and Internet-enabled
4. High wage differential compared to similar occupations in the destination country
5. Low setup barriers
6. Low social-networking requirement

In sum, offshoring is not as simple as it sounds. The design, manufacturing, and sales of a Hewlett-Packard (HP) laptop computer provide an informative example of the kind of global corporate infrastructure needed to operate successfully in the emerging, boundaryless world of international big business. Since the days of the first commercial computers in the early 1950s, almost all new computer models have been designed in the United States by U.S. companies (this is especially true for computers containing significant technology advances). But now, increasingly, the design of parts for HP computers is being outsourced and offshored. Hard-disk drives are made, and often designed, in Japan, China, and Singapore as well as in the United States. Memory chips now come from South Korea, Taiwan, and Germany, in addition to the United States—although the most important component, the microprocessor, is still primarily designed and manufactured in this country.

When a customer clicks on an HP Web site to purchase a laptop, the order is immediately transmitted to a factory in China managed by Quanta, a Taiwanese firm that supplies computers to several leading manufacturers. The final assembly of the computers is done in China because that is the source of the cheapest disciplined labor. Despite the complexity of this global process, the delivery of an HP computer to a customer in the United States is fairly rapid: within a week of the order being placed, the computer will arrive at the American purchaser's door, courtesy of FedEx or UPS air delivery.

Two factors allow HP to operate its laptop business in this global fashion. First, laptops have all the characteristics of products most-effectively sourced on a global basis: the PC business is highly competitive with both sophisticated engineering and low-cost manufacturing essential for success. As laptops are relatively lightweight, they and their components can be cheaply shipped around the world on Boeing 747s. Second, thanks to HP's information technology and management systems, the company can search the globe to find where a particular part of the production process can be accomplished best and then bring all the parts together in a seamless process. Without IT to connect those far-flung operations, it would be impossible to produce a laptop as quickly, efficiently, and cheaply as HP does today.

To position itself to benefit from the advantages of globalization, and to compete in a cost-sensitive manufacturing business, over the last decade HP has morphed from being one of America's leading High-Involvement companies into being the quintessential Global Competitor. The effect of that transformation on the company's American workforce has been staggering. A few short years ago, almost all HP workers were domestic, regular, full-time, and permanent, career employees. Today, about one half of its now-global workforce is composed of contingent, or contractual, workers.

Employees of technology companies are not the only ones affected by the convergence of IT and global sourcing. IT-based global product development also is used in the design and manufacturing of such products as automobiles and heavy equipment that used to be thought of in terms of rust-belt technology. Today, the software systems used in developing these products have become so sophisticated that design engineers can create three-dimensional product prototypes while, simultaneously, manufacturing engineers on a different continent are laying out the assembly lines and planning what tools will be needed in the manufacturing process. Whereas until recently almost all the major auto and truck companies—America's General Motors, Germany's Daimler Benz, Japan's Toyota, and France's Renault—were thought of as manufacturers based in a single nation, today they are all global players with operations and sourcing around the world. As a result, the entire design, manufacture, and delivery cycle of new cars, trucks, and tractors has been speeded up, and new products are brought to market in a fraction of the time it used to take, and at a reduced cost. Again, the effect of all of this on American workers has been mixed. Hundreds of thousands of domestic blue-collar and middle-management positions have been lost but, at the same time, some "good" new jobs in information technology (IT), engineering, marketing, and management have been created.

Of course, not every product lends itself to being produced on a global basis. Some simply have to be produced in the countries where they are sold, and others are best made in the single country that has an overall competitive advantage in producing them. Fortunately, many products need to be made and consumed in the United States. As noted, the provision of many services is purely domestic: houses, haircuts, and spas cannot be offshored. Some products are so large and heavy to transport that they can't be imported, for example, bricks and concrete. Products requiring timely delivery can't be outsourced; even with modern transportation and IT our daily newspapers can't be printed in China. Finally, labor represents such a small fraction of the total cost of some products that the price of shipping outweighs any potential savings from offshore production. This is particularly true for pharmaceuticals, processed foods, and packaged consumer goods like soap and personal-care products, which are manufactured by highly automated, continuous-process technology, and for chemicals and petroleum products where the main costs of production are raw materials and technology, not labor. In such capital-intensive industries, blue-collar workers are often paid high salaries and have good jobs. These jobs are likely to stay in the United States because exporting them provides no significant financial advantage.

While most of the stories in the press dealing with the consequences of globalization have focused on the offshoring of jobs by U.S. companies, a little-noticed countertrend of "onshoring" to this country by foreign corporations also has occurred. In 2002, onshoring foreign companies employed over 5.4 million American workers, about 5 percent of the nation's total private-sector jobs, and a significant increase from 2.6 percent in 1987.[6] Perhaps the most visible, and job-creating, onshoring has been in the automobile industry where all the major Japanese automakers have established major U.S. manufacturing facilities, as have Japanese auto parts suppliers. For example, Toyota, Honda, and Nissan operate some twenty-two major plants in North America, employing some 90,000 workers.[7] In contrast, one of the primary factors accounting for the increase in onshoring has been the foreign acquisition of U.S. companies in such industries as pharmaceuticals and farm equipment. In those cases, jobs may not have been created, but at least they weren't lost.

Onshoring often reflects a desire on the part of foreign corporations to capture the expertise and knowledge of American workers. The share of all

U.S. private-sector R&D accounted for by onshoring rose from 9 percent in 1992 to 14 percent in 2002. An indicator of the high quality of jobs being onshored is that the average annual compensation of an American working for a foreign-owned company in 2002 was over $50,000, some 31 percent higher than the average annual compensation in the U.S. private sector (and the premium paid by insourcing companies over salaries paid by domestic employers has risen by 20 percent since 1992).[8] In sum, foreign corporations are creating good jobs for Americans in the United States. What is worrying is that new, job-creating foreign investment in this country has declined significantly in the first half of this decade, but it is too soon to tell if this is a blip or a trend.

THE ERA OF HUMAN CAPITAL

One consequence of corporations becoming more services-oriented—and competing on the basis of expertise, knowledge, and advanced technology—is the increasing recognition by many employers of the importance of their "human capital." In manufacturing, employees' efforts may affect a company's bottom line, but the market value of the company nonetheless is determined mainly by its financial capital: such assets as its land, factories, machinery, vehicles, and cash in the bank. But, increasingly, the market value of a corporation reflects such "intangible assets" as its brand name, the organizational systems and processes it uses, and, perhaps most important, the quality of its workforce. Increasingly, this is true in both High-Involvement and Global Competitor companies where managers have introduced practices specifically designed to develop and effectively utilize their human capital—HI companies with a focus on developing and involving their workforces, and GC companies with an eye on obtaining the best talent available to perform whatever work needs to be done at a specific time.

In the late 1990s, the realization that human capital was increasingly important to corporate success led McKinsey and Co. consultants to coin the term "the war for talent."[9] At the time, competition among technology firms for people with technical skills was intense, and large firms, in general, were on the prowl for senior management talent. That stage of the "war" proved to be little more than a preliminary skirmish, however, ending abruptly in 2001 with the onset of the nation's most-recent economic recession. Nonetheless, competition for talent will doubtless heat up again because corporate executives learned a lasting lesson: it takes extremely competent people to manage global organizations and to create and deliver the complex services and products that are key to success in the global economy. For American corporations to be successful in the future they will need to develop systems and practices that attract, retain, and develop skilled, educated, and talented managers, professionals, and technicians. We are, in fact, at the dawn of the Age of Human Capital. That can be, and should be, good for American workers in the long run, *if* they are properly educated.

COMPLEX ORGANIZATIONAL STRUCTURES

The shifts to services, high-speed product development, global operations, and higher-value-added activities by large American corporations have led them to create ever-more complex organizations. Particularly in rapidly changing GC companies, employees no longer have clear, or static, job descriptions; instead, they are loosely organized into global teams, often with multiple and overlapping memberships.[10] In many cases these are "virtual teams" that interact by way of telecommunications. As a result, superior-subordinate relationships, if they exist at all, are not face-to-face. To complicate matters further, many members of a product development team often are not co-located or even on the same continent; instead, they may be employed by a company's cooperating vendors, customers, and strategic partners. Often it is not clear who is where, or who is what, in a corporate hierarchy. In general, these trends are confusing, but liberating, for most workers.

Many of the new organizational structures destroy bureaucracy and encourage speed and innovation. Besides having more virtual relationships, managers in GC corporations are likely to have more people reporting to them, to be reporting to two or even three different people themselves, and to have fewer organizational layers above and below them—all of which can free them (and their subordinates) to take initiative, be creative, and assume responsibility.[11] The disadvantage is that, without close supervision, some employees may feel a lack of direction and may not understand how their tasks contribute to the overall success of the enterprise. Hence, in a continuing effort to keep all employees informed and aligned with company goals, coordination and communication have become the prime tasks of management. This form of performance management is light-years removed from traditional supervision and the exercise of hierarchical control.

THE NATURE OF CORPORATE OWNERSHIP

We have mentioned in passing how the ownership of major U.S. corporations has changed dramatically over the last three decades. Increasingly, large institutional-investors hold corporate stock, and the managers of these financial institutions are extremely focused on the performance of the companies whose stock they own. When they become dissatisfied with the returns at a company in which they are a major investor, they often find themselves in a bind: they cannot readily sell their large blocks of shares because that would depress the price and cause them to incur a major financial loss. Thus, instead of selling shares in underperforming companies, institutional investors actively pressure corporate executives to make those firms more profitable. Some large pension funds, such as TIAA-CREF and CalPers, have such large and diverse portfolios that they concentrate on "lifting all boats" rather than risk depressing the entire market by scuttling a leaky vessel.

Performance pressure has led to increased turnover among CEOs and, in some cases, to the breakup of companies, their purchase by private equity firms, and the sale of major corporate assets. But the most profound consequence has been to shift the focus of corporate executives toward meeting investor demands for short-term profitability and away from planning for long-term corporate growth. Executives have had to change the way they think about their tasks, roles, and responsibilities and, that, in turn, has led to the creation of corporate structures and practices that were unknown in the slower-moving world of the 1970s.

FOCUS ON ECONOMIC PERFORMANCE

In particular, the changing nature of ownership has increased the pressure on publicly traded corporations to perform: investors demand it, and survival requires it. In many cases, good long-term performance is not enough;

investors closely track quarterly earnings, and stock prices reflect short-term performance against market expectations. This pressure heightens and intensifies the effects of globalization and technology, increasing the need for large corporations to respond rapidly to changes in the competitive environment. If a competitor introduces a technologically advanced new product—or even one with flashier bells and whistles—almost overnight a company can lose an entire line of business. When Sony introduces a new version of its electronic PlayStation, Microsoft's current version of its competing XBox becomes outmoded, and Microsoft must respond immediately with a new version of the XBox or get out of that line of business. Investors carefully monitor every move in this strategic, fast-paced chess match, and punish or reward companies based on their evaluation of the effects on next quarter's earnings.

Because the performance of large, global corporations can deteriorate rapidly, they have little slack in their operations and only a short period of time in which to correct problems. Often costs need to be cut quickly. As a result of the trend toward large corporations becoming more services oriented, employee rolls increasingly are the main places to cut costs. Hence, large-scale layoffs have become more and more common. Often downsizing occurs in response to demands made by the financial community. Corporate raider Carl Icahn has described his objective as eliminating "layers of bureaucrats reporting to bureaucrats." However, as MIT's Paul Osterman notes: "The trick in assessing claims regarding the impact of capital markets lies in distinguishing between firms who really need a wake-up call from cases in which capital markets are simply struggling for a higher share of profits at the expense of employment and wages."[12]

Since the 1980s, layoffs have involved not just production workers but, increasingly, employees at all levels, including managers. In some cases "downsizing" is undertaken simply to create a smaller, less expensive payroll. But today, particularly in GC organizations, force reductions are becoming the norm—part of a constant churning of the workforce targeted at continually fine-tuning the "mix of skills" needed to implement an endless stream of new strategies and products. As an illustration of how large the absolute number of reductions-in-force has become, U.S. corporations announced 538,274 job cuts in just the first half of 2005. Significantly, those cuts occurred in a so-called recovering economy. During similar times of economic growth in the past, corporations *added* people to their employment rolls.

There is considerable evidence that the combination of the three external forces for change—globalization, technology, and the focus on performance—have led to significant increases in national productivity. Economists calculate that U.S. productivity increased 72 percent between 1973 and 2003.[13] But this growth was not achieved at a steady rate. Productivity growth from 1973 to 1995 was relatively slow and then accelerated in the 1995 to 2003 period. The best explanation for the recent acceleration is the combined impact of information technology and the organizational changes we are discussing: machines have replaced workers in much of what is left of American domestic manufacturing; many lower-paid jobs have been eliminated and replaced by fewer higher-skilled, higher-paid jobs; and the number of employees on the payrolls of large manufacturing corporations has shrunk as business has increased.[14] Despite the recent surge in productivity growth, the United States nonetheless now ranks eighth in the world in national productivity, down from its commanding first place in 1973.[15] This drop is significant because productivity growth is perhaps the single clearest indicator of a nation's economic health: it is essential to the creation of new, higher-paid, higher-skilled jobs. Yet, while rising productivity is essential for the nation as a whole, not everyone benefits equally from it, especially not in the short-term—which may be the entire working life of a single American.

Although per-capita gross domestic product has risen by some 75 percent since the early 1970s, the median wage of working men, adjusted for inflation, rose by only two cents an hour, from $15.24 to $15.26 in 2004.[16] The average private sector worker's job security is also at greater risk today. These statistics do not mean that the efforts of large American corporations to remain competitive in world markets are wrong, or misplaced. Quite the opposite: the wealth generated by productivity growth is essential to fund future job creation and such national programs as Social Security and Medicare. The challenge is to upgrade the education and skills of American workers so that more can participate in the shift to the good jobs being created in GC and HI companies, and to improve the management of those companies so that they will create even more good jobs in the future. Steps also must be taken to address the basic needs of workers left behind in this era of transformation and disruption. We return to those tall tasks in detail in later chapters.

3

THE WORK ITSELF

The routine and repetitive jobs prevalent in the early 1970s were symbolized—not necessarily accurately—in the popular press by work on assembly lines. Research at the time showed that workers engaged in boring, overly controlled, and mentally unchallenging tasks tended to lack motivation, to quit their jobs frequently, to care little about the quality of the goods they produced, and to suffer from a variety of physical and mental ailments that had their origins in the workplace.[1] This situation was ripe for change. Over the next quarter century, multiple forces conspired to transform American manufacturing, the most profound of which was automation. In addition, three waves of domestic workplace reform—employee involvement, total quality management (TQM), and reengineering—were introduced at about the same time as manufacturing jobs that couldn't be automated or reformed were being exported.

Because these changes took place inside factory walls, and out of public sight, few Americans today realize how profoundly different modern manufacturing jobs are from those on traditional assembly lines. When we think of assembly-line work, we still tend to visualize Charlie Chaplin's tragicomic struggles in the classic movie *Modern Times.* But conveying an accurate image of today's modern manufacturing facilities would require futuristic computer-assisted graphics because the reality is closer to science fiction than most Americans realize. Moreover, the nature of a great deal of services work also is undergoing significant transformation. These changes may be more familiar to the general public, but they receive less attention than the manufacturing changes that preceded them.

AUTOMATION AND INFORMATION TECHNOLOGY

In the 1970s, the Philip Morris Company put an end to the traditional assembly-line manufacture of cigarettes when it opened one of the nation's first fully automated plants in any industry. That factory, located in Richmond, Virginia, looked more like a modern art museum than a traditional manufacturing facility in its extensive use of glass and polished hardwoods. Workers could meet and rest in quiet atriums adorned with sculpture, and employee training took place in a state-of-the-art auditorium complete with plush velvet seats (each equipped with a built-in ash tray!).

At the heart of the cigarette production process were several dozen noisy machines, each a little bit bigger than a lawyer's desk. Running into one end of each machine were funnels, shafts, and belts that continually fed the constituent ingredients of cigarettes—tobacco, paper, and filters—along with the wrapping, plastic, and cardboard used in packaging. Fully made, packaged, and cartoned cigarettes came out the other end. The labor content in the process consisted of a few people who stood by monitoring the machines in case they jammed and driving forklifts to haul the finished product to trucks for shipping. Far from being a classically grimy and dusty factory, it was clean and sterile; one literally could eat off the shop floor. The workers all were paid well for their efforts, and the only downside was that they had to wear ear protectors to muffle the clamor of the machines. The nature of work had come a long way since Carmen hand-rolled cigarettes in her storied factory in nineteenth-century Seville.

When Philip Morris's proud executives invited the nation's leading experts on work to visit the plant in 1979, these men and women from industry, labor, government, journalism, and academia were awed by what they saw. Many of them, futurist Isaac Asimov among them, concluded they

The New Faces of American Manufacturing

To Americans of a certain age, the name Schwinn once was synonymous with the word bicycle. In the 1950s and 1960s, for a parental outlay of a mere $35, a kid could feel like a million bucks sitting on the comfortable, well-padded seat of a shiny new bike found under the Christmas tree. For years, the Schwinn Bicycle Company of Chicago produced the "Cadillac of American bicycles"— heavy, steel-framed, balloon-tired models with streamlined fenders and chrome-plated headlights that had a lot in common with the big, finned, chrome-plated American cars produced in Detroit at the time. In fact, many of the bikes were built by members of the United Auto Workers employing much the same assembly-line methods used in making cars. In its record year of 1974, the company sold 1.5 million bikes.

But as cheaper, more-fashionable bikes made in Asia became widely available in U.S. stores, Schwinn found that its domestic-made bikes could no longer compete, and the company ultimately went bankrupt in 1992. Ditto Huffy, once Schwinn's major domestic competitor, which went belly-up in 2001. Now, only Chinese-made bikes are sold under the Schwinn and Huffy brand names at discount stores like Wal-Mart and Target. That's the bad news.

The good news is that the best bicycles in the world are now manufactured in America. Lance Armstrong rode to victory seven times in the Tour de France astride Trek bikes made in Waterloo, Wisconsin. Trek makes a product line of 138 different bikes, whose prices run as high as $9,500 for a model similar to the one Armstrong rode. The family-owned company reported sales on the order of $500 million in 2003. It employs some 1,200 workers in the United States (and another 200 in Germany). About 650 of those U.S. employees work in a state-of-the-art factory that doesn't have an assembly line and doesn't even feel like a factory. In this High-Involvement (HI) facility there are no class distinctions between workers and managers; indeed, they all share in a common "bike culture." Blue-collar workers don't wear blue, and most of them don't have collars on their work duds, preferring instead to wear cycling clothes on the job. That's because the vast majority of Trek workers are cyclists who often ride to work on the products they make and take spins on them at lunchtime (when the Wisconsin weather is conducive to doing so). The workers are skilled craftspeople who, working in teams, hand-make the bikes without the help of automation.

What is high-tech at Trek is its Research and Development (R&D). Trek can compete with bike makers from low-wage countries because it keeps a step ahead in the development of new composite materials and design innovations. In addition, the company stays close to its customers in terms of providing service and responding quickly to changes in product preference. That is easy to do in a company where all the employees are cyclists themselves. Trek demonstrates that U.S. manufacturers are able to compete with anyone in the world in niche markets for high-priced goods that have cutting-edge technology components. For this strategy to succeed, a manufacturer continually has to be able to offer the best, most innovative, highest-quality, and most technologically advanced products, and have a knowledgeable, committed, and well-educated workforce.

The other manufacturing strategy that works for American companies requires vast amounts of capital invested in production technology. GC-company Dell Computer is probably the world's most efficient computer maker, with giant, highly automated assembly facilities in Texas, Tennessee, and, soon, North Carolina. Dell is also the only remaining domestic PC manufacturer. To stay on top, Dell increases its annual output of machines at the staggering rate of some 30 percent per year. In 2000, two Dell workers spent fourteen minutes assembling a computer; in 2005, a single worker did the trick in about five minutes. As a result, labor amounts to only about 2 percent ($10 or so) of the total cost of a Dell PC.

Dell's comparative competitive advantage doesn't come from product innovation—it invests only 2 percent of profits in R&D, while industry rivals spend 5 to 8 percent—instead, its advantage comes from constant improvements in its process technology and manufacturing cost control. Speed is of the essence: orders received at the factory are out the door in four hours. Dell has mastered the just-in-time-delivery techniques pioneered by Japanese manufacturers, which saves the company millions of dollars annually in inventory costs, and hours in handling, storage, and retrieval that are made unnecessary. At the shipping end, a truck full of PCs leaves the plant within thirty minutes of its arrival at the loading dock. Like Hewlett-Packard, Dell uses offshore suppliers for many, if not most, components.

The pace of Dell's assembly-line is breathtaking, thanks to the kind of industrial engineering that would have warmed the heart of Frederick Winslow Taylor, father of "time and motion" studies. New York Times correspondent Gary Rivlin describes the process: engineers "wheel in video equipment to examine a work team's every movement, looking for any extraneous bends or wasted twists. Designers give themselves high-fives for eliminating even a single screw from a product, because that represents a saving of roughly four seconds per machine built—the time they've calculated it takes an employee, on average, to use the pneumatic screwdriver dangling above his or her head."[2] Such work is not for the old or the laid-back. Every worker's performance is continually timed and monitored, with the fastest and best dubbed "master builders" and rewarded by keeping some of the few well-paid assembly-line jobs left in America. In contrast, according to Rivlin, "The weak are told that it takes a special set of talents to cut it on the Dell factory floor—and are shown the door."

had had a glimpse of how Americans would be "working in the twenty-first century."[3] And by the turn of the millennium, a mere twenty years later, it became clear that they indeed had seen the future of work. Stepping inside an American manufacturing facility today, particularly one owned by a large Global Competitor (GC) corporation, is to step into the future promised by the Philip Morris plant.

Whether the product being made is autos, tractors, light bulbs, chemicals, chocolate bars, dog food, or computers, the overwhelming impression a visitor to a new U.S. factory receives is that machines are doing almost all, if not all, the work. No matter if the machines are robots, automated assembly lines, or continuous-process machinery run by employees in an information technology (IT) dominated control room (like ones used to make paper, chemicals, and soft drinks), few humans can be seen doing anything remotely recognizable as "labor." That generalization does not hold in all midsize or small companies, or in old-line industries like poultry processing, but it is true for every almost every large American GC manufacturer.

From the day cavemen used the first chisel, technology has had an enormous impact on the nature of work. Of all the technological changes that have occurred in this country since Henry Ford introduced the assembly line in 1913, recent developments in information technology have had the greatest impact on how Americans work. Although IT may still be in an early stage of development, it already has had greater impact on productivity, the nature of tasks, how workers interact with each other and their supervisors, and the quality of work life than the assembly line ever did.

The introduction of automation, and IT in particular, to the services sector has been more visible than it has been in manufacturing, but because the trend has been gradual and spread over a long period of time, it does not seem as dramatic and disruptive. But it has been, and is. The trend started with automatic elevators—yes, once upon a time humans operated almost every elevator in America, which prompted the very bad joke that "the job has lots of ups and downs." There were also gas station attendants who pumped gas for customers (and, hard as it may be to believe, cleaned their windshields). When a customer called a business, a real person answered—much as there were professional phone-answering services for individuals in the days before voice mail. Most managers and professionals had secretaries who typed their letters on manual, and later, electric typewriters (before we all learned how to type for ourselves on our own PCs), and banks had legions of tellers to serve customers before the days of the ATM. And before there was e-tailing, people went to stores where clerks helped them with their purchases. Now, of course, we go on-line and spend hours entering our pin number, credit card number, mother's maiden name, and all three of our phone numbers in order to make a simple purchase that once took minutes. (At least, that is how it feels to us sixty-year-olds.) All told, consumers today work harder, workers lose their jobs to IT automation, companies make more money, and economists call this a productivity increase!

Without doubt, technology is constantly changing the nature and mix of available jobs. For example, IT has changed the number and nature of two categories of jobs once-considered desirable occupations for high school graduates: bank tellers and secretaries. In the past, many bank teller jobs were available for those with high school diplomas; today, many of those jobs have been lost to automation. The remaining "customer service representatives" in financial institutions tend to have at least some college education, and their work now requires facility with IT and technical understanding of the services their employers offer. Similarly, in the past, most managers and professionals had secretaries who typed for them, answered their phones, and did their clerical work. Today those tasks are done by "bosses" themselves with their own cell phones, voice-mail boxes, and computers. If those bosses have any personal human support, it is "an administrative assistant" who does such higher-level tasks as scheduling and preparing reports.

While it is not absolutely clear that today's renamed tellers and secretaries have much better jobs, or just euphemistically improved ones, in both cases the upgrading has removed some of the social stigma associated with the old jobs and, in the case of secretaries, freed women from a gender-stereotyped category that was often seen as dead-end. What is absolutely clear is that there are far fewer teller- and secretary-type jobs. Indeed, almost every bank and office in America has been able to reduce its workforce significantly by the effective application of IT. In general, the net effect everywhere of IT is the same as it has been in banks and offices: reducing the number of jobs, changing the nature of those remaining—usually upgrading them—and creating a number of skilled IT service and consulting support positions.

There is little question that information technology, in general, improves the productivity of workers enormously in services as well as in manufacturing, and there is widespread agreement that a great portion of the nation's recent productivity gains are due to the significant investments corporations made in IT in the 1980s and 1990s. It is also clear that IT can help to eliminate many boring, repetitive tasks that workers in both manufacturing and services traditionally spent long hours doing—for example, time-consuming and mind-numbing data entry. Even more than eliminating routine tasks, IT enriches jobs by providing employees with improved feedback about their performance. For example, it can provide them with real-time quality and productivity data. It also can give them instant access to business financials and customer data.

When used correctly and creatively, IT is a tremendous enabler of employee self-management.[4] It can provide employees with information that allows them to make more and better decisions about how they work. IT also can help workers to implement decisions that previously might have required extensive and time-consuming paperwork. Sales can be completed instantly and information distributed to hundreds of thousands of employees. IT can give workers instant access to information about the overall operations of their organizations and how they fit into that big picture. And it may add meaning to their work when they come to understand what it takes to make their company successful, and how what they do personally affects the organization's performance. Sophisticated information systems that give workers access to operating information, and information about customers and products, can help employees at all levels to assume responsibility for decision-making, customer relations, and organizational effectiveness. For example, as Microsoft has demonstrated, allowing employees chained to computers to blog, and to bond with customers, enriches their jobs to the benefit of both employees and the corporation. Companies also increasingly use IT for employee training, providing online courses and just-in-time instruction with respect to the tasks they perform.[5] Providing employees with easy access to the knowledge they need to take on more responsibility enriches their jobs and increases organizational productivity.

Finally, the growing use of IT has made many kinds of work mobile, allowing individuals considerable choice about when and where they work: by signing-on to a company Web site, employees in many services occupations can work from virtually any location in the world. Sun Microsystems is one of many companies taking advantage of this by creating "hoteling" stations in all their facilities, and by encouraging employees to work from home. According to University of Michigan data, in 2002, 17.2 percent of American workers reported that they regularly work from home, up from only 5.9 percent in 1977. In sum, IT gives workers more freedom, more responsibility, and allows them to be trusted to act like responsible adults in the absence of close supervision.

IT also can be designed to make decisions for employees about issues ranging from the pricing of products to the approval of credit. Such "decision support tools" can be helpful to employees and can increase productivity—however, they have a downside in terms of motivation and job deskilling if they prevent workers from exercising discretion. Managers also can misuse IT to monitor, control, and micromanage the behavior of employees and thus decrease their autonomy (and productivity). Low-Cost companies, in particular, often use IT to gather instantaneous data about who is working where and when, what they are doing, and how well they are doing it. In some cases, this information is used to teach employees and thus to help them to do their jobs better; but it also can be used to control and punish people and, even, to invade their privacy. Ironically, misused IT can create the kinds of routine, overcontrolled, overmanaged, oversimplified, and repetitive jobs that appropriately applied technology eliminates. For example, it is estimated that something like 4 percent of all U.S. workers now are employed in call centers. On these "digital assembly-lines," as writer Simon Herd appropriately refers to them, workers phone potential customers and read to them from canned scripts on computer screens, the pace of their task controlled by the computer.

EMPLOYEE INVOLVEMENT

In the 1950s, the results of workplace experiments in Scandinavia and the United Kingdom demonstrated that tasks could be designed in ways to make them both productive and satisfying. The "secret" those researchers discovered boils down to worker self-management: that is, placing workers in teams and enabling them to decide how to organize themselves and how to do their tasks. When managers give workers authority over their work and then reward them for doing the right thing, they address basic human needs for recognition, control, and belonging, needs that are more important determinants of employee morale and performance than are the physical conditions of work. Particularly when people work together—as opposed to being separate cogs in a machine—social bonds are formed that lead to cooperation and a desire to help each other succeed.

Managers today often fail to realize that most successful efforts to increase worker motivation involve the design of work itself. From the European experiments with employee involvement in the 1950s, through hundreds of efforts in the 1970s and 1980s to involve workers in decision-making in American workplaces, whenever and wherever workers have been organized in self-managing teams, and given the authority and resources needed to do their tasks, they have been motivated and productive.[6] The ongoing involvement in decision-making addresses two of the three basic human needs that good work satisfies: to participate in meaningful tasks and to have supportive social relationships. (When the element of fair pay is added to this equation, all three needs are met, and the result is truly good work that is both productive and satisfying.)

The 1970s were a time of ferment and experimentation in European and American workplaces. Volvo led the way in Europe, abandoning the assembly line in several of its auto plants and organizing employees in teams to assemble cars delivered to them on moving platforms. In the United States, *Newsweek* ran a cover story in 1973 about General Food's Topeka, Kansas, dog food plant where employees were organized into self-managing work teams, thus eliminating the need for supervisors and reducing plant operating costs by 40 percent. Perhaps most significant was Procter & Gamble's company-wide adoption of self-managing work teams in the 1970s and 1980s, which led to marked reductions in its labor costs, improvement in product quality, and, ultimately, overall change in the company's approach to human resources management that reached far beyond the factory floor, and which is still in place today.

Throughout the 1980s and into the 1990s, most U.S. manufacturing companies—and many services providers, as well—adopted or experimented with self-managing work teams to cut payroll costs and/or to enrich jobs. Our Center for Effective Organization's triennial survey of the *Fortune* 1000 shows that the percentage of firms with self-managing teams rose from twenty-eight in 1988 to sixty-five in 2005, and job-enrichment efforts increased from 60 percent to 86 percent during the same period. These job enrichment efforts

What Works at Work

Since the mid-1970s, research evidence has been mounting that companies and employees both benefit when two conditions are present:

1. All employees participate in the decisions that affect their own work; *and*
2. All employees participate in the financial gains resulting from their ideas and efforts. [7]

Although profit sharing and employee stock ownership have long histories—going back over a hundred years at such well-known companies as Pillsbury, Procter & Gamble, and Eastman Kodak—and AT&T, General Foods, Xerox, and Honeywell experimented with employee decision-making in the 1960s and 1970s, labor organizer Joseph Scanlon first recognized the importance of pairing these two conditions in the 1950s. Several small- to medium-size companies operating with "Scanlon plans" have long been recognized as being both productive and good places to work, but until recently few large companies have made long-term commitments to employee involvement in *both* decision-making and financial gains. In the years since the 1973 publication of *Work in America* drew public attention to the value of employee participation—and thanks to the passage of employee stock ownership plan (ESOP) legislation in 1974, the introduction of 401(k) plans in 1981, and the widespread use of stock option plans beginning in the 1990s—enough Americans now are involved in one or both of these plans to allow researchers to draw meaningful conclusions about their merits.

In a special analysis undertaken for this study, researchers Joseph Blasi, Douglas Kruse, and Richard Freeman examined data from the U.S. Census Bureau's 2002 General Social Survey of three thousand adult Americans which contained a special segment on workplace issues. The researchers found that about 30 percent of American workers employed in the private sector participated to one degree or another in one of several forms of "shared capitalism": Twenty-one percent received profit sharing or gain-sharing bonuses, 15 percent owned shares in the company where they worked, and 13 percent held stock options (the percentage adds up to over 30 percent because some workers participated in two or even three of those programs). The returns to these workers, above their regular salaries, ranged from infinitesimally small for some to an enormous part of their total income for others.

The researchers were able to document that the larger the share of workers' income that came from the results of "shared capitalism" the better their relations with employers: the more workers felt like owners, the higher their levels of job satisfaction, the better their relations with supervisors and coworkers, the greater their pride in their company, and the more satisfied they were with their pay and benefits. In particular, they were more likely to agree that they "have a say about what happens on my job" (76 percent of "shared capitalists" versus 64 percent of all other workers) and to say that they often or sometimes "take part in making decisions that affect" them (84 percent versus 74 percent). In essence, from both the employee and employer perspectives, the more shared capitalism, the better. However, workers who had to buy their own shares in company stock—that is, to put their own income at risk in order to participate—did not realize these positive effects. The researchers conclude that "analyses suggests that employee stock options are far more likely to drive responsible worker behaviors when they are structured like 'pure profit sharing,' namely, they represent additional incentives on top of a fair wage rather than some kind of wage substitution."

The positive benefits of shared capitalism are multiplied when combined with true worker participation in decision-making. Again, the extent to which workers participate is key: the more, the better. To measure this effect, survey respondents were grouped into four categories: A (workers with low levels of participation in both decision-making and financial gains); B (workers with low levels of participation in decision-making who nonetheless participated in financial gains); C (workers with high levels of participation in decision-making but who did not participate in financial gains); and D (workers who had high levels of participation in decision-making and participated in financial gains). When the respondents in each category were asked, "If you were to see a fellow employee not working as hard, or as well, as he or she should, how likely would you be to do nothing?" their likelihood of doing nothing was a clear function of the degree of their participation in decision-making and company gains: only 17 percent of high-participation group D said they would do nothing, as opposed to 32 percent in low-participation group A.

The same two factors also increase employee loyalty. When workers in the four groups were asked how likely it is that they would look for a new job with another employer within the next year, 29 percent of low-participation group A said they were very likely to do so, compared to only 9 percent of high-participation group D. Again, on all measures relating to relations with supervisors and coworkers, and satisfaction with coworkers, the more deeply workers are engaged in self-management, the better for them and their employers. When that participation is coupled with significant stock ownership and profit sharing, the positive effects are markedly greater.

While none of this should come as news, it should be seen as a call for change. Only a small percentage of American employers make concerted attempts to provide high levels of worker participation in decision-making along with, and linked to, high levels of worker participation in their company's financial returns.[8] But it makes sense economically, psychologically, and practically that, the more that employees are as fully engaged as executives in the most important managerial aspects of the company, the more they will think and act like those executives. And, morally, the two conditions are inextricably linked:

participation in decision-making without participation in financial gains is unjust because others (executives and shareholders) reap the fruits of employee contributions. And participation in a company's financial gains without participating in decision-making also is unjust because workers are powerless to influence the conditions that determine the size of their paychecks.

included such things as allowing a single employee to handle a complete service transaction and permitting workers who assemble a product to certify its quality. In most cases, such efforts led to increased employee motivation and to lower levels of turnover, absenteeism, and stress-related illness.

There is evidence that the growth in employee involvement has slowed, if not stalled completely. In part this slowdown can be attributed to the success of the movement: many aspects of this people-centered approach to management have become ingrained in the way HI employers treat their people. These companies no longer view the substitution of employee self-management for the outmoded processes of command and control as innovative; instead, it is implicit in all their human resource practices. And for some GC companies, the question often is not "Does employee involvement work?" but "Where is it applicable?"

While it is true that not all jobs can be enriched—it is hard to make collecting tolls on highways an interesting task undertaken by self-managed teams—jobs that cannot be enriched are increasingly rare. At least some form of worker participation is appropriate in every manufacturing setting. Even LC organizations can use problem-solving groups, and there is never a case where it is inappropriate for managers to listen, explain, and give feedback to employees. In this regard, companies increasingly have adopted what are called parallel participation practices—processes that operate separately from a worker's regular job—the most popular of which are suggestion systems, attitude survey feedback, and discussion groups. According to our research Center's 2005 survey, over 90 percent of *Fortune* 1000 companies used one or more of these methods.

TOTAL QUALITY MANAGEMENT

The total quality management movement, TQM, had its origins in American munitions factories during World War II and, ironically, was adopted later by Japanese manufacturers: thus, what came to be known as "Japanese management" in the 1970s and 1980s was actually a variation on the far-sighted quality techniques developed in the 1940s by American statisticians Joseph M. Duran and W. Edwards Deming.[9] By sharing operating information with shop-floor workers and teaching them the statistical techniques needed to be self-managing with regard to quality control, "Deming's way" encouraged workers to think like managers, thus creating a sense of mutual interest between the two.

In the 1950s and 1960s, when America dominated the world economy while its main competitors were recovering from extensive war damage to their industrial infrastructures, American executives rejected TQM techniques. However the Japanese, desperate to find an advantage that would allow them to regain their competitive position, embraced Deming's way. They had been introduced to it in the late 1940s and early 1950s during the American military occupation of their country. Eventually the Japanese government offered the Deming Prize to firms that implemented the techniques most effectively. By the 1980s, America had reimported these techniques, even creating our own national prize (the Baldridge Award) to encourage U.S. corporations to adopt them.

In the 1970s, the Japanese auto industry demonstrated to skeptical American managers that TQM methods are useful in producing high-quality goods. Toyota, Honda, and Nissan all turned out cars with higher quality ratings than cars produced in the United States and Europe, and Sony did the same with consumer electronics. At first, American executives argued this success was attributable to the fact that "hungry" Japanese workers—who, only a few years earlier, had been unemployed in a war-ravaged economy—simply were more committed to their tasks than were "soft and spoiled" American workers. This argument lost credibility when Honda and Toyota opened plants in the United States that turned out cars with the same high quality as those they made in Japan. Eventually the accumulated evidence forced American managers to draw a simple conclusion: it was the system, not the workers.

The TQM system involves a number of practices that influence the nature of work, the most highly publicized of which is "quality circles," a method designed to facilitate employee problem-solving related to the development and implementation of quality processes. Popular in the United States in the 1980s, quality circles are a form of employee involvement;

however, the level and scope of that involvement falls far short of the authority invested in the self-managing work teams described above. Whereas self-managing teams typically have authority to manage their total workflow, quality circles can only make suggestions about improving the work processes designed by management. Nonetheless, TQM greatly improved the nature of work because it involved large doses of employee training—including lessons in statistical processes, quality control methods, and the installation of inventory management and production flow systems.

The Six-Sigma approach to quality—originally developed at Motorola and later used extensively at GE and elsewhere—is an American derivative of TQM. Six-Sigma enriches jobs by providing feedback to employees in forms that allow them to learn from their mistakes and successes. Significantly, GE has developed ways to apply Six-Sigma to services businesses. However, as typically implemented, this method, too, does not provide opportunity for true employee self-management. Recently, as the result of its success, TQM has become less of a "movement"; although fewer organizations have total quality management *programs* than they did in the 1990s, many TQM *practices* have been incorporated in the standard operating procedures of most large manufacturing companies.

REENGINEERING

In the 1990s, the reengineering movement focused on reducing costs by eliminating unnecessary steps in work processes and, in particular, by eliminating unnecessary layers of management.[10] This approach to rethinking corporate staffing practices and overhead levels is often depicted as an updated variety of "Taylorism," the infamous "time and motion study" method of job simplification that swept through American industry in the 1910 to 1920 era. Both approaches revolutionized American industrial practices in their respective eras, and both left such nasty aftertastes that their names became synonymous with bad news for American workers. At one point in the 1990s, the very mention of reengineering sent ripples of anxiety throughout a corporation because, in too many cases, it meant doing the same amount of work in the same way, but with fewer people.

Reengineering was particularly useful at companies seeking to become LC organizations. It made large corporations "lean and mean," and that was its intent. However, one unintended, and fortuitous, side effect of eliminating unnecessary layers of supervision was that the jobs remaining in a reengineered company often were improved compared to how they previously had been designed. Surviving employees often ended up having greater autonomy than before and, as a result, their work was enriched. But the useful idea that organizational structures could be redesigned to be made more efficient got lost in the search for reduced costs and, in the end, reengineering simply came to mean downsizing. Like employee involvement and TQM before it, reengineering faded partly as a result of its success: reducing unnecessary layers of management has become an accepted practice in almost all large organizations today.

OFFSHORING

U.S. companies offshore key operations to: (1) take advantage of lower wages paid in other countries, (2) do tasks Americans are unwilling to do, (3) make use of special skills found elsewhere, and (4) gain access to local markets. Regardless of why companies offshore, the practice almost always affects the nature of work remaining in the United States. In addition to causing work that cannot be enriched to be exported, it also can generate greater use of IT and often requires the use of virtual teams in which Americans work with, manage, and are managed by individuals from other countries whom they may not have met or ever will meet. Offshoring also may create management and technical jobs in the United States to coordinate the work done abroad—and sales, marketing, and services jobs in this country to deal with American customers for the foreign-made products.

There is a clear rationale for moving jobs offshore when the work involved requires special skills that can be obtained readily overseas and at a low wage. Chinese factory workers have the skills and dexterity necessary to do the small-finger assembly work that Americans will no longer do, and they are willing to do so for ten percent of what Americans would earn for the same work, if they were willing to do it. As mentioned, American toy companies have moved almost all their work offshore, mainly to China, and clothing manufacturers are offshoring to less-developed countries around the world. In fact, almost all simple and repetitive manufacturing jobs in most industries have been offshored to places where they can be done at the lowest cost. As mentioned, in most cases, these are jobs that cannot be automated efficiently. They also are jobs that cannot be enriched, or made more interesting, for an educated workforce. Because they cannot be upgraded to add more value or to utilize higher skills, objectively, they don't warrant being done in a high-wage economy. Thus, there is a somewhat positive side to exporting low-value-added jobs: in many, if not most, cases these jobs are not particularly satisfying or rewarding for American workers. While such jobs doubtless could provide employment for low-skilled Americans, there is another and better solution to their employment needs: increase their skills so that they can add higher amounts of value and thus have better jobs and lives.

Not all offshoring involves low-wage, low-value-added work. As noted, some American GC corporations are moving engineering and software jobs offshore. Typically, there are three reasons for this:

1. People can be found abroad who can do these jobs as well as Americans, but for a much lower wage.
2. When manufacturing labor is done abroad, it is also necessary to have local engineers and managers.
3. Moving work offshore may allow for a twenty-four-hour workday and, as a result, quicker development and delivery of products. For example, heavy construction and engineering firms can have employees working eight-hour shifts at three different places around the world, tripling the speed of design completion.

When design work is shifted offshore, America loses interesting and challenging jobs. Yet, to the degree this leads to a competitive advantage for a U.S.-based corporation, it may end up generating more "good jobs" in this country. At a minimum, globalization may allow a U.S.-based corporation to win contract work it otherwise might lose, and thus at least some good U.S. managerial and technical jobs are preserved.

The 2005 strike by members of Boeing's main union illustrates the complex issues raised by offshoring. As Boeing has found engineers and other skilled workers overseas who are willing to work for less than Americans, there has been increasing pressure on U.S. aircraft unions to reduce their members' wages. But that issue is just the tip of the iceberg. For years, Boeing has been among America's leading exporters, and traditionally most of the parts in its commercial aircraft were made in the United States. But recently, the company announced that 60 to 70 percent of the components in its new 787 Dreamliner will be sourced overseas: wings in Japan, engines in England, passenger doors in France, central fuselage in Italy, and parts of the rudder in China. A large part of the company's decision to offshore this work was not to save money but to respond to pressures exerted by foreign governments who insisted on getting jobs for their own workers as a condition for allowing their national airlines to buy the "made-in-America" planes. European manufacturers have had to make similar concessions to sell their Airbus planes. The lesson here is of central importance: *America is not alone: all advanced industrial nations are experiencing the loss of manufacturing jobs as the result of offshoring.*

TOTALING UP THE CHANGES

In sum, offshoring, when coupled with the effects of information technology, is having a profound effect on the nature of work being done by Americans. And when those effects are added to the cumulative impact of employee involvement, TQM, and reengineering, the result is a reshaping of many, if not most, domestic jobs. There is some evidence that the combined effects of these changes has been to improve the nature of work in America. The accompanying table presents data from the University of Michigan's 1977 and 2002 national surveys of American workers. Note that items having to do with the work itself indicate a positive trend: Americans today feel they have more freedom and opportunities to learn on the job and to do more meaningful work than they did in the 1970s:

Percent of workers responding "strongly agree"	1977	2002
I have the freedom to decide what I do on my job.	18.1	24.1
My job requires that I keep learning new things.	45.4	62.3
It is basically my responsibility to decide how my job gets done.	32.3	54.6
I have a lot of say about what happens on my job.	20.8	31.9
I decide when I take breaks.	22.6	53.1
My job requires that I be creative.	20.4	45.2
The work I do is meaningful to me.	26.9	66.0
My job lets me use my skills and abilities.	27.8	68.5

These data come from a cross-section of the entire U.S. workforce. Doubt-less, the results would be different if the information was disaggregated by industry or by company size. Since those distinctions were not made, these numbers may understate how positively better-educated, professional, tech-nical, and managerial workers feel about their jobs and, in particular, how employees in GC and HI companies evaluate theirs. And, likewise, the numbers may overstate how less-educated people in poorly paid jobs at LC companies feel about theirs.

Despite the overall positive change between 1977 and 2002, there still are significant numbers of bad jobs in the United States. It is hard to docu-ment precisely what those jobs are and where they are found, but they are predominately in organizations that offer services to domestic customers. That conclusion is based on economic reality: employers who can do so will offshore (or automate) low-value-added jobs; otherwise they would end-up paying those who do them more than they receive in economic benefit. Hence, the bad jobs left in the domestic economy are ones that can't be au-tomated or offshored: people are still needed to take tickets at movie theaters and sports stadiums, serve food and wash dishes in restaurants, haul bags of cement at construction sites, clean toilets and mop floors in offices and ho-tels, pick fruit and vegetables on farms, and mow the lawns at suburban homes. These and other routine and laborious tasks cannot be done abroad, and so far no technology has been developed to do them effectively. For as long as that is true, the domestic U.S. economy will have some jobs that do not require high levels of skill, are not particularly interesting or rewarding, but are paid relatively well compared to the value they add (pay that, at the same time, is too little to support a family). Thus we will continue to live in an advanced economy that pays relatively high wages for some jobs that are simple, repetitive, and low-value-added, and that work will continue to at-tract immigrants, legal and illegal.

The need for people to do the bad jobs Americans won't do—or won't do for the wages employers are willing to pay—is the major attraction of low-skilled workers to the United States. While the many and complex issues in-volved in immigration policy are beyond the scope of this book, it is clear that no discussion of legal and illegal workers in this country can ignore the fact that they are here doing jobs Americans want them to do, and are paying them to do. At a minimum, recognition of that fact highlights the hypocrisy of mis-treating alien workers and denying them basic social services.

REDUCED SUPERVISION

Historically, the most important relationships in corporations were hierarchical: all workers reported to bosses who told them what to do. Lateral relationships were unimportant because bosses coordinated the efforts of workers' peers as well. The problem with such traditional, hierarchical management is that it is neither efficient nor effective. Indeed, rectifying those fatal shortcomings was at the heart of employee involvement, TQM, and reengineering—all of which were predicated on the assumption that workers in teams can add value by managing their own work processes and relationships with fellow employees. As a result of those reforms, American workers, particularly in HI and GC companies, increasingly find themselves organized in teams responsible for establishing and managing their own lateral relationships. The net results are less need for supervision and greater value-added by employees.[11]

WL Gore and Associates is a sterling example of an HI organization with minimal supervision. This $1.5 billion company with six thousand employees makes a thousand different products, ranging from such well-known fabrics as Gore-Tex to synthetic blood vessels used in surgery. Since its founding in 1958, the company has operated pretty much without bosses, rules, hierarchy, rank, titles, or job descriptions. To nurture a sense of community and to facilitate communication, the organization is broken down into numerous separate facilities, usually with 150 to 200 workers at each one. The company practices what its founder, the late Bill Gore, called "non-management": new hires are assigned to a team and then simply told, "Go find something useful to do." Each year, all team members evaluate each other's performances to determine compensation.

Various factors have led to a reduction in the number of levels of management in organizations and, especially, in the number of supervisors. Decades of experience at WL Gore, Lincoln Electric, and other HI companies demonstrate that supervisors are simply overhead and do not add value to what workers do. In traditionally managed companies, front-line supervisors play the role of traffic cops: they enforce rules and give out tickets (punishment) to offenders. By analogy, workers in those organizations are constantly looking over their shoulders to see if a cop (supervisor) is getting ready to swoop down and issue a ticket (a bawling out, or reprimand). Such behavior is not only nonproductive; it leads to conflict: workers hate the supervisors who, as a result of being viewed as martinets, suffer from low self-esteem, which they then take out on the employees.

Today there is a greatly reduced need for "cops" in workplaces, as IT has contributed to the flattening of organizations and the reduction of supervision, providing the communication links and access to knowledge and skills integral to effective self-management. Even in large companies where the face-to-face communities of workers found at HI companies don't exist, IT facilitates the ability of team members to coordinate their own efforts. When team members have instant access to the information they need to manage their own processes, they don't need supervisors. A virtuous circle is established: when employees use IT to get information and knowledge, they need less supervision, which gives them more control over their tasks which, in turn, increases the degree to which their jobs are motivating and satisfying and their efforts are productive.

DECLINE OF "JOBS" AND RULES

Until recently, organizations depended on formal job descriptions to manage and control worker behavior. That approach is fairly effective in stable times and in predictable environments, but it doesn't work in a highly competitive arena characterized by constantly changing demands and challenges and in which knowledge is the core capability needed for success.[12] Now the traditional notion of a "job" is changing, if not disappearing. Jobs and job descriptions are no longer the basic molecules of the way many American businesses organize and manage tasks; instead, companies often use flexible work-assignment descriptions, such as the titles of the projects an individual is working on, the "deliverables" of those projects, and how the individual's contributions will be measured. These dynamic descriptions change as projects are completed and employees are given new responsibilities and assignments.

As hierarchies, close supervision, and job descriptions are disappearing at the most progressive employers, the rigid rule-books that once were the governing bibles of American workplaces also are on the path to extinction. Rules are the backbone of bureaucracy, stifling initiative and handcuffing employee efforts to respond to customer demands. Because the creation of knowledge knows no rules, companies like WL Gore—whose basic business is innovation—have sought to liberate their employees to solve problems, invent new products, and make fast decisions without needing approval from layers of management. In place of rules, WL Gore has four governing principles:

1. Try to be fair with all associates, suppliers, and customers.
2. Allow, help, and encourage all associates to grow in knowledge, skill, and scope of responsibility.
3. Make commitments and keep them.
4. Consult with others before making high-risk decisions that would endanger the enterprise.

When the company's founder, Bill Gore, was a young research scientist at DuPont, he discovered how to color code wires by dipping them in plastic, an invention that facilitated the electronics revolution of the last fifty years. However, because of layers of bureaucracy and reams of rules at DuPont, he could not get a hearing for the idea and had to leave the company to develop it. The lesson he learned was that scientific knowledge was not enough: success depends as much on having effective organizational structures to implement new products as it does on the genius of inventors. Gore vowed to create an organization that would encourage, rather than stifle, employee initiative and innovation.

Today, all WL Gore employees are encouraged to spend about 10 percent of their time developing long-term, speculative ideas, and everyone is free to launch a new team to commercialize an idea whenever they are able to attract followers. Gore's practices are structured so that no employee suggestion is ever rejected with a flat "That's a bad idea." When the company decides an employee-generated project isn't going to succeed, it has a champagne celebration and then funds the next new idea. The entire company is a kind of R&D lab in which production workers, researchers, and sales people work side by side. Today, as knowledge has become key to America maintaining its leadership in the world economy, an increasing number of organizations are drawing on the liberating managerial ideas and practices Gore (and other farsighted executives at such HI companies as Nucor in the steel industry and Whole Foods in retailing), put into practice in the last half century. Those ideas are slowly changing the nature of work in America.

What slows the transformation is fear among traditional managers that they will lose control of their organizations if employees become self-managing. In practice, the grounds for such fear turn out to be both true and false. Organizations do risk getting out of alignment if something isn't put in the place of traditional controls. That something can be guiding values like WL Gore's principles, or methods that encourage employee self-control and accountability. For example, in some large corporations, managers give employees regular and constant feedback about how well they are performing and hold them accountable for results. And IT makes measuring the results of individual and small-team efforts increasingly practical. Once a system of measurement is in place, workers can be made responsible for whole tasks, given autonomy from close supervision and feedback about their performance, and then held accountable. When managed correctly, this process increases employee motivation and satisfaction and creates the possibility of evaluating and rewarding people more effectively and fairly. Effective worker self-control then replaces initiative-stifling micromanagement.

There is little question that work today is different from what it was thirty years ago. On balance, the changes have been positive. The work Americans now do is more likely to be enriched, challenging, and controlled by employees than it was in even the quite recent past. Workers also are more likely to get feedback about how well they and their organization are performing. As a result, many experience greater autonomy and accountability on the job. The major shortcoming of these positive changes is that they have not been as broadly or deeply implemented as one would expect given their positive benefits. Their application too often has been sporadic and inconsistent and, in too many jobs in the services sector, they have not been applied at all. The challenge moving forward is to create more good work for Americans to do.

4

THE EMPLOYMENT RELATIONSHIP

The relationship between employees and their employer is a kind of contract or agreement—sometimes formal, more often implicit—in which each party makes commitments and, in return, expects to receive something of value.[1] In recent years, the terms of the contracts corporations are offering their employees are intended to lead to a number of positive behaviors related to performance, attitudes toward customers and coworkers, and learning and creativity. The many and varied rewards corporations offer may serve as attractors and retainers of talent, prime sources of motivation, and even public messages about what a company stands for and hopes to accomplish. For example, if a company offers employees the opportunity to develop a new set of skills, it is establishing a "brand" as an employer seeking workers with a desire to learn. In sum, the employment relationship today has become complex, nuanced, and strategic.

Looking back three decades, we can see that the way large American companies dealt with their side of the employment contract was rather straightforward and relatively similar in most industries. Pay rates were determined largely by an analysis of the content of jobs and by a comparison with what workers in similar jobs in other companies were paid. Based on that analysis, workers were assigned a pay grade, and the amount of pay they received from there on depended on how long they were in a job and, to a lesser degree, how well they performed it. Annual pay increases were based largely on inflation and changes in overall labor market demand, and the only way to get a large raise was to be promoted. Benefit packages were standard and typically included health insurance, a pension, disability pay, and some paid vacation and illness days. Some companies also offered life insurance and discounts on company products. In 1973, the cost of benefits in U.S. firms was 32 percent of the cash compensation of a typical worker.[2]

An important part of the reward package for many white-collar and managerial workers was the promise of a career with a company, combined with a virtual guarantee of a job for life or, at least, until age sixty or so. That promise often was backed by a well-funded pension plan that included comprehensive medical insurance. At major corporations like IBM and AT&T, managers and professionals had every reason to believe that—unless they were outrageously disruptive, irresponsible, lazy, or engaged in criminal behavior—they could count on a job for life. Above-average performers also could expect upward mobility and increasingly higher pay at each step up the corporate hierarchy. Corporations signaled to their "exempt" (managerial and professional) employees that they had careers, not just jobs, by rewarding their seniority. In many respects, companies protected these employees from risks associated with unemployment, ill-health, and aging. A company even sheltered exempt employees from the effects of its, and their, poor performance. In sum, the employment relationship that prevailed in America was based on "loyalty": as long as employees were loyal to the organization, the organization would be loyal to them.

However, there was a second, and considerably different, contract for hourly, or "nonexempt," employees. Although these workers often enjoyed relatively high salaries and generous benefits—particularly if they were represented by a union—they did not have job security. When business declined, they were subject to seniority-based layoffs or could be assigned to less-than-fulltime work. Further, their careers were limited to hourly jobs, with only the remote chance of promotion to first-level supervisor.

FORCES FOR CHANGE

As the capacity to make rapid change has become increasingly central to the survival of corporations, loyalty is giving way to contingency at the heart of the relationship companies have with all their employees. Because the old employment contract proved to be too inflexible in the face of growing competitive pressures, it has become an endangered, if not extinct, species. The practice most associated with hindering change was corporate commitment to career and job security. Because this commitment made it difficult for an organization to change the skill mix and size of its workforce, today it is seen as the fatal flaw in the traditional employment contract, particularly in Global Competitor (GC) companies. Because the capacity to change requires mobile human capital, GC companies now recruit employees who are willing to learn, reward them with pay increases for learning new skills, bring in new talent if the existing workforce can't be upgraded, and dismiss those who are unwilling to, or cannot, learn the skills the organization needs in order to compete effectively. Corporations no longer make excuses for downsizing their workforces when a decline in business volume or shift in technology requires a reduction in costs or a change in strategy.

The increasing need for rapid organizational change also makes it difficult for organizations to deliver on the old promise of company-managed careers. In most cases, organizations find they can't predict what skills they will need in the future; thus, they can't do a good job of managing employee learning or career development. As a result, executives have concluded that the old approach of systematically moving workers from job to job every few years (so that they develop a variety of skills over the course of their careers) simply doesn't fit the exigencies of a rapidly changing business environment. Hence, for the most part, employees in today's Low-Cost (LC) and GC companies are on their own: no matter how loyal they may be to their companies, their companies say they can't promise loyalty to them in return. Executives do not believe they are being cold-hearted; rather, they say they have "no choice" if they are to ensure the survival of their organizations.

COMPENSATION COSTS

As we have seen, globalization has put significant pressure on U.S. organizations to reduce their costs. Because wages, salaries, and benefits now account for such a high percentage of the cost of doing business in knowledge-based and services industries, those expenditures have become prime targets for cost cutting. This trend also is found in manufacturing where foreign competitor companies usually have lower total labor costs than do American firms. And, because U.S. companies bear most of the direct cost of such benefits as retirement and health insurance, they are at a distinct disadvantage when competing with companies from countries where governments provide those benefits to all their citizens.

Moreover, the costs of both retirement and medical insurance have grown significantly over the last several decades. In fact, benefits expenditures in U.S. companies are now equal to 42 percent of payroll costs.[3] The rapid increase in the costs of benefits is, of course, driven by the out-of-control economics of the nation's healthcare system. To cope with the skyrocketing costs of insurance, more employers are cutting back on the healthcare benefits they offer employees, and more are choosing to outsource tasks and to use contingent and contract employees who are not covered by company benefit plans. Meeting retirement commitments also has become increasingly expensive for many companies, particularly those with aging workforces and large numbers of retirees with "guaranteed" levels of pensions and other benefits.

INEFFECTIVENESS OF TRADITIONAL PRACTICES

In the 1970s, most "exempt" employees at large American companies were paid fixed salaries. Thus labor costs could be lowered only by reducing the total number of people on a payroll. As the financial performance of companies became more volatile in the 1990s, some GC firms began to realize that simply laying off people across the board was not the most efficient way to vary labor costs: reductions in force were slow, retaining the "right" people and getting rid of the "wrong" ones was difficult, termination costs were significant and, often, there were continuing benefits liabilities. In short, corporate executives saw they needed a more flexible employment relationship.

At the same time, there was growing realization among employers that their standard salary and benefit programs were not motivating employees to perform. Research on the effects of compensation clearly shows that paying a fixed salary with annual merit increases does not have a positive effect on employee performance: particularly in times of low inflation, merit salary increases don't offer a sufficient incentive to change behavior. In addition to being poor motivators, traditional salary plans also are weak in terms of getting employees to support the implementation of corporate strategic change, and they do little to align employee interests with company success; worse, they support stability and the status quo, a serious handicap in a world where the capacity for change is a key to organizational performance. And while standard approaches to pay and benefits help companies to retain employees with high seniority, all-too-often they turn out to be the very people companies want to terminate. Worse, traditional pay systems do not serve to retain high performers.

Most traditional benefits also prove to be poor investments from the perspective of employers. Part of the problem is that many benefit packages are uniform, allowing little room for employee choice, whereas individual workers value different things. Some, particularly older workers, are attracted to organizations that have generous retirement plans, but others, especially younger workers, prefer cash now. Similar individual differences exist when it comes to health and life insurance, vacations, family leave, and other benefits: what's good for the goose may be valueless to the gander. In the end, research findings show that workers "value" benefit packages at only about 70 percent of their cost to a company—in noticeable contrast to cash, which they value at 100 percent.[4] Not surprisingly, many organizations today try to reduce their overall labor costs by cutting back on the benefits they offer. Given the increased cost of medical insurance and fixed-income retirement plans, organizations with aging workforces, such as Ford and General Motors, have been particularly eager to cut benefits. The same is true at LC companies: for example, supermarket chains in southern California recently underwent a lengthy and bitter employee lockout in an effort to win union wage and benefit concessions.

All of these factors conspire to make the key elements of the traditional American employment relationship outdated, at least in large corporations.

Such once-hallowed practices as seniority-based pay, lucrative benefits, and job and career stability are widely viewed as unaffordable luxuries in a hypercompetitive global economy. GC and LC companies have rushed to rewrite their employment contracts in ways that are better aligned with the realities of today's business environment. The bottom line: good-bye to loyalty, stability, security, and entitlements.

THE NEW EMPLOYMENT CONTRACT

The corporate commitment to lifelong careers began to fade in the 1980s, and had all but disappeared everywhere in corporate America (surviving only at a few High-Involvement [HI] companies) by the 1990s. Layoff after layoff at such major corporations as IBM and AT&T brought home the fact that not just blue-collar workers, but white-collar and professionals as well, were at risk of dismissal. As mentioned, until the 1980s, American corporations treated their hourly employees as "variable costs" (reducing the hours they worked or laying them off when revenues went down), but they did not treat their salaried managerial and professional workers in the same way. That all changed when reengineering was applied across-the-board. Heads sticking out above white collars were lopped off with the same efficient scythe used to sever those wearing blue.

Some corporations issued policy statements announcing the terms of a "new employment contract," although most simply changed their practices without fanfare. The effect of this new deal has been significant: employees at all organizational levels now realize they need to be concerned about their future employability. What has emerged is a social contract in which employees understand they have jobs for as long as they have the right skills and for as long as the organization has the resources to pay for them. Moreover, corporate executives have become the sole decision makers with regard to determinations about both criteria. "Employment at will" is now a fact of organizational life for almost every worker in the private sector. (And this fact of life is supported by law: in forty-five of the states, employers have the right to terminate employees without cause.) In general, when the provisions of the new employment contract are one-sided, established by employers alone and not in negotiation with employees, this amounts to a redefinition of the nature of contracts. As the eighteenth-century philosopher Jean-

Jacques Rousseau noted in *The Social Contract,* the absence of mutual give and take makes a contract illegitimate, if not meaningless: "It will always be equally foolish for a man to say to another man or to a people, 'I make with you a convention wholly at your expense and wholly to my advantage; I shall keep it as long as I like, and you will keep it as long as I like.'"

According to our research Center's 2005 survey, 49 percent of *Fortune* 1000 corporations have issued formal statements of their employment contracts. Most state that workers are responsible for making themselves employable and that the company will provide jobs only for as long as employees successfully keep up their skills. The following table, based on our survey data, shows how executives describe the terms of their companies' employment contracts. In stressing the importance of employee performance and the need for individuals to take care of themselves, corporate executives have moved a long way away from offering the loyalty-based, career-oriented employment relationship that prevailed in the 1970s.

Terms of Company Employment Contracts	Percent Saying True to Great or Very Great Extent
Rewards are tied to seniority	5
Loyalty to company is rewarded	16
Outstanding performers have jobs for life	27
Continued employment is based on workers' developing their skills and knowledge	29
No one has a secure job	31
Career development is the responsibility of workers	46
Rewards are tied to individual performance	60
Rewards are tied to group and/or company performance	68
Continued employment is based on workers' performance	77

According to some reports, these changes have been nothing short of monumental. A late 1980s Conference Board survey of managers of large corporations found 56 percent agreed that "employees who are loyal to the company and further its business goals deserve an assurance of continued employment." A decade later, agreement with that statement dropped to 6 percent. Yet not all companies have abandoned the notion of loyalty. Particularly in industries where business demand is predictable enough to gain from a long-term employment relationship—for example, in public utilities—there is still commitment to lifelong careers or, at least, to "employment stability." Even among companies facing rapidly changing competitive environments, there is considerable difference in how rapidly they actually will engage in layoffs and employee churning: HI organizations move slowly, if at all, while LCs move with head-spinning rapidity. Even among GC companies, there is significant variation in terms of employment contracts. In fact, most large GCs offer their employees two tracks: a core of jobs at the center that are seen as critical to the long-term future of the organization and, therefore, warranting special rewards and career treatment, and a larger number of contingent jobs at the periphery that are treated as "variable costs." Significantly, few companies offering such dual contracts have addressed the effects on productivity and morale of having two classes of employees, each with different benefits and degrees of job security.

There is also considerable difference in how much support organizations provide for individual learning and development. For example, HI organizations often provide financial support to employees who attend college classes, and provide information and advice about what new skills they should learn and what they can expect in the future in terms of the company's strategic plans; some expect all employees to spend a week or more every year in training programs. In contrast, GC companies—focused on getting the "right" talent today—are less likely to help employees navigate through the labyrinth of information needed to make long-term personal career decisions. The 2002 University of Michigan survey indicates that 70 percent of employees work for companies that pay for job-related training; 64 percent report their employer offers training opportunities, but only 18 percent say they are currently participating in a training program. We return to the latter figure in a subsequent chapter because it is one of the most alarming statistics we found in our study.

Again, the most significant single fact that emerges from an examination of data about the modern American workplace is *its incredible diversity*. Companies today offer almost every variety of employment relationship imaginable. Even within the same industry, and facing the same competition, it is common to find great variation among companies in terms of their employment contracts. For example, even in the most rapidly changing and highly competitive industry, high technology, a few companies do not subscribe to the industry-prevalent view that employees are expendable resources. In an industry dominated by competitors with large numbers of

contingent employees, Cisco, SAS, and Xilinx have chosen to a
resource policies to make them attractive as *career* employers. I
son, they potentially gain an advantage in the competition for ta

While recognizing the enormous variations found among companies,
we provide a brief overview below of some of the most important recent
changes in the ever-evolving relationship between American employees and
their employers. The devil, we find, is in the details of these various and
varying practices.

PAY FOR PERFORMANCE

Although most companies continue to offer traditional merit increases, and
some employees still receive small increases in pay based on the results of
their performance appraisals, there have been radical changes in the compensation programs at many corporations. Recently almost all large companies have made serious attempts to design pay systems with significant
performance incentives. These systems vary greatly in terms of the percentage of annual salary that is variable ("at risk") and in the degree to which
they focus on rewarding the performance of individuals, teams, or the total
organization. As shown in the next table, our research Center finds that an
increasing number of *Fortune* 1000 firms have adopted a variety of per-
formance-based pay plans, including profit sharing, employee stock ownership, stock options, and individual and team-based bonuses.

Percent of Fortune *1000 Using:*

Pay Plans	1987	1990	1993	1996	1999	2002	2005
Individual incentives	86	90	90	91	93	92	95
Profit sharing	64	63	66	69	70	72	61
Gain-sharing	26	39	42	45	53	51	39
Work group/team incentives	n/a	59	70	87	80	82	85
Employee stock ownership	62	64	71	68	71	74	72
Stock options	n/a	n/a	85	87	91	84	88

The most visible shift to variable compensation has occurred at the senior-executive level: the amount of bonus pay executives receive has increased significantly, and even that large sum has been dwarfed by a more remarkable increase in their stock-based pay. Starting in the early 1990s, in many companies the number of stock options and outright grants of stock executives received surpassed the value of their base compensation. There is reason to believe the trend to pay for performance has not ended: the many corporations that still rely primarily on merit pay may now adopt variable pay; and organizations that offer only one form of variable pay are potential adopters of others (for example, a company can offer stock grants, give bonuses to teams, *and* have incentive plans for individuals). Indeed, in practice, all forms of variable pay can coexist, and the case for using them is compelling with respect to the ability of each to motivate performance and make total labor costs more variable.

Variable compensation plans are as attractive to HI companies as they are to GC companies. In the former, they contribute to the effectiveness of self-managing teams, making it clear what a team's deliverables are, what a company's expectations are about its performance, and offering incentives to perform at a high level. Similarly, widespread stock ownership reinforces employee involvement in the management of a business, making concrete the important role workers play in an organization's success and encouraging their loyalty. That is true even when shares are not publicly traded. For example, although WL Gore is privately held, 15 percent of associates' salary comes in the form of stock that they can cash in when they retire or leave (few quit; the turnover rate is only about 5 percent).

A growing body of research suggests that profit sharing, employee stock ownership, and other forms of compensation that tie rewards to company profitability contribute to performance. While this is particularly true for HI organizations, it seems to hold for other types of companies as well. Where they can measure performance, even some LC companies use variable pay because it helps them to keep their labor costs flexible, and, more important, it is the only incentive they can offer to motivate employees whose jobs are intrinsically uninteresting. Almost all companies are discovering that the key to creating a successful pay system is to find the right combination of practices and incentives that align the interests of workers with their potential contributions to the organization. When firms do so effectively the financial returns can be great. Thus, there is every reason to suspect that more organizations—particularly human capital-intensive ones—will adopt variable pay and ownership systems based on performance.

PAY FOR SKILLS

In 1987, 40 percent of *Fortune* 1000 companies in our Center's survey paid some employees based on their skills (as opposed to paying them for the jobs they were doing); by 2005, this practice had spread to 62 percent of such companies. This shift is less dramatic and, perhaps, less significant than the parallel shift to pay for performance during the same time period, but it has challenging consequences for workers. It has occurred for a number of reasons, the most important of which is the growth in knowledge work. The skills of knowledge workers have market value that needs to be rewarded, or else those workers will take their skills to other employers who will pay for them.

The creation of self-managing work teams in HI manufacturing and services organizations also has led to the adoption of skills-based pay. The success of such teams often depends on having a carefully designed pay system that supports the behaviors needed to make those teams effective. When team members have a variety of skills, not only can they cover for each other individually, they can better manage a total work process. Moreover, paying workers for what they can do, as well as what they actually do, is applicable to a variety of organizational challenges, for example rewarding learning when the traditional practice of giving workers raises when they are promoted is impossible or impractical. Skills-based pay makes particular sense in research and development labs and in management development programs where individuals are encouraged to make lateral career moves. Thus, as traditional upward-mobility in hierarchical organizations disappears, motivating workers to increase their skill-sets builds the overall talent capacity of companies and serves as a powerful attraction and retention device for key talent. When a company pays its most-skilled individuals more than it does less-skilled workers, the most-skilled ones are not as likely to be lured away by competitors.

BENEFITS

The entire concept of benefits has undergone a radical transformation as their costs have increased and their return on investment has dropped. What used to be called "fringe" benefits (when they were a low percentage of total labor costs) are now often at the center of major corporate decisions, such as whether to create a new internal job or to outsource the work. Below are some major trends in the increasingly important arena of benefits.

Flexible Plans

In the 1970s, organizations slowly began adopting "cafeteria-style" benefit plans in recognition that employees have different wants, and that one size doesn't fit all with regard to family needs. Under these plans, individual workers are given a set amount of benefit dollars and are then free to "spend them" by choosing among a smorgasbord of benefit options—for example, a pension here, dental care there, and no thanks to elder care. The initial acceptance and growth of these plans were slow because of regulatory issues and concerns about how to price benefits accurately, but they since have become popular. In 1989, 34 percent of the *Fortune* 1000 companies we surveyed offered flexible plans; by 2005, 73 percent of them did.

In the original cafeteria concept, workers could take all cash if they didn't want any benefits or could opt for a small set of core benefits that constituted a safety net; most plans today require individuals to spend a fixed amount on benefits, typically requiring everyone to enroll in basic retirement and healthcare programs. Thus, even though much of the promised flexibility of these plans never was realized, workers nonetheless still have some ability to choose benefits that they value. This approach saves companies money—they don't have to give benefits to those who don't want or need them—and the plans can help attract and maintain workers who want more control over their own lifestyles.

Retirement

Traditionally, company-sponsored retirement meant a pension, what today is called a defined-*benefit* plan. When employees retired, usually at age sixty-five, they were paid a set amount based on their last salary and the number of years they had worked for the company. Typically, long-term employees could count on receiving monthly incomes at levels somewhat below their last salaries, but high enough to enable them to retain a "comparable lifestyle" with the help of Social Security checks. In the 1970s, some 40 percent of private-sector employees were covered by fixed-benefit plans; however, by the late 1990s, the figure had dropped to about 20 percent.[5] That decrease in coverage continues even among large, established employers who are either freezing or terminating traditional pensions because they are extremely costly and their long-term obligations under them are unpredictable.

Today, approximately a quarter of the workforce is covered by defined-*contribution* plans. Under these plans, a company commits to paying a certain dollar amount into a retirement account to which a worker also can contribute.[6] Each worker "owns" all the money in his or her account and often has a say in how it is invested. For corporations, the obvious advantage of such plans is that the total amount they must contribute is clear and fixed: companies don't have to worry if retirees outlive actuarial predictions, if inflation drives-up future costs, or if investments made by the plan perform poorly. Also, companies don't have to fret about government funding requirements.

The shift to defined-contribution plans has been aided by legislation that encourages the creation of tax-free retirement accounts to which employers and employees can contribute, the best-known of which is the 401(k) plan. Defined-contribution plans also allow companies to encourage workers to set-aside savings and assume more responsibility for their own retirement. If employees leave before working four or five years for a company, they may forfeit the amount the employer has contributed; if they leave after that time, they maintain ownership of all the money in their retirement account and the accounts are said to be "portable" to their next jobs.

Perhaps the greatest increase in risk workers are running today is that their company's pension plan may default. The federal Pension Benefit Guaranty Corp. took over nearly 600 insolvent corporate pension plans between 2000 and 2004. The underfunding of pension plans has become endemic in corporate America, with thousands of companies closing their plans, freezing benefits, and denying participation to new hires.

Medical Insurance

Many corporations are trying to control the runaway costs of health insurance by adopting "cost sharing" with their employees. In other words, workers increasingly are paying larger portions of the total costs of their insurance and medical services. At the same time, an ever-growing number of companies simply are not offering medical coverage as an employment benefit or are postponing eligibility until an individual has worked for them for six months to a year. And an alarming number of employed Americans now are on their own in terms of paying for medical insurance: in 1971, 69 percent of private sector employees were covered by company medical plans; today the number has dropped to 56 percent.[7]

Many companies also have backed away from providing retiree medical insurance. In the early 1990s, nearly 50 percent of companies with more than five hundred employees offered that benefit; today less than 25 percent do so.[8] Largely as a result of the decreased willingness of companies to provide employees and retirees with medical insurance, recent estimates indicate that over 50 million Americans are without it. Some workers—young ones in particular—who are not covered by medical insurance see themselves at low risk and are willing to gamble on going without. The opposite is true for older workers, especially those with histories of health problems, who feel they need insurance and are willing to pay for it, but sometimes cannot obtain it because of their medical records. In both cases, the way for such workers to obtain medical coverage is through working for an employer who automatically insures all its employees. Unfortunately, since such employers are increasingly rare, the American healthcare system is burdened with individuals who cannot pay, and the costs of their medical care are then passed on to such government programs as Medicaid and Medicare. For example, in late 2005 it was revealed that 46 percent of the children of Wal-Mart's employees were on Medicaid or uninsured.

Family Benefits

While employers have been cutting back on most benefits, some have become a bit more generous when it comes to helping the families of employees. For example, a 2005 study found that more than 20 percent of employers with at least one hundred employees offered some child day care assistance.[9] However, the quality and quantity of those benefits varies enormously, ranging from first-rate company-run and paid-for day care centers, to providing lists of "acceptable vendors" where employers are willing to share costs with employees. As expected, big companies tend to offer the best benefits: 19 percent of *Fortune* 1000 companies our Center surveyed offer on-site child care.

Thanks to recent federal and state legislation, employee leave to provide care for newborns and for elders is now a common benefit; but, again, the range of these benefits varies widely from the short, unpaid leaves mandated by law, to longer ones in which employers pay the full salaries of workers on leave. In a 2005 survey identifying thirty-nine different "family friendly" benefits—including scholarships for children, paid family leave, and domestic partner benefits—the Society for Human Resource Management found that most benefits were offered by only some 20 percent of companies.[10] Less than 10 percent of companies offered another dozen benefits, and none of the 366 organizations that responded offered paid child care and elder care.

Overall, the range and type of employment benefits have changed significantly over the last thirty years, and employees today have more choices—and much more responsibility for choosing among them—than they once did. Workers now have greater opportunity to contribute to their own retirement accounts, and the ability to manage those funds, but they face greater risk if they fail to contribute to, or mismanage, them. In terms of medical care, even where employers offer it, workers often have to choose among a wide variety of plans and options for which they need to pay a part of the cost—and the risks associated with making the wrong choices are enormous. The net result is that most American workers are at greater risk today than they were several decades ago: if they make the wrong choices with regard to their benefits, they can easily end up with no medical insurance and little or no retirement money.

CONTINGENT JOBS

A "contingent job" is one with an asterisk after it. Although hard to define precisely, the term is commonly used with regard to temporary, part-time, and contract employment (in contrast with "regular" full-time, full-year jobs in which employees are counted on a company's employment rolls and are eligible for whatever benefits that entails). Most American companies employ some temporary and part-time workers, and most contract-out for services, at least from time to time. These workers have different legal standing from full-time, regular employees and are not covered by many federal, state, and local labor requirements and standards, such as those relating to layoffs and firings.

Contingent work is becoming increasingly common because of the flexibility it affords employers, enabling both LC and GC corporations to alter their workforce mixes quickly and to reduce labor costs as circumstances require. In response to employers' changing needs, the "temporary-help" industry has grown significantly since the 1970s, shifting its initial focus from providing office temps to now brokering the services of workers with a wide range of professional skills, including accounting and computer programming. According to the U.S. Labor Department, in 2005, 25 percent of those employed by temporary staffing agencies were office workers, 37 percent blue-collar workers, 20 percent in management and professional occupations, and 18 percent in services and sales.[11] In some instances, temporary agencies provide contract and contingent workers with benefits and even with some employment stability. Despite the growth of this industry, only 1 to 2 percent of the entire U.S. workforce is officially counted as temporary employees, although the percentage is greater in the private sector, particularly in high technology where contract workers are common, but not considered to be temps. Contingent workers also are prevalent in such seasonal industries as tourism, construction, and agriculture. Since many workers temp only for short periods, the total percentage of the workforce temping in any one year is doubtless higher than official numbers indicate.

There is evidence that organizations increasingly hire workers on a temporary basis in order to "screen" them for possible permanent jobs. (Less commonly, workers use temporary status as a way to screen possible employers.) However, in most cases, employers simply want the flexibility of not having a large number of employees for whom they have to provide benefits, and individuals use these jobs as sources of short-term income before moving on to their "next permanent job." (More than half the people temping in a given year end up in regular jobs during the next year.) Hence, in a paper commissioned for this study, labor economist Alec Levenson concludes that temping is not a trap from which people cannot extricate themselves; overall, it seems to benefit those who are engaged in it voluntarily and for short periods.[12] Although temping has a number of obvious shortcomings—low salaries, few benefits, and no security—it provides workers entrée to companies where they often will be offered regular jobs. In this regard, it is useful to distinguish between temporary workers placed through agencies and those who are "on call" by corporations. On-call workers are estimated to amount to 1.8 percent of the workforce and the hours they work are typically at the discretion of their employers. Significantly, the majority of on-call workers say they would prefer to have regular jobs.

Because temporary work is not necessarily part-time work, these two forms of nonstandard employment should be distinguished from each other, not least because they serve quite different needs and populations. A part-time job is defined as one in which people work less than thirty-five hours a week. Although such jobs typically do not provide benefits, they meet the needs of workers who have substantial responsibilities and interests outside the workplace: for example, those with small children or elderly parents at home and those attending school. They also meet the needs of older workers who wish to remain active in the workforce but do not want to work full time.

Part-time work accounts for something like 13 percent of total employment in the United States, and 68 percent of part-timers are women. The Organization for Economic Cooperation and Development reports that most developed countries make use of part-time employees to a greater extent than does the United States: 35 percent of all workers in the Netherlands and roughly a quarter of all workers in Switzerland, Japan, and Australia are part-timers.[13] There is no evidence that part-time employment is increasing in the United States, but some 92 percent of the *Fortune* 1000 we surveyed report they offer it. That fewer workers take advantage of part-time opportunities in the United States than elsewhere is due in part to the typical practice in this country of linking health insurance to full-time employment. In this regard, Starbucks has turned part-time jobs into "good work" by offering its part-time employees decent benefits.

In the last few years, the business media and academic researchers have focused increasing attention on the role of independent contractors. Until recently, this group was a hidden minority, even though they represented 7.4 percent of the workforce in 2005, and 62 percent of the *Fortune* 1000 companies our Center surveyed employed them. Contractors differ from temporaries in that they are much more likely to be older, white, male, and college-educated, and the terms of their employment relationships are far more positive from an employee perspective. Contract workers are twice as likely to be managers and professionals and four times as likely to be in construction and extraction industries than are temps. And contractors are far more likely to be satisfied with their status: 80 percent of them say they prefer to be independent contractors rather than regular employees.[14]

Contract employees often receive somewhat higher wages than do regular employees, but they are on their own when it comes to benefits and, by definition, their job security is limited to the length and conditions of their contracts. Contract employment appeals to some workers because of the independence it gives them from organizational politics and bureaucracy, as well as the freedom to move quickly and easily to the "next interesting job." The risk career contractors run is that they must maintain readily marketable skills to get that "next" job, which also requires them to maintain a broad network of well-placed contacts so they can be made aware of employment opportunities as they arise.

The entertainment industry offers an example of how contract employment can benefit both labor and management: the model serves studios and producers who need to employ skilled individuals for short periods of time, and it serves "the talent" (writers and actors) who are free to participate in productions of their choice. (In "the old days," talented actors were contracted to studios and often were prohibited from taking attractive roles offered by competing producers.) The system works to the benefit of all today because a variety of trade and professional unions give support to most workers in the industry. Unions representing actors, musicians, writers—and a host of technical jobs and professions—negotiate contracts with studios and producers. What is most unusual, these unions provide a number of services normally provided by employers: health insurance, retirement benefits, even retirement homes, and, for some professions, they collect royalties and fees (in the music industry, the union monitors the use of music on the air to ensure its composer/musician members get their fair royalties). Talented, contract computer programmers and designers in Silicon Valley are evolving similar types of institutional support, akin to traditional guilds, to reduce the risks they face in their industry.[15]

CHANGES, CHANGES, CHANGES

Recent changes in the structure of employer organizations, the nature of work and jobs, and the terms of the evolving employment contract add up to a radically transformed American workplace. As the hierarchical, bureaucratic, and monolithic manufacturing corporation has given way to dynamic new forms of business organizations, traditional notions of jobs and careers have disappeared. What has emerged is a complex new set of relationships between employers and employees. In general, if yesterday's working conditions were characterized by stability, predictability, and security, today's world of work is about variety, choice, and change:

◻ Technological change, in particular the increased use of IT, is radically altering work conditions.

◻ Work is becoming more knowledge-intensive and services-oriented.

◻ Today's workers face increasing risks in terms of job security, salaries, the availability and levels of benefits, and the need to manage their own careers.

◻ The emerging transactional employment relationship is based more on current performance and skills than on long-term loyalty.

◻ Large American corporations offer increasingly varied conditions of work: some provide good, high-paying jobs and others no more than a day's pay for a day's work.

We now turn to a detailed examination of the consequences of these trends on the increasingly diverse American workforce.

PART III

CONSEQUENCES FOR THE AMERICAN WORKER

As the workplace has been transformed over the last three decades, the consequences for American workers have been as mixed as the nation's workforce is diverse, as these examples illustrate:

- With regard to their chances of finding good jobs and careers, there is a growing chasm between those workers with higher educations and those who are less-educated. The changing relative fortunes of African American workers are reflective of these changes in the overall workforce. In 1985, 12.1 percent of American workers were black, of whom 4.6 percent were in managerial jobs. In 2003, blacks comprised 13.8 percent of the workforce and 6.5 percent of managers (including three CEOs of *Fortune* 100 companies). The gain in the percent of African American professionals was slightly greater. At the same time the employment status of those better-educated managers and professionals was improving, the gap between their incomes and those of the least-educated African Americans grew markedly.[1]
- Older and less-educated men experience shorter job tenure and lower relative compensation than in the past. In contrast, better-educated women are earning more and have improved career prospects.
- The incomes of people with similar demographic characteristics now vary considerably, in contrast to the small differences found in the recent past.

☐ Many workers are reporting greater satisfaction with their work, more rewarding careers, and increased opportunities for mobility; at the same time, many others are experiencing greater on-the-job stress, increased tensions between work and family responsibilities, and a loss of meaning and community in the workplace.

☐ Even after eliminating 3.4 million factory jobs in the United States between 1998 and 2005, domestic manufacturers are reporting a shortage of skilled machinists and other qualified production technicians.

In the chapters that follow we explore how workplace changes of the last thirty years have affected the careers, jobs, health, and family lives of American workers, identifying the benefits that have accrued to the winners and the costs borne by the losers.

CAREERS

1970's
→ education did not have to direct into a particular career
→ careers are ≠ interconnected

A career involves an individual's progress over the course of his or her occupational life. When they are asked, less than 50 percent of workers think of themselves as having a career; instead, most say they have a *job*.[1] Indeed, people in poorly paid, unattractive, dead-end jobs truly don't have careers; at best, over a long period of time they may have a series of jobs that pay decent wages. With some exceptions, the concept of a career is applicable mainly to technical, managerial, and professional workers. Since the early 1950s, almost all workers who have thought in terms of having careers have needed at least some higher education; in recent years, a college degree has become a minimal requirement. Today, even a college degree doesn't guarantee a good job, let alone a rewarding career. A lot has changed since the 1970s, and the changes have not been good for everyone.

When college seniors prepared to look for their first jobs in the thirty or so years following World War II, they had confidence in finding starting positions at "good employers" such as IBM, AT&T, Dow, and Polaroid. These young people usually had some choice among employers, and there was relatively little problem if their college majors didn't match up with the business needs of the companies recruiting them. The companies treated these young workers as "trainees" and their starting jobs were merely the first rungs on career ladders they could expect to climb if they worked diligently and were loyal. The trainees might not have been paid spectacularly in their first jobs, but almost immediately they became eligible for a generous package of benefits, including healthcare and a pension. If all went well, sometime in their mid-forties they could expect to enter top management and, perhaps, even gain a company-paid membership in the local country club. Their futures, in effect, were laid out before them. In this career model, as we have noted, workers gave a company their loyalty, and they were repaid with security and predictability.

For those young people in the postwar era who were interested in pursuing a profession rather than a business career, entrance into graduate school was not as difficult as it is today. Universities were rapidly expanding their professional schools and were eager to fill them. Those who obtained advanced degrees in law, dentistry, and other professions were able to choose from a variety of job offers. However, for the most part, a university graduate didn't need an advanced degree to obtain a "professional" job. Typically, a bachelor's degree from a good college or university was sufficient and the degree holder could expect to be launched successfully on a predictable career path within a few months after graduation.

Although college graduates at that time—especially men—didn't have to worry much about finding a good job, the norms of society and institutional inflexibility limited their options in other ways. Corporate employees often were expected to become "organization men" and to adapt their lifestyles to conform to company values. Gender stereotyping considerably narrowed the choices available to professional women, and the options open to African Americans were even more limited. Indeed, much of the social protest that occurred in the 1960s and 1970s in this country was in reaction to such social and institutional restrictions.

Shortly after the *Work in America* report was published in 1973, the Aspen Institute created a study group to explore the effects of the symbiotic relationships among work, education, and the quality of life. At the first group meeting, one member went to the chalkboard and drew an illustration of "the canonical life and career path of American men," representing the typical stages in neat little boxes:

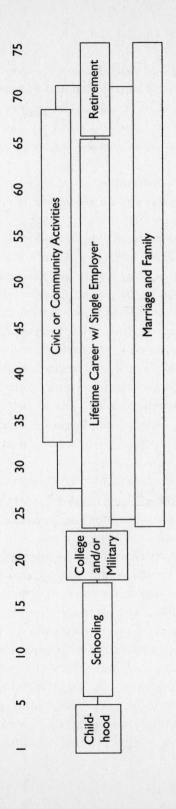

| 1 | 5 | 10 | 15 | 20 | 25 | 30 | 35 | 40 | 45 | 50 | 55 | 60 | 65 | 70 | 75 |

Child-hood

Schooling

College and/or Military

Civic or Community Activities

Lifetime Career w/ Single Employer

Retirement

Marriage and Family

As he finished drawing the chart, he said, "There's the problem: A satisfying life isn't lived in little boxes! Men and women today want freedom and flexibility; they want to be able to choose how to live and, in particular, how to allocate their time and effort among various activities over the entire course of their lives. But our institutions are too rigid to allow for that."

Indeed, the most important message in *Work in America* was a reminder that the main activities of life—work, family, education, health, and so forth—are interconnected. The prescriptions advanced in the report were based on the assumption that all those domains are complexly interrelated, each with significant spillovers to and from the others; hence, decision makers were urged to design policies systemically rather than programmatically. In the 1970s, institutional interconnectedness was not widely understood, a fact reflected in the nation's discretely designed, and ineffective, health, education, and welfare policies. Most employers also ignored the interconnectedness of work and life, and sought to confine their thinking about jobs and careers to activities contained in a single box—their business—as if that arena had no connections to other institutions or to other aspects of an employee's life. Indeed, at that time almost everyone—policy makers, educators, employees—tended to think of careers, and to organize work and life, as if "the canonical path" was and should be the dominant pattern.

Since the 1970s, both careers and society have changed in myriad and significant ways: No longer are the career paths of most women dramatically different from those of men. No longer do typical Americans work for only one employer throughout their lives. (Indeed, they are likely not only to have multiple jobs but multiple careers.)[2] In this era of lifelong learning, education is not reserved for the young. And today some people retire early, some never retire, and some mix work with retirement (and with education).[3] Still, when we discuss careers today we resort too often to thinking in terms of confining boxes. As if to underscore the point, when managers communicate with each other via PowerPoint presentations, as they do increasingly, they almost invariably use boxes with connecting arrows to show how one discrete activity influences or "drives" another. These charts can become quite complex—and the boxes and arrows can proliferate beyond comprehension—as executives seek to explain how a multifaceted social system works (as the new saying goes, "Power corrupts; PowerPoint corrupts absolutely"). They seldom see that the reason their charts are so complexly unfathomable is due to the very nature of social systems: *the constituent parts are seamless.*

Businesspeople are not uniquely at fault in this; we all tend to forget that the parts of a social system are complexly interrelated and mutually influential in countless and often unchartable ways. But today employers, shapers of public policy, and American workers themselves finally must recognize that things have fallen apart and the "traditional career" no longer holds. Today, most Global Competitor (GC) and Low-Cost (LC) corporations do not offer traditional career paths; when they do so it is to an increasingly small minority of their workforces. And today most Americans are no longer willing to be put into boxes. In general, employers want more flexibility, and employees want more freedom.

The simple fact is that careers and career opportunities have changed enormously since the 1970s, particularly for professional and managerial employees who now have many more career choices than several decades ago. The exponential increase in technical and scientific knowledge in recent years has led to a concomitant proliferation of areas of expertise and, thus, to a greater number of professional specializations. Individuals also can choose to work at an ever-increasing variety of organizations. There are many new services businesses, more foreign companies that employ large numbers of Americans, and an increasing number of small-business and self-employment opportunities today. Who had heard of e-tailing even half a dozen years ago?

Perhaps the most important change is in the freedom individuals now have to structure their own career paths. As the traditional "loyalty" model of spending an entire working life with one company began disappearing in the 1980s, individuals began seeing themselves as having a transactional relationship with an employer or, rather, with a series of employers. As a result of more frequent job changes, responsibility for career planning, guidance, and skill development has shifted from the organization to the worker. In many cases, it is now up to individuals to define what career success is and then to take their own steps to achieve it.[4] For many workers, particularly young ones, this shift from organization-determined to self-defined careers is liberating. As the restraints that once confined the careers of "organization men" have fallen off, workers increasingly have become able to make choices based on "individualism, personal fulfillment, and passion,"[5] values in keeping with the zeitgeist of the times. And the new model can be far more cost-effective and efficient for employers: as the human resources strategy of many companies has changed from "promote from within" to "find the best talent," employers are able to acquire workers with needed skills quickly, to free themselves of workers with obsolete skills, and to cut back on training and development expenditures.

But this flexibility and freedom comes at a cost to employers and employees, and to the nation as a whole. Employers lose worker loyalty, employees face increased risk, and both lose predictability. And, unless the nation puts in place an appropriate infrastructure of private-sector practices and public-sector programs to support the emerging reconceptualization of careers, no one will realize the potential benefits. Although individuals now have greater freedom to design their own careers and to define what success means to them personally, they face more substantial challenges in successfully carving out those careers. The greatest challenge is unpredictability. Today's job skills are unlikely to be in demand in the future, and many of today's jobs probably won't exist tomorrow. As one organization now tells its employees, "Every job has an expiration date." With the rapid growth of knowledge, most Americans can no longer safely assume that the skill sets they have are going to be good enough, or needed, in the future. Hence, they must constantly ask themselves: "What's next in terms of technology and business growth?" "What do I now need to learn?" "How should I develop myself so I can make a contribution to a company?" Indeed, they increasingly have to ask, "What is my next *career?*" Some workers can count on help from their companies in answering those questions, most cannot. As we have noted, more and more GC and LC organizations simply say to their employees, "Figure it out for yourself: you must design and direct your own career."

Even though workers are increasingly left to their own devices, the effects of the new employment contract have been positive for many. In the days of the "loyalty" career model, individuals had relatively little freedom to move from one organization to another. If their career dead-ended at one organization, often it was difficult to move to another. As a result, their upward career trajectories were permanently stymied—particularly if they had changed jobs once or twice before. In that case, they often became suspect goods, "unable to handle a job" or "not valued where they used to work," and hence unemployable elsewhere.

Workers at all levels now can, and do, move freely from organization to organization, particularly among GC companies. Instead of being seen as disloyal and undesirable, individuals who make many moves often are seen as being "in demand," while those who have spent a long career with a single organization may be seen as "too set in their ways" or lacking the talent or drive to move elsewhere. Another advantage today for young college graduates is that their first career decisions no longer constitute lifelong commitments. If their initial job choice was not a good one, they can move on. Of course, there are costs associated with changing jobs: individuals may have to forgo the retirement nest eggs that they accumulated, they may have to "go naked" (at least for a time) with respect to health insurance, and they may have to return to school to learn new skills.

Increasingly, it has become possible not only to change jobs readily but to leave the paid workforce entirely for a period of time and then reenter it successfully. This opportunity is available to those who choose to take time out to raise children and then go back to paid employment when their children begin school. The U.S. Census Bureau reports that in 2003 the number of American mothers who were putting work on hold had grown to 5.4 million, an increase over the 4.5 million who chose to stay home to raise children in 1994.[6] While more men today discuss that possibility, if they are in fact doing so they aren't showing up in national census data.

Part-time and contract work is another area where career choices are increasing. Historically, temporary work and contract labor were seen as undesirable and low status, the societal assumption being that no one who wanted a successful career would engage in such work; today that perception has changed significantly. For a variety of reasons, contract work in particular has become an acceptable career options. In a paper commissioned for this study, Stephen Barley and Gideon Kunda summarize their in-depth interviews with seventy-one high-tech contract professionals, most of whom called themselves "freelancers" or "consultants." In Silicon Valley, where they represent between 15 to 30 percent of the total workforce, contractors who independently sign-on with high-tech firms are called "1099s" (after their income tax form) and those who work through agencies are called "W2s," but individuals in both categories make "from 1.5 to 3 times the hourly wage of a permanent employee doing the same job," even accounting for the value of lost benefits. The overwhelming majority of these contractors would have it no other way: they are proud of their autonomy and control over their own time. Their independence, especially their freedom from organizational politics, is a source of self-respect. As one information technology contractor explained to Barley and Kunda:

> One thing I can do as a contract employee that I couldn't do as a full-timer is to be honest, straightforward and upfront. I can say, "Here are the facts." I don't have to worry about politics. On the way in, I say, "I am going to tell you exactly the way I feel about everything. You can take it or leave it. That's why you hired me, to give you my opinion."

One major career choice widely available today was not even considered by most Americans forty years ago: the option *not* to retire at sixty-five or, for that matter, at any age. The Age Discrimination in Employment Act of 1967 forbids organizations from forcing individuals to retire at any age, a dramatic change from the time when most organizations pushed people out the door by their mid-sixties. It is difficult to estimate how many individuals will choose to work past the age of sixty-five in coming years, but there is good reason to believe many will. For economic reasons, many Americans will be forced to continue to work: a 2005 *Wall Street Journal*/Harris Interactive poll found that only 34 percent of working Americans expect to have enough money to retire comfortably, 35 percent said their employers didn't offer retirement savings plans, and 14 percent chose not to participate in plans even though they were available.[7] Worse, the United States government's Pension Benefits Guaranty Corporation reported in 2005 that 60 percent of private sector pension plans are underfunded, up from 19 percent in 2000.[8]

But that is only part of the story: because men and women are living longer, and staying healthier, they can work longer. Attitude surveys indicate that many baby boomers are planning to keep working, at least on a part-time basis, simply because they enjoy it. According to a Rutgers University national survey, nearly 70 percent of Americans expect to continue working full- or part-time after they reach retirement age, with 15 percent planning to start their own businesses.[9] And there is evidence that companies are beginning to see the value of retaining older workers. In our Center's 2005 survey of *Fortune* 1000 companies, some 30 percent reported that they were offering part-time or contract employment to potential retirees in order to keep them on the job, and 80 percent of those say their efforts are successful.

Are Americans better off in today's world of increasing career choices than they were in the more option-constrained 1970s and 1980s? In part, the answer depends on which workers we are speaking of, and what their personal needs, values, and goals are. Research shows that some Americans are overwhelmed by the variety of options they face and the number of choices they must make. Stress and anxiety often result, and some workers have responded to increased career uncertainty with maladaptive behavior, for example, by clinging to their employers when the healthy thing to do would be to quit their jobs. The answer largely depends on the quality of decisions that individual workers make and, of course, the amount and kind of resources they have available. Obviously, those who are not free to choose for economic and educational reasons—and those who make poor decisions about where they work, what skills they develop, and how they define their careers—are worse off.

In all, the self-directed career model offers the potential for more people to develop satisfying careers than the traditional lifetime-loyalty model did. Because the new model allows individuals to define success for themselves and offers them many more career options, there is a far greater chance that the wide range and variety of career interests found in the workforce can be met than under the traditional model. The traditional model worked for many, and no doubt it is missed by some today, but it could not accommodate those who did not want to pursue the monolithic path of slow, upward mobility in large organizations. Countless individuals who were not successful climbing the corporate hierarchy, or in finding a good fit in their first jobs, were defined as "unsuccessful" for their entire lives. Now everybody defines success for himself or herself and, in this relativistic age, that is what passes for an increase in freedom.

Theoretically, the additional freedom for skilled people to choose among careers, jobs, and employers should lead to higher levels of upward economic mobility for some and for greater variability in the mobility of individuals, in general, in the long term. Whatever the economic effects, greater choice and flexibility doubtless will have important social benefits in an America in which more and more people want "to have it all," *but only if work organizations and social policy properly support the new model.* IBM, Capital One, Deloitte and Touche, and UTC are among the corporations that have introduced new development practices appropriately tailored to the emerging career model. Instead of simply moving their employees around according to a staffing master-plan, these companies use their in-tranets to inform employees about what jobs are available and what skills are required to do them, and employees are invited to submit applications for transfers and promotion. And the next step in making the new career model work is for the federal government to fine-tune its training, retirement, and healthcare policies, as we discuss in later chapters.

If the needed private and public policy changes are made, more workers will be able to take time out for educational retooling and sabbaticals, fewer workers will be trapped in dead-end careers, and greater numbers of older Americans will be freer to choose when, and if, to retire. And those Americans who wish to spend more time in leisure and community activities, and less at work, will be able to do so. We expect the new model will allow more Americans to have the kinds of careers and family lives they want. Although the unpredictability of the new career model—or perhaps we should say *models*—can be stressful, even traumatic, on balance it promises to give many men and women greater and better life and career choices than work-ers have enjoyed in any society at any time.

6

WORK/LIFE BALANCE

The poet Grace Paley writes, "The word 'career' is a divisive word. It's a word that divides the normal life from business or professional life."[1] Indeed, as we have seen, the main domains of life are not confined to discrete boxes: people can be, and most often are, simultaneously workers *and* spouses, workers *and* parents. A father doesn't cease being one when he steps into a factory and an executive doesn't cease being one when she is home with her children. Not surprisingly, then, 38 percent of Americans report some tension between their work and home lives.[2] Today's highly publicized work/life balance conflicts are multiple, and their nature differs significantly depending on the jobs individuals have and on their family situations.

☐ Many single parents can't afford to raise their kids properly. Their jobs don't provide adequate resources for day care, family health insurance, and education. For example, only 9 percent of individuals earning less than $15 per hour have access to employer-provided child care assistance, compared to 22 percent of those who earn more.[3]

- ☐ Middle-class, two-income couples have to work long, hard hours to make ends meet, and they struggle to coordinate their schedules to make sure their kids are cared for during the hours when they aren't in school. Some 14 percent of workers report they need to hold two different jobs to provide for their families.[4]

- ☐ Professionals find themselves on the job 24/7 and increasingly must choose between spending time working or with their families. Some professional and managerial couples report working more than a combined hundred hours per week.[5]

It is important to recognize that work/life balance is not "a woman's issue," nor is it necessarily a new one. (Unions have demanded shorter workdays for decades.) However, the issue has come to the fore at the time greater numbers of women with children have entered the labor force and, especially, as more women have been pursuing professional and managerial careers. Since 1975, the labor force participation rate of women with children under the age of eighteen has increased from 47 to 72 percent, and since 1977, the percentage of American women holding professional and managerial positions has increased from 24 to 39 percent.[6] Even as we acknowledge these significant changes, we must also recognize the fact that women always have worked. They worked in textile mills during the Industrial Revolution, and they worked in munitions factories during World War II. Traditionally, they worked as domestics. In the mid-twentieth century, they dominated nursing and school teaching. (The latter career was considered particularly well-suited to a woman who was both a mother and a professional because the work hours coincided with the hours their own children were in school.)

What has changed is that women increasingly have broken out of the boxes of "women's work" and entered the full range of professions, and they have done so just at the time when the traditional concept of the nine-to-five workday is growing obsolete, particularly in Global Competitor (GC) and Low-Cost (LC) companies: the sun never sets on global corporations, retail chain stores are now open all hours seven days a week, and call-centers don't distinguish night from day. Yet kids need to be fed three times a day at regular hours, need to sleep regular hours at night, need to go to school promptly in the morning and come home to adult supervision in the afternoon, and need someone to care for them on weekends and during vacations.

Some data about the American family help to put these conflicts in perspective: Between 1977 and 2002, the average combined weekly work hours of dual-career couples with children under eighteen living at home increased from eighty-one to ninety-one hours.[7] The 2002 University of Michigan survey of the American workforce shows that 80 percent of workers have daily family responsibilities, 43 percent of working adults have a child under eighteen living at home, and over a third have significant elder care demands. Further, dual-wage earners are now the modal American family: only 17 percent of families are comprised of a male "breadwinner" and a stay-at-home wife, and about half of all new mothers go back to work almost immediately.

What is particularly striking is that nearly half of all American children live in a single-parent (usually female) household before reaching the age of eighteen. One reason for this is that approximately a third of all births in the United States are outside marriage, and another is that the divorce rate is over 50 percent. Overall, these changes raise significant issues not only for workers and their families, but for the long-term welfare of the nation as well: somebody has to care for the next generation and, as usual, the burden continues to fall on mothers. A quarter of all American women hold part-time jobs, or jobs with reduced schedules, as opposed to only 9 percent of men.[8]

The boundary between work and home has become increasingly blurred for many American workers, in particular those employed by GC companies. Technological change has made it possible for off-the-job employees to connect to their workplaces at all hours and from all venues. Whether they are at home, in the car, or out to dinner, employees can be reached electronically, and they can work wherever they are found. In the 2002 University of Michigan survey, 23 percent of Americans reported that working at home after hours is expected of them, and 19 percent reported that they received job-related e-mails at home. Moreover, workers are likely to have even more intrusions on their private lives in the years ahead: 57 percent of the *Fortune* 1000 employers in our Center's 2005 survey say they have flex-location policies that include work at home. For some employees and couples this can lead to effective multitasking with respect to work and family, but it also can lead to unsatisfying interference with both realms of life.

Several important legal changes since the 1970s have altered how organizations deal with workers who have family responsibilities. The federally mandated Family Medical Leave Act of 1993 allows most employees to take up to twelve weeks off, unpaid, to care for a new infant or to deal with a family medical situation. Some state laws require employers to offer even more-generous benefits to employees, but only California has adopted a paid leave program.

Voluntarily, some large corporations have designed practices to make their workplaces "family friendly," offering health and education benefits for children and spouses, day care, elder care, extracurricular activities for school-age children, and flextime. Even though such programs often give these employers an edge in recruiting, research shows that they are not being widely used. In particular, smaller organizations are much less likely to offer such benefits. As noted, 25 percent of employers with one hundred or more workers provide some assistance for child care, compared to only 5 percent for firms with fewer than one hundred employees.[9] The 2005 Society for Human Resource Management's benefits survey found that 50 percent of large companies offer parental leave with benefits above the federal requirements; only 30 percent of small companies did. Perhaps the most positive family-friendly trend is growth in the use of flexible hours. The 2002 University of Michigan survey found that 73 percent of workers say it is not hard, or not *too* hard, to take time off during the workday for family matters. Our own 2005 *Fortune* 1000 survey found that 75 percent of those large companies offer flexible work schedules to at least some their employees. Further, the number of companies reporting employee satisfaction with work schedule flexibility rose from 46 percent in 1989 to 62 percent in 2004.

Offering a "family-friendly" benefit is not the same thing as solving the problem the benefit was designed to address. Many benefits go unused because employees believe that exercising them comes with significant career costs. For example, a man who takes a parental leave risks signaling the end of his career with that employer. In this arena, reality is not what employers say but what they do. Today almost all employers say the right things about work/life balance, and many even encourage reluctant employees to take the full vacation time they are allotted to be with their families. But prospective employees must be careful not to take too literally the fine words about generous benefits found in company recruiting brochures. One leading professional services firm offers its partners unlimited vacation time at their personal discretion, but it does so safe in the knowledge that none would dare to exceed the cultural norm of two weeks. And if they did exceed the norm, the firm's high "billable hours" requirement would negatively affect their compensation and career chances.

Numerous factors mitigate against organizations (and workers) doing what they say they believe, and want to do, with respect to work/family balance, including: the peculiar American cultural ethic of taking few vacation days, organizational reward systems that motivate workers to put in long hours, economic pressure on companies to reduce headcount (which means the remaining workforce has to work harder and longer), and the simple fact that many ambitious people prefer work over the alternative uses of their time. We would expect research data on work/family issues to help resolve the contradictions between what people say, on one hand, and what they do, on the other. But, in fact, it is often difficult to square the results of attitude surveys with observed behavior. For example, a 2000 Radcliffe Center and Harris poll found that some four-fifths of men in their twenties and thirties reported that having a flexible work schedule to permit them more family time was of greater importance than a challenging or high-paying job.[10] The 2002 University of Michigan study found that 38 percent of respondents reported having to make the difficult choice between career/job advancement and family and personal life, with little difference between the responses of men and women. Yet many American workers, particularly men, are not being *forced* to make these choices: in fact, they freely choose to work rather than to spend time with their families. To help us to understand this behavior, it useful to review what Robert Crandall, former CEO of American Airlines, has to say about the requirements of corporate success in America:

> For all the years I was working, I was trying to achieve a particular goal. So I wasn't interested in balance. I didn't sail very much. I didn't play any golf. I didn't take much time off. I ran American Airlines and it pretty much took up my entire life. Which suited me fine. I was having a great time. . . . Now you read a lot about balance. In today's world people say, "I have to have a more balanced life. I have to have time for my kids, my job and my hobbies." That's all well and good. But people who worry about balance have no overriding passion to achieve leadership.[11]

In his book *Winning,* General Electric's former CEO Jack Welch echoes Crandall:

> For 41 years my operating principle was work hard, play hard and spend some time as a father. It is clear that the balance I chose had consequences for the people around me and at the office. For instance, my kids were raised, largely alone, by their mother, Carolyn. And from my earliest days

at GE, I used to show up at the office on Saturday mornings. Not coincidentally, my direct reports showed up too. . . .

There's lip service about work-life balance, and then there's reality. To make the choices and take the actions that ultimately make sense for you, you need to understand the reality: your boss's top priority is competitiveness. Of course, he wants you to be happy, but only inasmuch as it helps the company win. In fact, if he is doing his job right, he is making your job so exciting that your personal life becomes a less compelling draw.[12]

Welch then offers some astringent advice to young managers who fret about work-life balance:

☐ Most bosses are perfectly willing to accommodate work-life balance challenges if you have earned it with performance. The key word here is: *if.*

☐ Bosses know that the work-life policies in the company brochure are mainly for recruiting purposes and that real work-life arrangements are negotiated one on one in the context of a supportive culture, *not* in the context of "But the company says . . . !"

☐ People who struggle with work-life balance problems and continually turn to the company for help get pigeonholed as ambivalent, entitled, uncommitted, incompetent—or all of the above.

☐ Even the most accommodating bosses believe that work-life balance is your problem to solve. In fact, most know that there are really just a handful of effective strategies to do that—staying focused on what you're doing and saying no to demands outside your work-life balance, for example—and they wish you would use them.

Welch's comment about his (first) wife having raised their children almost single-handedly illustrates the challenge that many women executives and professionals are experiencing today. One of the most striking things about the biographies of CEOs of major corporations over the last fifty years is that most of these men (as almost all of them were) were married to women who were lifelong homemakers: it took a team of two to make one successful top executive. In those traditional marriages, the man was free to concentrate all his time and effort on his career, while the woman served as his director of logistics: managing the family, running the household, planning and executing entertainment events, dealing with personal business, checking Junior's homework, attending PTA meetings, driving Sis to soccer, and the 6 million other practical chores that add up to a full-time job. Single dads and moms didn't apply for executive jobs.

During the last decade or so, most women executives who made it to the top tier in large corporations also have tended to have long support lines: stay-at-home husbands or rich husbands (or parents) who were able to hire "a wife" to assist them with their personal business over the many years it took them to climb the corporate ladder. And among the ranks of highly successful professional women in the twentieth century—doctors, lawyers, scholars—a great many were single, childless, or superhuman. In sum, until very recently, women were forced to make the difficult choice that men did not have to make: either a family *or* an executive/professional career.

Today, thanks to the opening of graduate and professional education to women, changing social values about gender roles, and the availability of day care and other family-friendly corporate practices, women are entering the ranks of top management (in 1980, the percentage of women corporate executives in America was effectively zero; in 2001 it was 11 percent).[13] The bad news is that they are doing so just as corporations are facing two nearly incompatible pressures: to produce greater short-term profits *and* to provide employees with better work/life balance. It is difficult to make these two demands complementary, at least in the short term, and definitely not given how most business models, careers, and jobs are currently constituted.

But there is some promising news. In the past, researchers assumed a negative trade-off between the demands of work and the demands of family, implicitly concluding that energies invested in one realm were subtracted from the other. But now some studies indicate that work and family activities actually may enrich each other. Survey data from the 2002 Michigan study show that over 55 percent of the members of the workforce feel they "at least sometimes" have more energy to do things with their family as a result of their work. Researcher Ellen Kossek reports evidence that a growing portion of the workforce is "dual-centric," treating work and family as equal and complementary activities, and feeling they can be successful in both.[14]

While there's no definitive answer to the question of how compatible today's work and family demands are, survey data provide one clue. When University of Michigan researchers asked Americans "How much do your job and personal activities interfere with each other?" the answers they received were essentially unchanged from 1977 to 1997: approximately 20 percent answered "not at all," another 34 percent answered "not too much," and only 15 percent said "a lot." Clearly a problem exists for a minority of workers, but that percentage does not appear to have worsened greatly since the 1970s. One possible explanation is that although the demands of work may have increased, workplaces in fact have become more family friendly (or, at least, workers have gained more control over their schedules and can now avoid some work/family conflicts). Only time, and the choices workers and employers make over coming years, will tell if the conflicts between work and family are being reduced.

From the perspective of analysis and prescription, work/family balance is today's most maddeningly elusive workplace issue. Tensions between work and family life clearly have implications for the well-being of individuals and their children and ramifications for society in general. Yet because the personal needs, desires, motivations, and economic circumstances of Americans are so varied, there appears to be no single way to resolve these tensions, no universal best practice with regard to work/life balance. For example, while both may say they want more time off work, the desires of a young, unmarried, high-paid professional for more leisure time are not the same as the work-hour flexibility needs of a middle-class couple with a disabled child or parent.

Moreover, as Winston Churchill observed, broadly speaking there are two classes of people: "First, those whose work is work and whose pleasure is pleasure; and secondly, those whose work and pleasure are one." We too must recognize that there are some people who live to work and some who work to live, as there are some for whom their profession is their identity and the source of meaning and purpose in their lives, and others who seek balance among many activities and relationships. It is simply impossible for anyone to say what is right for others. Ultimately, then, individual workers and their families must resolve these issues.

Individual choice aside, employers nonetheless have a moral imperative to be honest and clear about the conditions and expectations attached to the jobs they offer. Employers need to define the limits to their family-friendly policies: the trade-offs employees are expected to make when business and family interests come into conflict. It is probably too much to expect employers to refrain from abetting employee self- and family-destructive habits—some employers reward those who sacrifice personal relationships for the sake of careers—at a minimum, though, they should be clear in their recruiting about what their organizations' expectations are. Our most disturbing finding in this regard is the subterfuge of some employers who offer benefits they do not expect their workers to exercise. Without question, employers should do what they say and say what they do.

HEALTH AND SAFETY

As far back as the eighteenth century it was recognized that the lung disease silicosis was linked to dust inhaled by quarry workers and stone grinders. In the twentieth century, numerous other occupational health problems were identified and efforts begun to reduce, prevent, and cure the worst ones, most notably carcinogenic diseases caused by working with, inhaling, or being in contact with lead, coal dust, and asbestos. In 1970, President Richard Nixon signed the Occupational Safety and Health Act (OSHA), designed to reduce workplace injuries, accidents, and exposure to disease-causing toxic materials and airborne contaminants.

THE GOOD NEWS:
OCCUPATIONAL SAFETY AND HEALTH

Thanks to the incessant nagging of OSHA regulators and to preventative steps taken by farsighted employers (detailed in Part IV), the worst of the safety and health issues that plagued industrial workplaces for over a century are now memories. Since the 1970s, nonfatal injuries in manufacturing and construction are down by about 50 percent (some of this reduction is due to the decline in the number of manufacturing jobs).[1] But with the possible exception of dangers from exposure to beryllium (used in the manufacture of a wide variety of currently popular products, including cell phones, computers, cars, and golf clubs), workplace exposure to most toxic materials has been brought under control or eliminated entirely. In general, American workplaces are far less dangerous today than they were thirty years ago, and most of the worst occupational diseases have been or are being eradicated.

American corporations have saved billions in lawsuits, workers' compensation, and insurance premiums over the last few decades thanks to preventive health and safety measures, which, more importantly, have extended the lives of countless blue-collar workers. The biggest threat is now a lack of commitment to the ongoing task of monitoring for existing hazards and vigilance in terms of responding to new threats that come with the changing nature of work and the materials used in new products.

THE BAD NEWS: STRESS, STRESS, AND MORE STRESS

A rough profile of typical American workers and workplaces in 1973 compared to their counterparts in 2005 might note the following: the 1973 worker was more likely to be a man, a union member, and engaged in a routine manufacturing task requiring manual skill or physical strength. He worked a clearly demarcated forty-hour week, was likely to have a backache at the end of the day, and may have been at risk from a toxic contaminant in the factory. When he went home, this blue-collar worker climbed into a hot bathtub to find relief from his work-induced aches and pains. The 2005 worker is more likely to be a woman employed in the services sector and using information technology. She probably has more responsibility and flexibility on the job and far less security and predictability than her counterpart did thirty years ago. She and her spouse may work three jobs between the two of them, not counting child and elder care, and they both take the headaches of their work home with them. Today's services worker may be unaware of the physical toll her work is exacting on her arteries and heart, a condition commonly known as stress.

As early as the 1970s, social scientists and medical doctors were offering persuasive evidence that job-related stress is related to elevated risk of cardiovascular disease. The results of their research was so convincing that, shortly after *Work in America* was issued in 1973, representatives of the tobacco industry contacted the Department of Health, Education, and Welfare to see if it could be proved that the causal effects of cigarette smoke on heart attacks and strokes were small in comparison to the effects of stress. (It could not be proved.) Even then it was understood that the nation was paying an enormous total medical bill and that many of the costs—for research, treatment, hospital care, Medicare, private insurance premiums, workers' compensation, and days lost at work—were generated on the job. Because prevention is cheaper than cure in almost all instances, *Work in America* argued that improving health conditions on the job could save the nation billions in the long term.

In particular, there was growing evidence that if unnecessary job stress could be reduced, workers would suffer fewer heart attacks and strokes. Although stress seldom leads directly to disease or death, it greatly increases the risk for individuals with certain identifiable characteristics, such as Type-A personality and obesity. Moreover, a growing body of data suggested that many mental health problems have their genesis at work, and excessive drug and alcohol use are linked with certain occupations and conditions of employment.

Put positively, in the 1970s, there seemed to be an untapped opportunity to improve physical and mental health by changing working conditions. What gave health researchers particular hope was that the nascent efforts to redesign jobs by giving workers greater autonomy and control over their tasks appeared not only to improve their job satisfaction and productivity, but also to reduce their stress. But over the next few years, a closer look at the research revealed that there was a fine line between a challenging job and a stressful one; worse, it appeared that efforts to increase worker involvement and self-management might actually increase stress. That would have been a significant finding: if job enrichment created harmful stress, then the quality of work-life movement would have been laid to rest. However, later research showed that when workers were given more responsibility and, at the same time, more authority, tools, resources, education, and control over their tasks—as they typically are at High-Involvement companies—the actual effect was a reduction in dysfunctional stress. Hence, it was learned that the key to healthy workplaces was to carefully redesign work tasks to provide a supportive environment.

However, by the mid-1990s, the emerging high-tech, global economy had increased stress levels in most private sector workplaces at all organizational levels and for both genders. The manufacturing shift work that upsets circadian rhythms, and had long been associated with a variety of physical and psychological symptoms, was now being mimicked in services workplaces and at home workplaces. Modern 24/7 services work put the majority at risk for health problems once experienced only by the few: where once only top managers were "on call" at all hours of the day and on weekends, the exigencies of global operations and the ready availability of new technologies now allowed nearly every employee to be linked in a single telecommunications network. As such, privacy and sleep were put at risk . . . and leisure time and family life as well.

And stress, which used to be thought of as "man's disease," proved to be an equal opportunity risk as women entered the labor force in greater numbers and worked their way up hierarchies from clerical to managerial posts. The pressure to be on call added stress to the already complicated task of balancing work and child care responsibilities. The supportive husbands some women were lucky enough to find were also increasingly on call and experiencing stress themselves. Recent studies show that the leading causes of absenteeism in the United States today are family-related, and the one out of six people who fail to show up for work offer stress as the reason.[2] Jobs have changed, but stress has remained and spread like a contagion throughout the ranks of the workforce.

The symptoms of stress are clear: anxiety; increased heart, blood pressure, and breathing rates; and increased muscle tension and levels of cortisol (a hormone produced in the brain). The challenge in eliminating the risk of stress is that it isn't a disease, and it even is hard to define clinically in a way that isn't circular. In fact, a little stress is a natural, functional, and even necessary part of human physiology. Stress is the body's response to threatening conditions; it is what helped our ancestors run to safety when threatened by a saber-tooth tiger and what helps us today to get out of the way of an onrushing car when crossing a busy street. Not everyone reacts to stress at work in the same way. At one extreme, a few individuals seem never to exhibit symptoms of stress no matter what happens on the job; at the other extreme, a few individuals get "stressed out" by what most people would dismiss as minor annoyances. The majority, the bulge in the middle of the bell curve, experience stress at work from a common set of readily identifiable factors that correlate highly with the risk of several physical and mental health problems, most notably cardiovascular disease (heart attack and stroke). Even if we could discount the terrible human toll of disease and death, these workplace health problems are expensive: a 1999 study of 46,000 workers showed that the healthcare costs of those at risk from stress-related disease were 147 percent higher than for other workers. [3]

Fortunately, there has been definite improvement over the last thirty years in knowledge about what causes stress at work. We now know that workplaces characterized by conflict and abuse "get under our skin" and we now know how those factors ultimately lead to health problems. For example, researchers say that workers who don't have the resources needed to do their assigned tasks experience "role conflict." A 1997 study documents how the anxiety created by such conflicts activates "the sympathetic-adrenal-medullary system and the hypothalamic-pituitary-adrenocortical axis," which, in turn, may lead to cardiac illness.[4]

It is also now known how to ameliorate the working conditions that cause such physical reactions. For example, studies show that social support can moderate elevated blood pressure. Hence, healthy workplaces are environments that provide ample opportunities for social interaction. In this regard, the Dilbert cartoon strip is good science: a nonsupportive supervisor can make one sick, and the opportunity to schmooze with coworkers at the water cooler is a useful—perhaps necessary—element of a healthy workplace. Workers' ability to control their tasks also is associated with healthy workplaces. Jobs that are unrealistically demanding—ones in which workers have little or no control over their workload or performance—are highly stressful, whether they are in factories, offices, or call centers. A 1991 study showed that workers in situations over which they had low control suffered from catecholamine/cortisol imbalance, a predictor of stress and health problems.[5] Perhaps the strongest point to emerge from recent research is that employees who are able to control the demands of their work are much less likely to experience stress than those who are not.

A lack of work, or inadequate work, also can be stressful. It has been understood for years that unemployment, particularly involuntary job loss, is associated with a variety of physical and psychological problems. Recently, the University of Michigan's Richard Price and his associates have found that job insecurity and jobs offering inadequate income and benefits are linked to the same problems. Underemployment—working at a job below one's educational level or making insufficient money at one's job—is linked to anxiety, depression, alcohol abuse, hypertension, child mistreatment, and marital disruption. Similarly, overwork—working more than forty-five hours a week when one wants to work less—is associated with much the same set of ailments.[6] The Japanese even have a name for it: *karoshi* ("death from overwork"). Significantly, the average American works about 350 hours more per year than the average German and slightly more than the average Japanese. Ironically, working without health insurance is one cause of the stress that leads to physical and psychological health problems requiring medical care.

In sum, role conflict and the related feeling of loss of control—for example, having a job with high performance demands but little decision-making authority, or not having enough coworkers to get a task done—appear to be at the core of most stress-related workplace health problems. Not surprisingly, research shows that socially supportive High-Involvement workplaces tend to be the healthiest for most workers.

8

JOB AND LIFE SATISFACTION

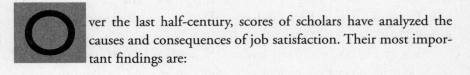

ver the last half-century, scores of scholars have analyzed the causes and consequences of job satisfaction. Their most important findings are:

☐ Low levels of job satisfaction lead to turnover and absenteeism.

☐ The effect of job satisfaction on job performance is weak; in fact, job performance is more likely to be a *cause* of job satisfaction.

☐ Job satisfaction is determined primarily by the type and amount of rewards people get at work (as compared to what they feel they should receive). And workers develop their perceptions of what they should receive by comparing their rewards to what others like them receive.

☐ There is a positive relationship between employee satisfaction and customer satisfaction in some services situations.

☐ There is an inverse relationship between job satisfaction and the desire of employees to form a union.

Oddly, given all the research on job satisfaction, there is no standard measure of it. Thus, it is difficult to compare the results from one study of job satisfaction to another. In addition, since only a few studies have measured the attitudes of a national, random sample of workers, it is hard to draw meaningful conclusions about the degree to which Americans are satisfied with their work, and who is and is not satisfied. While many surveys of job satisfaction have been conducted over the years, they seldom have been repeated. Hence, there is little solid, scientific information on the degree to which levels of job satisfaction have changed. One exception is the 1977 and 2002 University of Michigan surveys, which document an interesting change in the levels of job satisfaction reported by American workers: in 1977, 41 percent of a random national sample of employed adults reported they were *very* satisfied with their jobs; in 2002 that number increased to 51 percent. Overall, in 2002, 92 percent said that they are either somewhat satisfied or very satisfied with their jobs. The Gallup organization also enquired about job satisfaction over the same time period. Changes (albeit minor ones) in the questions the Gallup pollsters asked at different times affect the validity of their findings, but they too found a slight increase in job satisfaction.[1] And the 2002 U.S. General Social Survey of twelve hundred adults working in the private sector found levels of job satisfaction in roughly the same range as the Michigan and Gallup surveys.[2] The 2002 survey also found a small positive change in job satisfaction compared to data from the early 1970s.

Other studies showing lower levels of job satisfaction have put the question to workers in somewhat different ways. Since there is no standard or "right" way to ask the question, and since survey researchers get different levels of satisfaction when they ask different questions, it is impossible to state definitively what percentage of the American workforce is satisfied with their jobs. But it is possible to reach a meaningful conclusion about the degree to which job satisfaction has changed: the Michigan study, and the U.S. General Social Survey, asked exactly the same question of a true random sample of the U.S. population at two different times. Thus, they provide the most valid evidence related to change: job satisfaction shows a slight increase over the last three decades.

There is further supporting evidence that a significant percentage of people feel their jobs are good. When Americans are asked whether they would take their present job again, the responses in the Michigan survey also are favorable: in 1977, 60 percent said they would do so without hesitation; 69 percent said so in 2002. Further, only 6 percent of workers in 2002 said they would definitely *not* take their same job. Consistent with these results are data about the likelihood of workers looking for new jobs: in both 1977 and 2002, about 64 percent replied that *it is not at all likely* that they would look for a new job. This statistic supports the positive findings about job satisfaction and underscores that, if anything, things are getting better in this regard. The only caveat is that, because 2002 was a recession year, after looking around them and seeing many others out of work, some employed people may have been satisfied to have any job at all.

Perhaps the most interesting finding in the 2002 University of Michigan survey is that 54 percent of Americans said they were very satisfied with their jobs, but only 34 percent reported similar satisfaction with their family and personal lives. Moreover, while job satisfaction increased slightly since 1977, satisfaction with family and personal life declined. Of course, job and family life satisfaction are not independent factors—the demands of one can interfere with the demands of the other. Nonetheless, it is striking to find Americans claiming to be more satisfied at work than in off-the-job activities. This fact may help to explain why increasing numbers are so willing to work long hours and say they plan never to retire.[3] When workers in the U.S. General Social Survey were asked if they would continue working even if they had enough money to live as they liked for the rest of their lives, 70 percent of Americans responded yes.

Overall, despite the many observed changes in their employment contracts, compensation packages, and other salient features of work, employees seem to be more satisfied with their jobs today than they were in the 1970s. Whether this positive trend will continue depends on the key choices individuals and organizations must make in the near future. Unfortunately, in the absence of a periodic, scientific, national survey of Americans' attitudes about their work, it may be as difficult in the future as it is today to tell if progress is being made with regard to job satisfaction.

SATISFACTION IN BIG VS. SMALL COMPANIES

In 2005, the Harris Interactive/Age Wave survey of 7,718 adult Americans found several key elements of job satisfaction to be higher in small companies (49 employees and fewer) than in large ones (those with over 5,000 workers).[4] The table below shows the percent of employees at small and large companies who in 2005 agreed with these statements about their work.

	Small Company	Large Company
"I often feel energized"	44	28
"Inspires the best in me"	44	24
"I'm willing to put forth more effort"	61	43
"I feel passionate about my job"	53	36

Workers in the small companies also reported that they received significantly fewer financial benefits than did their counterparts in the large ones. The table below shows the percentages of employees at small and large companies who say their employer offers specific benefits.

	Small Company	Large Company
Bonus compensation	24	44
Stock/options/grants	7	50
Retirement savings plan	29	83
Annual pay raise	34	74

Although this study sample was extremely large, it was not random; hence, the findings should be interpreted with some caution. Yet they are consistent with those of many academic studies conducted over the last four decades and with the results from Society of Human Resource Management focus groups convened for purposes of this study in 2005: in general, employees in the best small companies experience working conditions more positively than do employees in the best big companies. Since more money and better benefits cannot explain this difference, it seems that workers in smaller organizations are more satisfied because they are members of supportive communities in which they know their bosses and coworkers and in which they are treated as individuals. The focus groups noted that employees in small companies feel valued and their bosses are more willing to tailor work conditions to their personal needs and interests. Workers in small companies also seem to gain greater satisfaction because they are able to see more directly how their efforts influence organizational performance. At the same time, research indicates that employees in the worst small companies tend to experience working conditions more negatively than do those at the worst big companies. This is logical; in a small company employees will feel the effects of poor or insensitive leadership more directly than they would in a large company where the effects are buffered by layers of management and ameliorated by public scrutiny.

9

PERFORMANCE PRESSURE

It has been said that Americans are increasingly "overworked." The claim turns out to be true—for some workers, in some jobs, some of the time. A key indicator of overwork is unrealistic pressure to perform. Whip-cracking supervisors can create undue performance pressure, as can demanding customers, incentive pay practices with unmeetable expectations, insufficient staffing levels, and the fear of failure. Such excessive pressures can cause anxiety, leading workers to perform poorly, particularly when doing intricate or complex tasks. (As we have seen, workers who feel they can't meet performance expectations report a variety of stress-related physical and mental health problems.) Under extreme pressure, some workers simply stop trying.

In addition, pressured employees also are more likely to cut ethical corners, say by cheating and falsifying reports. Many of the problems that led to the scandals at Arthur Andersen, Enron, and other companies appear to have been generated by excessive performance pressure on managers and professionals. To meet unreachably high standards, and in response to a combination of financial incentives and cultural norms, employees cut corners and engaged in illegal tactics to "make their numbers." This is a tricky issue to analyze because performance pressures are both bad and good things. No one benefits from lax management: if everyone in a company is coasting, ultimately it will fail and workers will lose their jobs. Organizations cannot succeed unless their employees feel some urgency to work hard and effectively. The best managers thus challenge their employees and reward them when they meet and exceed goals and expectations. When stretched, workers develop and grow, and organizations benefit as well. Moreover, workers who feel they are performing well, particularly when they also feel that their companies are high-performing ones, report high levels of job satisfaction. Hence, there seems to be an optimal amount of performance pressure: if workers feel they can meet standards with a bit of stretching and extra effort, the pressure is functional and healthy; if workers feel expectations are at levels beyond what they are ever capable of achieving, the pressures lead to dysfunctional behavior and negative health outcomes.

Because the experience of pressure is very much a psychological factor, there is no objective way to say what the right amount of performance pressure is, or to measure the amount of pressure employees are under. The best proxy measures are found in survey data in which respondents self-report on their working conditions. In 1977 and 2002, the University of Michigan national employment survey asked two questions relevant to the issue: when workers were asked how hard their jobs required them to work, 58 percent said they had to work very hard in 2002, up from 25 percent in 1977. When asked whether they have enough time to get everything done on the job, 13 percent agreed that they "never seemed to have enough time" in 1977, while 25 percent so indicated in 2002. Further confirmation that some employees feel overloaded at work comes from a 2004 survey by the Families and Work Institute in which 27 percent of respondents reported feeling overwhelmed "often" or "very often" by how much they had to do on the job. Overall, survey data suggest an increase in pressures to perform, with 25 percent of the workforce saying the pressures are excessive.[1]

An indirect indicator of performance pressure is the number of hours worked. American men work about one hour more per day than women (although, among employed couples, women typically do 60 percent of the work at home). A recent Bureau of Labor Statistics (BLS) study found that Americans, on average, work 8.1 hours per day, a little longer per *day* than people in most western European countries. What is clearer is that Americans work more hours per *year* than Europeans (1,792 hours per year versus

1,453 hours in France) and take shorter vacations.[2] This partly reflects the fact that the nation's 12.2 million self-employed do not get paid vacations (self-employment is more prevalent in the United States than in Europe), nor do 37 percent of the American women who earn under $40,000 per year. Although there are no solid historical data on the number of hours Americans worked in the past, there is reason to believe that hourly employees are working less today than thirty years ago because of laws limiting overtime and raising the cost of overtime pay. Yet the BLS finds that one in five Americans do some paid work while at home, particularly those who are better educated. And it is likely, but hard to prove, that telecommuting (working at home and communicating electronically) causes people to work longer hours than they would if they punched in at traditional workplaces.

From what we have documented about changes in the American workplace, it should come as no surprise that a significant number of workers are experiencing increased performance pressure. A quick look at data about the performance of large American corporations reveals that almost all have increased their sales over the last half dozen years or so, but few have added significantly to the size of their payrolls. For example, one *Fortune* 500 firm that we have studied recently doubled its sales and halved its workforce in less than five years. This increase can be accounted for by gains from automation (especially from information technology), more efficient management, outsourcing and offshoring, and eliminating redundancies after mergers and acquisitions. But even when added together, the positive productivity effects of those factors cannot account for all the gains. Some of it came from employees working harder.

There is a little good news about the nature of the pressures people feel on the job: the University of Michigan survey found that the percentage of workers who *disagreed* with the statement that they "had to do things that went against their conscience" on the job increased from 24 percent in 1977, to 69 percent in 2002. That is a remarkably positive finding—even though there is still a problem when over a quarter of Americans report they are facing ethical dilemmas at work. More negatively, the recent spate of corporate ethical lapses appears to be indirectly increasing performance pressures on employees in large corporations. A 2005 research study indicates those publicly traded companies that restated their earnings during 2001 and 2002 collectively eliminated some 250,000 to 600,000 jobs in the months immediately following the restatements, numbers that would account for a significant percentage of all jobs lost in the nation during that period.[3] Embarrassed executives at those companies appear to have been eager to find ways to improve productivity and burnish their financial performance quickly, and nothing is faster than workforce reductions. The employees remaining at those companies would have little choice but to work harder in order to compensate for the staff reductions.

Given the changes in the nature of organizations, work, and reward systems that we have outlined, it is hardly surprising that Americans feel they have to work harder and faster: in both manufacturing and services, jobs now are designed so that fewer people will produce more; pay-for-performance systems provide incentives for extra effort; and changes in the employment contract lead workers to conclude that they have to perform or lose their jobs. Global competition also has caused Americans to understand that, if their companies don't perform, eventually they will be out of work. In many ways, then, working harder is a rational reaction to an economic and business environment far less tolerant of slack than it was in the past. But if these factors conspire to make Americans overworked and stressed, paradoxically, lower levels of commitment and productivity may result. It is almost certain that health problems will.

10

COMPENSATION

Here's the headline: Median family income in the United States grew about 22 percent from the mid-1970s to 2004.[1] And there's an important subhead attached to the story: productivity grew 65 percent during the same time period. Looked at another way, a larger economic pie was created as productivity growth outpaced growth in wages and incomes, and the gains in corporate profitability went mainly to shareholders and executives. One result is that there is far greater income inequality in the United States today than there has been in decades. As the relative incomes of the top quintile of Americans improved dramatically, one in four American workers in 2004 were earning $18,800 or less per year.[2]

There is also less economic mobility: among families starting out in the lowest income quintile in the late 1980s, more than half were still there in the late 1990s.[3] Two key drivers of lower mobility are that now-familiar duo: the shift to knowledge work and the increase in global competition. There also is an increasingly strong correlation between the education level of workers and their incomes: those with less than a college education tend to earn lower wages and have greater difficulty moving into higher-paying jobs.

This may be an inevitable by-product of a knowledge economy in which people are paid for their skills and expertise rather than for their physical labor, but the trend most certainly is exacerbated by globalization, as low-skilled, relatively high-paying manufacturing jobs are now exported. The net result is that the wages of those who have the least bargaining power are stagnating, and there is little reason to believe that situation will change in the near future.

GENDER GAP

On the bright side of the income ledger, over the last three decades there has been a marked closing of the male-female wage gap, in part as a result of women spending a greater part of their adult years in the paid workforce. The narrowing is most noticeable among younger women who, by the late 1990s, earned 94.2 percent of the wages earned by younger men.[4] Strikingly, the gains made by women were achieved at a time when the overall distribution of wages was shifting against people in low-paid occupations. Hence, significant changes in women's wages have resulted from federal legislation with respect to gender equity and the concomitant movement of women into jobs that were traditionally the province of men. In particular, women are far more likely to be in higher-paid managerial, technical, and professional occupations as a result of increased levels of education: the percentage of MD degrees earned by women rose from 6.7 percent in the 1960s to 38 percent in the late 1990s, and similar increases have occurred in the graduate law, business, and dentistry degrees.

WAGE VARIATION

Increase in the variation among the incomes of workers with similar demographics and in comparable jobs has been a relatively unnoticed trend. In one respect, the data appear contradictory: On one hand, job level, type of work, and, especially, education continue to be major predictors of how much one will be paid; on the other hand two people (in the same firm or in different companies) who do the same type of job and have the same level of education are increasingly likely to receive different amounts of pay. The best explanation for this phenomenon is that wages are increasingly being determined by pay-for-performance practices. The implication for workers is clear: as corporations shift toward greater use of bonuses, incentives, and skill-based pay, there will be increasing dispersion of compensation among those who are similar in everything but their performance. In business terms, companies are doing a better job managing their rewards systems. From a societal perspective, rewarding people based on their relative performance is an indicator of a healthy meritocracy.

EXECUTIVE PAY

Trends in executive pay seem anything but healthy if the measure of fair compensation is the degree to which it is linked to relative contribution to organizational performance. In 1970, average *total compensation* (in 1998 dollars) for the CEO of a *Fortune* 100 corporation was $1.3 million, which was thirty-nine times that of the average worker's ($32,522) at the time.[5] Thirty years later, the average CEO was pocketing about $10.8 million per year, some four hundred times what their front-line workers earned ($35,864). During the 1990s, CEO pay increased by 571 percent while the average worker's grew by 37 percent. No matter how one cuts the figures, even moderately well-paid CEOs of large corporations make about as much in a day as their average employee makes in a year.

Even if the point of reference is the more modest salaries of CEOs of midsize American companies, the average for them in 2004 was some thirty-four times that of industrial workers. (Comparable ratios were 13 to 1 in Germany and 11 to 1 in Japan.) In evaluating these salaries, keep in mind the $35,864 *total compensation* earned by the average American worker is exactly that, *an average* that includes the astronomical bonuses of CEOs, sports figures, and Hollywood celebrities on the high end, and the take-home pay of $5.15 per-hour minimum-wage earners on the low end who, if employed full time, make about $10,000 a year. The pay of CEOs in the United States is high not only relative to the pay of American workers, it is high relative to the earnings of executives in the rest of the world, even when corporate size and profitability are taken into account. In England, where the economic system is much like ours, million-dollar executive salaries are rare. Depending on the countries being compared, American CEOs make at least six times more than their international counterparts; in some cases, they earn twenty times more.

As a result of increasing CEO pay, there also has been a concomitant boost to the incomes of other members of the executive suite and, in turn, those of other top managers in corporations—although these trickle-down increases have been far less dramatic than the raises at the very top. Two explanations offered for the explosion of executive pay in America are inadequate oversight by board compensation committees and the creation of numerous innovative compensation "vehicles," such as the granting of restricted stock and stock options.

While some economists argue that many executives more than earn their extraordinary incomes (and a host of perquisites, including private jets, personal loans, and assorted "lifestyle" benefits) as just rewards for the wealth they create for shareholders, in a recent issue of the Conference Board's *Across the Board,* business writer Jim Krohe asked, "Why, in a nation that thinks of itself as a bastion of the common man, do people tolerate social stratification more typical of eighteenth-century France?"[6] Krohe calculated that "if wages overall had risen at the same pace as that of CEOs since the 1980s, the average worker would today be pulling down more than $184,000 a year, rather than today's not quite $27,000, and the minimum wage would now be almost $45 an hour." (Note: Krohe's figure of $27,000 is the average *salary;* the $35,864 figure cited above is average *total compensation,* including benefits and bonuses.) One obvious reason why the astounding increases in executive compensation haven't caused more of a backlash among shareholders is that they represent a relatively small percentage of total corporate expenses: given the total dollar cost of doing business in a giant corporation, even large changes in executive compensation have only a small effect (typically a few pennies a share) on company earnings. It is easy to see why directors, and even large shareholders, have not made a greater effort to keep executive salaries under control.

A rarely researched issue, and one more germane to this study, is the degree to which executive pay has a negative influence on the morale and behavior of corporate employees down the line. If such a reaction exists, it might surface as resentment among the lowest-paid members of the workforce. Instead of seeing their senior executives as leaders committed to the organization—and credible when they speak about what is good for everyone in the company "family"—workers might see the people at the top as self-serving exploiters of the efforts of those down the line. Although a 2002 Gallup poll found that 87 percent of Americans agreed that executives had "gotten rich at the expense of ordinary workers," we could find little hard evidence that the compensation gaps between those at the top and bottom of large corporations do in fact lead to low morale or strong protests among the rank and file, except perhaps in unionized companies. The best explanation for this, offered by Arthur Okun, the late chairman of the President's Council of Economic Advisors, is that most Americans believe in the "jackpot theory" of career success. The essence of that belief is that luck is the main difference between those who "hit it big" and those who don't, and therefore those who are luckiest are to be envied, not resented.[7]

As a footnote, we would be remiss in not mentioning the 1990s practice of granting stock options widely, often across the board, in an effort to create alignment between company goals and employee behavior. In plain English, it was argued that everyone would work harder if all employees made money when the price of the company stock rose. (This belief was stimulated by the dot-com phenomenon in which workers at all levels at such companies as Amazon and Yahoo! became millionaires.) But the practice seems to have ebbed with the recent accounting requirement that corporations "expense" options. While executives in 2005 still received their options—although perhaps less frequently and in smaller numbers—many companies eliminated or greatly reduced employee grants. The result once again was a gap between what is good for executives and what is good for their employees.

EMPLOYEE STOCK OWNERSHIP

Since the 1970s, there has been a major increase in employee stock ownership. It is estimated that roughly twenty-three million Americans own stock in the companies at which they are employed; perhaps ten million hold stock options (these are not necessarily separate groups).[8] Workers own company stock in several ways, increasingly through 401(k) retirement plans (to which their employers make fixed contributions) and through employee stock option plans (some 11,000 U.S. companies have ESOPs, covering 8.8 million workers, or about 6 percent of the private sector workforce). Perhaps two to three million Americans work in companies that are wholly or majority employee-owned. It is further estimated that over two thousand companies, employing some eleven million workers, are primarily invested in their own stock in the 401(k) plans they offer as benefits.[9] And about four thousand companies offer stock purchase plans to help employees buy their stock at a discount, including Wal-Mart, UPS, IBM, Kroger, and Home Depot, covering some 15.5 million employees.

Hence, large and growing portions of the American labor force are practicing capitalists, at least to some degree. A great deal has been made of this fact, and it is often said that it has enormous implications for the attitudes and behavior of workers. Indeed, some evidence does link the amount of stock owned by employees to company performance, although no causal relationship between how hard employee-owners work and the price of their company's stock has been proven. Nonetheless, as noted previously, employee-owners are more inclined to exhibit positive behavior on the job, to stay with a company as a result of their equity interest, and to pay more attention to its financial performance, all of which are positive behaviors from a company point of view. Yet, as we discuss later with reference to United Airlines, few large corporations have taken advantage of the promise of employee ownership by changing their organizational practices to reflect the desire of employee owners to assume greater responsibility for the management of their enterprise.

For workers, there are pluses and minuses associated with ownership. On the plus side, the United Airlines example notwithstanding, significant degrees of employee ownership often increase the likelihood that workers can influence how their company operates. On the negative side, the main problem with employee ownership is that it concentrates employees' risk: not only do their jobs depend on the continuing success of their employing company; their retirement depends on it as well. In sum, we conclude that the attractive promise of employee stock ownership is largely unrealized, both for workers and for companies; its coverage is still limited and it has not yet had a significant impact on the way most American corporations are managed.

11

EMPLOYEE "VOICE"

In the 1970s, the trade union movement provided a voice for the American workforce. Through collective bargaining, unions won wage and benefit premiums for their members and provided a vehicle for them to pursue grievances against employers with regard to working conditions and the nature of supervision. Approximately 25 percent of the U.S. workforce belonged to unions in 1973, and many more were positively affected by the contracts unions negotiated and the political actions they undertook on their behalf. Indeed, powerful unions were an omnipresent influence, affecting the votes of legislators and the practices of almost all employers. The mere threat of being unionized caused many nonorganized companies to raise the pay of their workers and to put grievance procedures into place.

A major decline in union membership began in the early 1980s and has continued ever since. By 2004, only 12 percent of the U.S. workforce was organized. The decline has been particularly steep in the private sector, where less than 8 percent of workers are now in unions.[1] While the public sector remains a labor stronghold, with 36.4 percent of government workers unionized, even there union membership is decreasing as a percentage of the total public-sector employment. A number of factors have contributed to the dramatic drop in union membership, most notably the decline in the manufacturing sector, which had historically been the base of union membership in the United States. For example, as the result of a sharp decrease in the number of production workers employed by American car manufacturers, membership in the United Auto Workers (UAW) has dropped from a high of over 1.5 million thirty years ago to less than half a million today. The automobile industry also provides a clear illustration of the second major factor in the decline of the union movement: the inability to organize new facilities and companies. The UAW has not succeeded in organizing workers in U.S. auto plants owned by Toyota, Honda, and Nissan. In addition, most of the fastest-growing domestic industries in recent decades have remained nonunion: Silicon Valley, for example, is virtually without unions.

The *Work in America* report identified a third reason for the decline of the union movement: inexplicably, union leaders did not play a significant role in the efforts from 1970 to 1990 to improve the quality of work life in America. Although the report cited a few sterling examples of successful union/management joint efforts to foster employee involvement and to redesign jobs to make them more satisfying, by and large, unions took a pass on what proved to be the most significant workplace reform movement of the last half of the twentieth century. And unions largely have stayed on the sidelines during the growth of employee stock ownership.

The failure of unions to participate in the quality of work life (QWL) movement, let alone their refusal to lead it, has undercut their power and credibility. Many of the "green-field" High-Involvement factories built in the 1970s and 1980s—such as the pathbreaking General Foods plant in Topeka, Kansas, featured in *Work in America*—have been able to remain nonunion precisely because most employees have felt that their jobs would get worse if they joined a union. In the team environment at the General Foods plant, employees had greater autonomy, freedom, and opportunity to learn than did workers in a typical union plant. When interviewed about their own interest in union membership, many replied that a union would not provide the kind of "voice" that they wanted. In fact, many felt it would take away from their ability to influence managerial decisions.

The failure of unions to support efforts to improve the quality of work life coincided with, or perhaps was the result of, their unwillingness to speak out on the broader issues of business effectiveness and performance. When foreign competition threatened the survival of American manufacturers, unions chose to continue to voice traditional employee demands for higher wages, better benefits, and safer working conditions. By and large they succeeded in those areas, but they failed to provide an effective response to the challenges of globalization. To be fair, the American trade union movement suffers from a major disadvantage in dealing with the effects of globalization: unions are local, but an increasing number of major corporations are global. Thus, when faced with tough union demands, employers increasingly move jobs to other countries. Unions do not have the option of following the companies, nor can they negotiate globally since, in most cases, they are purely domestic organizations.

Nonetheless, union practices and policies contributed, to at least some degree, to the decline of many U.S. rustbelt industries—steel, chemicals, and autos. The promising union/management cooperation programs started in the 1970s originally had been intended to give unions a voice in improving manufacturing company operations on the theory that workers can't thrive unless their employers survive. The hope at the time was that unions would come to see that the issue wasn't simply what companies could do for union members but also what workers could do for their employers, so that the company then would be able to do more for them in the long run. But union leaders did not see cooperation with management as a part of their role, and they walked away from the programs. The most recent casualty in this regard was the cooperative effort by General Motors and the UAW to create "a different kind of car company" at GM's Saturn division. After years of backtracking by both the company and the union, in 2005 Saturn was finally and fully reabsorbed as just another part of GM, subjecting the division's employees both to conventional working conditions and to adversarial labor-management relations.

Another reason why unions have declined is the advent of alternative voices for workers, starting with the fact that many employers at long last have learned to listen to their people. As corporations have increasingly recognized that their employees are not only keys to the success of their operations but, in fact, real and valuable assets, managers have become more willing to pay attention to worker needs, wants, ideas, and suggestions than they were thirty years ago. Today almost all major corporations conduct annual employee surveys to gather information about attitudes and morale. And the most progressive employers have learned that if they give their employees what unions provide—good salaries and benefits, safe working conditions, and a grievance procedure—most will not want a union.

Lawyers also have become voices for employees. Many issues that used to be handled by grievance procedures now end up in the hands of lawyers who file individual or class action suits on behalf of employees who claim they have been unfairly paid, dismissed, or harassed. Because the settlements lawyers win often are larger than those won in traditional grievance procedures, to some degree lawyers have become an effective substitute for unions. Finally, the loudest voice for employees on many issues is the federal and state legislation that now covers many of the practices for which unions once bargained.

In most other developed countries, it is much easier for unions to organize plants, offices, and stores than in the United States, where courts and legislatures have made it difficult for unions to expand their membership. While there is no doubt that American employers have succeeded in their legal and political efforts to make union organization difficult, the trade union movement mainly has itself to blame for failing to change in response to a transformed social and economic environment. Many of the issues they bargained for in the 1950s and 1960s have become standard operating procedure in large, progressive corporations. As a result, workers today often see joining unions as an unnecessary expense. In the 1970s and 1980s, unions could have reinvented themselves to provide new services to workers but, in general, they chose to continue doing what had worked for them in the past. For example, the voice of the UAW has been absent in calls for reform of the nation's health insurance system. Much like companies that do not change, unions run the risk of self-inflicted extinction. If that were to occur, the American economic and political system might become seriously out of balance, because unions are the most effective check on corporate power, much as the private sector in our democracy is a necessary check on the power of government.

Although unions are weakened, they are not moribund: they continue to be strong in the hotel and restaurant industries and especially in the public sector, where employers cannot move operations overseas to avoid organization. In some ways, the union bargaining situation with government agencies today is similar to what existed when the UAW was the sole union dealing with all American auto companies. At that time, the union could assure carmakers that, if one granted a contract concession, its competitors would have to pay the same labor costs. Unions representing government workers don't have to worry about creating competitive disadvantages among the agencies from which they win concessions. The issue of competition mainly arises when an agency has the option of outsourcing a service to a private employer; typically that isn't feasible with such government services as schools and police.

Overall, it is difficult to know whether employees have a clearer, louder, or stronger voice today than they did in the 1970s. As a result of declining union membership, workers now have a much weaker voice in the political arena. Because they have lost so many dues-paying members, unions simply don't have the funds they once had to lobby the Congress and state legislatures on matters important to all American workers, particularly on matters affecting the poorest-paid and least-educated. In today's workplaces, where bargaining power is based on an employee's skills, knowledge, and access to management rather than on membership in an organized group, employee voice is more individualized. Those employees who can directly address their own personal needs, or the needs of their small workgroups, as opposed to the general needs of fellow union members, benefit. But, for many workers, particularly those in the worst jobs, lacking the collective power of an effective union has meant that not only are they stuck in minimum-wage jobs without benefits, they no longer have the strong voice they once enjoyed in Congress and state legislatures.

Significantly, research shows that most American workers continue to say they like the idea of organized representation, in particular the advantages of collective bargaining, but they are unwilling to join and pay dues to a union.[2] In essence, they are voting with their feet against unions, at least as currently constituted. This leaves open the prospect that, if unions improve their "products" and more effectively address the real concerns of workers in the future, they might be able to regain some of their lost membership and the strength of their voice. But to do so, they will need to rethink their positions and roles relating to such issues as education and training, the individualization of work relationships, and, especially, cooperation with regard to improving business performance.

12

TRAINING AND DEVELOPMENT

I n 1973, the *Work in America* task force concluded that many sources of the job dissatisfaction identified at the time were related to worker perceptions of being trapped in jobs, and that feeling "locked-in" often was due to the lack of marketable skills. To address this issue, the task force outlined an ambitious national "Worker Self-Renewal Program" designed to meet the midcareer retraining needs of those left behind as the result of technological and competitive change. The proposal was never implemented, but the need it sought to address has intensified over the intervening decades.

Particularly in the last decade, an observable convergence of trends has heightened the need for more, and better, job training: the increasing speed of technology change, the increasing sophistication of foreign competitors, the export of manufacturing jobs, downsizing due to pressures to increase productivity, shortcomings in the quality of formal education (particularly at the high school level), and the aging of the workforce. All told, those trends amount to an almost perfect storm, creating an ever-increasing need for workers to update their skills regularly and, often, to develop entirely new ones.

On the face of it, there shouldn't be a problem with skill development in America. After all, almost all American employers train their workers. By one crude measure they spend about $60 billion annually on a range of programs and activities falling under the general heading of "human capital investment." The relatively little longitudinal data available on the actual amount companies spend on training and education indicates a potentially alarming trend, however. *Training* magazine's annual survey of U.S. employers indicates that in the early 2000s there has been a significant decline in company education and training expenditures, the first such decrease since 1982. And workers feel their employers are not committed to training them: a 2005 Harris Interactive/Age Wave survey found that only 29 percent believe management cares about advancing employee skills.[1]

Training expenditures vary widely from company to company, and large corporations are particularly likely to support all forms of employee development. The Society for Human Resource Management's 2005 benefits survey found that 88 percent of large employers provide tuition support for all or most employees. Yet only 62 percent of small companies (those with fewer than fifty employees) offer such support. But, again, there is a disparity between companies offering a benefit and employees exercising it. As previously noted, in the 2002 University of Michigan survey when workers were asked if their employer offers training opportunities, 64 percent answered yes, and when asked if their employer pays for job-related training and education, 70 percent responded yes. But when asked if they were currently taking classes in school or participating in training programs at work, only 18 percent answered affirmatively.

In late 2005, the National Association of Manufacturers released a study showing that 83 percent of American manufacturing companies reported that they could not find enough qualified machinists, technicians, and engineers to meet their production needs. Of the eight hundred companies surveyed, 13 percent reported severe shortages, and 68 percent experienced "a moderate shortage."[2] Reductions in federal spending on training programs in recent years compound the problem. Given the nation's growing competitive challenges and the need to create greater mobility (and good careers) for workers, the decrease in the amount spent on training—coupled with the number of employees who apparently are not participating in training programs—leads us to conclude that the already undereducated American workforce also is being undertrained. This undertraining is surprising, especially given the tremendous increase in the number of e-learning programs companies now offer, as well as the increase in other forms of remote-learning such as the many video courses that are widely available. And, during the last decade, almost one thousand corporate "universities" were established.

In practice, the size, scope, curriculum, quality, and purpose of corporate training and development activities vary dramatically. At one end of the spectrum, some companies place employee development at the heart of their enterprise. For example, at NRC Holdings (formerly SpringfieldRe), all blue-collar workers, even those without high school diplomas, are exposed to the equivalent of an MBA curriculum, and UTC offers extensive subsidies to all employees who pursue degrees, rewarding them with stock when they graduate. At the other extreme, many companies teach only narrow, job-specific, nontransferable skills out of fear they will incur the expense of training workers who then will take what they have learned and apply it at a competitor. In between are companies that teach basic literacy skills, teach functional business skills (such as sales techniques), provide college tuition remission, offer leadership training to managers and executives, and so on, ad infinitum.

The beneficiaries of training programs can be represented along a continuum from, at one end, only employees, to both employees and the company in the middle, and to only the company at the other end. Unfortunately, the training activities of too many companies appear to be clustered at the company-only end just when there is increasing need to move toward the center of the spectrum. Most companies simply teach their front-line people how to do their current jobs or how to do them better. For example, McDonald's management has no choice but to teach the young people who work for them how to be proficient burger flippers. The company does this exceptionally well. In fact it does it in a way that practically guarantees all employees will do it "right" in terms of health and safety, waste reduction, and efficiency. The amount the company spends teaching employees this relatively nontransferable skill is a component of that $60 billion national training bill, but little of the benefit goes to workers preparing for their next and, it is hoped, better jobs.

While many companies are proficient at employee *training,* too few are committed to employee *development.* The *Work in America* report cited the words of a corporate executive who, in 1972, spoke about his responsibilities for employee development. "The employer's obligations to society, stockholders and workers [are] intricately interrelated. One cannot, in effect, serve society at all if it does not serve its people. One cannot serve shareholders effectively if he does not act to make business itself an agent for human growth and fulfillment." This executive put his principles into practice by creating a program that financed the general education of his poorly educated workforce so they would have enhanced opportunities for career and social mobility. Today, if employers have any social or moral responsibility beyond what they owe their shareholders, we believe it is to provide developmental opportunities for their employees to learn and grow. Jefferson's majestic words in the Declaration of Independence proclaiming every American's right to pursue happiness refers directly to the opportunity for all to develop the potentials with which they were born. Today, for most Americans, the workplace is the primary or only venue in which they can realize that personal potential. Hence employers face a heavy responsibility: in Jefferson's philosophical construct, to deny people the opportunity to develop is to deny their humanity.

Obviously, worker development costs money. There are three basic sources of financial support for education and training activities: workers themselves, their employers, and the government. Given the shift from company-focused to individual-centered careers, it is not surprising to find that there has been a reduction in company support for training and development. As corporations now expect individuals to take more responsibility for their own development, they also feel it is reasonable for workers to pay more of the costs of their own training and education. The issue is drawn most clearly at Low-Cost companies where employers have little incentive to invest anything in training beyond the minimum workers need to do their jobs (which often are designed to be done by the least-educated, and least-trained, members of the labor force).

What is more surprising, and disappointing, has been the inconsistency of the commitments of Global Competitor organizations to the development of their employees. A key provision of their new employment contract is that, in lieu of job security, GC companies promise to provide opportunity for their workers to develop their skills so they will be employable in the event their jobs are eliminated. Nonetheless, when the recession hit hard in 2002, the first cuts many of these companies made were expenditures in training and education. But treating development investments as discretionary and, therefore, revocable may not turn out to be in the self-interest of GC companies in the long term. In a paper commissioned for this study, researchers Elizabeth Craig and Douglas Hall document how "prioritizing learning" is essential *if* companies wish to make the new employment contract work. Even in companies where employees have assumed the risks associated with managing their own careers, Craig and Hall conclude that "learning and career development are experiential and rational and cannot be effectively accomplished by a lone, self-directed individual."[3]

Companies fully committed to providing continuing opportunities for employee learning, growth, and development—even when those companies make no long-term job or career commitments—generate returns on their investments in terms of increased employee initiative, motivation, trust, and reduced turnover. GC companies committed to worker development—including Dell, Cisco, Boeing, Millennium Pharmaceuticals, Procter & Gamble, Intel, and PepsiCo—seem to benefit as much as employees from investments in training and education, particularly in terms of having a recruiting edge with the most qualified job candidates.

13

COMMUNITY AND COMMITMENT

When Americans are asked what working conditions are most important to them, they often cite "relationships with coworkers" near the top of their personal lists. As *Work in America* documented, the workplace always has been where people meet, converse, connect, and form friendships. Indeed, relationships at work are the most meaningful ones for most adult Americans outside of our families. While these bonds may not be as deep or lasting as those formed with childhood friends and schoolmates, work relationships are of tremendous immediate importance because they directly affect the quality of our daily existence. Often a serious argument with a coworker spills over to our life at home, adversely influencing the way we interact with our spouse and children and perhaps even affecting our health.

Conversely, good relations at work are a source of satisfaction, even healing. For example, as discussed in the chapter on work and health, research shows that high-blood-pressure levels can be moderated by social support at work. The CEO of a large U.S. corporation offered an explanation for why this is so. In the 1980s, he reported he was surprised to learn from his employees that their jobs were places of succor (even escape) for those with abusive family relationships, for those who cared for gravely ill or disabled relatives, and for those who simply lacked a warm and supportive family.[1] Countless people look forward to going to work if for no other reason than that is where their closest friends are. For them life is at work. Indeed, as we have mentioned, one of the most remarkable recent survey findings is that more Americans today say they are satisfied with their lives at work than say they are satisfied with their personal lives.

THE WORKPLACE AS A COMMUNITY

Social scientists find that people derive a strong sense of community from interactions with their coworkers, and the absence of community at work is a source of job, and life, dissatisfaction. After all, humans are social, not solitary, animals, the few "lone wolves" notwithstanding. The search for community has been particularly strong in America for over two centuries. Because we are largely an immigrant nation, and because we have the most geographically mobile population of all developed countries, we often find ourselves strangers in new neighborhoods. To compensate for this rootlessness, Americans actively look for places in which to form social relationships.

In the early nineteenth century, the landmark study by France's Alexis de Tocqueville, *Democracy in America,* noted a strong sense of community in the New World, the bonds of which were strengthened by membership in the kinds of voluntary associations seldom seem in Europe at the time: civic organizations, charitable institutions, clubs and lodges, community hospitals, and nongovernment schools and colleges. But as sociologist Robert Putnam recently documented in *Bowling Alone: The Collapse and Revival of American Community,* Americans today participate in fewer and fewer of the voluntary associations Tocqueville so prized.[2] They are also less likely, as we have noted, to be members of unions.

Moreover, in recent years, Americans are more likely to be working alone: self-employment, working at home, contract work, telecommuting, and other fast-growing forms of solo and isolated jobs are replacing employment in the traditional workplaces with water coolers and cafeterias where employees once gathered and bonded. The high rates of turnover in Low-Cost companies, coupled with ever-more frequent mergers, acquisitions, plant closings, offshoring, and outsourcing in industries across the board, have conspired to make it increasingly difficult for many Americans to form communities at work. "Hollow corporations" and "virtual organizations" are not likely to be communities.

It is probably not coincidental that the recent decline in the bond of community in neighborhood associations and workplaces has coincided with an increase in participation in religious institutions in America. Members of churches are, after all, called communicants, and members of a religious group are called a communion, words with the same Latin root as "community." There also has been increased interest in spirituality at work, which often seems to represent as much a desire for a supportive community on the job as it does formal religious activities.

In explaining the strong sense of community he found in this country, Tocqueville noted that, unlike the socially stratified nations of Europe, a particular strength of America was that it was a "classless" society. Slavery aside, he noted that American bosses and workers were political and social equals. That meant American employers were more likely to show respect and concern for their employees than was the case in Europe. Yet he warned that an American "aristocracy" might one day "naturally spring out of the bosom of democracy" as a by-product of the factory system burgeoning at the time. In this system—characterized by impersonal organizations employing larger numbers of workers than in the small, traditional face-to-face businesses that had been the previous norm—the owners tended to segregate themselves from their workers residentially, socially, and politically. Tocqueville warned that this separation of "the workman" from "the manufacturer" would have negative consequences for the commitment of the former to the business interests of the latter. Equally important, class stratification could destroy that all-important American sense of community and might even undermine democracy itself:

> These two men meet in the factory but know not each other elsewhere; and while they come into contact on one point, they stand wide apart on all others. The manufacturer asks nothing of the workman but his labor; the workman expects nothing from him but his wages. The one contracts no obligation to protect, nor the other to defend; and they are not permanently connected either by habit or duty. . . . An aristocracy thus constituted can have no great hold upon those whom it employs; and even if it succeed in retaining them at one moment, they escape the next. . . . Between the workman and the master there are frequent relations, but no real association.

The ensuing Industrial Revolution proved Tocqueville's prescience. In the last half of the nineteenth century and the first three decades of the twentieth, the gulf between American workers and owners of large companies widened markedly, creating a gap perhaps even larger than Tocqueville had anticipated in his most pessimistic moments. Less than a hundred years after he described a classless society, early-twentieth-century America was divided between the extremes of an aristocratic class of industrial moguls living in European-style mansions, at one end of the socioeconomic spectrum, and a mass of immigrant workers huddled in urban tenements, at the other.

The democratizing shocks of the Great Depression and World War II helped to close the gap between those two extremes. As discussed earlier, during the 1945–1975 postwar period, most corporate executives were employees themselves, many of whom had worked their way up the organizations they headed. If they hadn't started in the mailroom, they had begun in middle management and spent their careers in the companies they now led. Many executives in those days knew their workers, if not by name at least by sight, and many had fought beside their front-line workers in World War II and Korea. The managers and workers, and their children after them, attended the same public schools. They thus felt a common bond of membership in the same corporate community. Laying off fellow employees was a sign of failure on the part of executives, and it was viewed as unseemly for them to be paid fortunes while their fellow workers earned minimum wages. In sum, in the 1950s and 1960s, the social and economic distance from the executive suite to the shop floor was relatively small, at least compared to the earlier era of industrialization.

The always-fragile sense of workplace community received a reinvigorating boost in the late 1970s thanks to Japan's challenge to America's manufacturing supremacy. American executives, trade unionists, business journalists, and professors rushed to Japan to learn from, and copy, the secrets of Japanese management. But most American corporations—with the notable exception of a few High-Involvement organizations—did not adopt one key element of postwar Japanese management: a shared concept of community, or what the Japanese called *amae*, which literally means "to depend and presume on another's benevolence." No single English word carries this sense of a mutually trusting relationship, but "fraternalism" comes closest. If "paternalism" means that management knows what is best for workers—and gives it to them, whether they want it or not—the fraternal sense of community in

Japanese management is about a reciprocal, trusting relationship in which all members of an organization feel they are in the same boat and, consequently, they search together for what is good for them all.

In the United States, this communitarian aspect of Japanese management often has been viewed as both counter to American individualism and economically inefficient. As Jeffrey Pfeffer writes in a paper commissioned for this study, "instead of building closer, more communal-like relationships with their workforces, over the past couple of decades most organizations in the U.S. have moved systematically to more market-like, distant, and transactional relationships with their people." Executives at many American corporations clearly believe they have benefited from this choice in terms of greater organizational flexibility, innovation, and competitiveness. But, as Pfeffer documents, their choice also has carried some costs for corporations. He cites surveys showing low levels of trust, engagement, and commitment among American workers: fewer than 40 percent say they trust their company to keep its promises, 67 percent say they do not identify with, or feel motivated to achieve their company's goals, 50 percent say they feel disconnected from their employers, and 25 percent of them say they are showing up just to collect a paycheck. Only 30 percent of the companies that participated in the 2005 Society for Human Resource Management benefits survey had communities that provided significant help to employees in need, and an even smaller percentage used social and service events to build a workplace community.

Over the last quarter century, a small minority of corporate executives have acted on the belief that it is possible to be flexible, innovative, and competitive while at the same time creating supportive communities inside their workplaces. Among them have been leaders at Southwest and Continental in the airline industry; Costco, Whole Foods, and Men's Wearhouse in retailing; SAS and Xilinx in computer software; Herman Miller, Nucor, and NRC Holdings in manufacturing; UPS in shipping; WL Gore Associates and Medtronic in medical technology; DaVita in healthcare; Starbucks in food services; and AES in the energy industry. Executives from these HI companies have argued that creating a strong sense of mutual obligation is neither countercultural in America nor inefficient; instead, they say it enhances a company's productivity and profitability in the long term because it addresses the basic human need for community. We explore the difficult challenge of creating community in Global Competitor and Low-Cost companies in part IV.

14

WINNERS AND LOSERS

An inevitable consequence of a major social transformation is a shift in the fortunes of the players, the creation of a new cast of winners and losers. The last three decades of remarkable change in the American workplace are no exception to that rule: every significant demographic segment of the workforce has experienced either a significant gain or a loss in terms of its relative income, status, and prospects for the future. By way of review, we now turn to a brief accounting of the nation's biggest winners and losers in the workplace. In this record, we find portents of the challenges of tomorrow. To make wise choices in the future, we must understand how the lives of individuals have been affected by past decisions made by private employers, public policy makers, and by workers themselves. By considering what has happened to various segments of the workforce, we can better understand what needs to be done to make tomorrow's workplaces more effective and fair for all.

SENIOR EXECUTIVES

As we have documented, over the last thirty years the senior executives of major American corporations hit the jackpot, particularly during the casino economy of the 1990s. To cite just one example, William McGuire, CEO of the United Health Group, the nation's leading health insurer, was ranked third on the *Forbes* 2004 list of highest-paid executives. His take-home pay of $124.8 million could cover the average health insurance premiums of nearly 34,000 people. Significantly, the pay of top American executives does not correlate with the financial performance of the companies they head, nor is it closely related to overall economic conditions. Average executive pay did dip slightly during the 2001–2002 recession, when corporate profits dropped 20 percent, but in every other year over the last decade, CEO salaries rose by much more than the compensation of their employees or the value of their companies' stocks. A Mercer company study shows that, in 2004, CEO compensation increased by 15 percent, while salaried employees' compensation moved ahead at a 4 percent rate, a pattern typical of the last decade.

As Peter Cappelli has documented in a paper commissioned for this study, the career paths of senior executives have shortened considerably in recent years. It now takes considerably less time for successful men and women to climb to the top, and the rewards associated with getting there are much greater. As the old hierarchical "loyalty" model has disappeared, the average journey up the organization for the ten highest-ranking executives in large U.S. corporations took four fewer years in 2001 than it did in 1980. And, many executives today lead lifestyles of celebrities, with company-paid perks that would embarrass a pasha, including executive jets to wing them from Aspen to Davos (in some cases, even after they have retired). In dramatic contrast with the 1970s, some CEOs have achieved star status, appearing on the covers of newsmagazines and penning best-selling how-to leadership books. Observers recently have claimed that the era of the "imperial CEO" is ending, but if that is true, it is not yet reflected in their compensation.

These days, job insecurity seems to be the only downside to being a CEO: according to a recent study, 14 percent of the chiefs of the world's 2,500 largest corporations left office in 2004.[1] Of those 355 CEOs, 111 were forced from office for performance-related reasons, the highest level of forced resignations since researchers started keeping track in 1955, and a 300 percent increase over the number of executive cannings in that year. In the United States, annual turnover among big company CEOs in 2001 was 9.2 percent, a 53 percent increase over 1995, during which time the average tenure of CEOs declined from 9.5 to 7.3 years.

Undoubtedly, the current, accelerated rate of turnover is due to increased performance pressures on CEOs. While being a CEO is a lot more challenging today than it was in the past, before shedding tears for those who have recently been shown the door it is worth noting that many, if not most, have received lucrative golden parachutes and termination payments. When Hewlett-Packard's Carly Fiorina exited the executive suite in 2005, she walked out the door with a package of $14 million in severance, a $7 million bonus, and $23 million in pension payouts and restricted stock options. Disney's Michael Ovitz notoriously received a $100 million–plus severance package, and he wasn't even the CEO. GE's Jack Welch came under considerable criticism when the size and nature of his retirement package was made public in his divorce proceedings, causing him to shamefacedly forgo such necessities as lifetime choice seats at Yankee Stadium. Despite these occasional setbacks and embarrassments, overall, the recent past hasn't just been good for senior executives, it's been great, and they are the biggest winners in the new American workplace.

WOMEN WORKERS

The marked increase in the labor force participation rate of women—from about 40 percent in the 1970s, to 60 percent today—has dramatically transformed their lives and changed many things about work in America in the process. But this phenomenal increase in their labor force participation isn't what has made women winners at work; that has come from their increasing say in the workplace and the more equitable pay they now receive. Women are entering senior management ranks in major corporations in greater numbers—a few are now highly visible as senior executives—and they have experienced a notable increase in their average compensation. In 1973, the ratio of the median wage earned by women to that earned by men was 63.1 percent; the gap closed to 81.0 percent in 2003.[2] The closing of that male-female wage gap occurred primarily between 1979 and 1995, during which time the male median wage declined slightly while the female median wage rose significantly. There is no single reason why this phenomenon occurred, but the decline in manufacturing, where blue-collar men historically enjoyed high-paying jobs, and the rise of services, where women are more likely to be employed (particularly in well-paying professional and managerial jobs) account for significant parts of the change. The rest is due to a host of social, economic, and political factors, including the effects of gender discrimination laws.

Perhaps the biggest factor in the improved employment opportunities of women has been the gains they have made relative to men in terms of education. The gender mix of Americans enrolled in college has changed dramatically: the percentage of young men ages twenty-five to twenty-nine completing a degree has been almost stagnant since 1980, edging up from 24 to 26 percent, compared to a growth of nearly 50 percent in the number of young women obtaining a BA degree, up from 21 to 31 percent in that age group.[3] Women of all ages now make up 56 percent of all college grads, up from 42 percent in 1970.

And the great majority of women are not trapped in low-paying jobs to the extent they were in the past. In 1973, almost 50 percent of working women earned poverty-level wages; that number dropped to approximately 30 percent in 2003, while the percentage of men in poverty-level jobs remained essentially unchanged, at 20 percent, during the same time period.[4] Between 1983 and 2000 women also closed the job tenure gap: For example, the median job tenure of men ages forty-five to fifty-four declined during that period from 12.8 to 9.5 years, while the tenure for women in that age group increased from 6.3 to 7.3 years. Women also no longer bear the brunt of layoffs and recessions. In 1973, the unemployment rate among American women was 6.0 percent, as opposed to 4.2 percent among men. That pattern continued through much of the 1970s, but today there is no noticeable difference: in 2003, the rate was actually higher for men than it was for women; in 2004, the unemployment rate for men and women was exactly the same.[5]

University of Michigan survey data comparing 1977 to 2002 provide an insight into how working conditions have changed for women. In 1977, the responses given by men on most items relating to work and job satisfaction were noticeably higher than those offered by women but, by 2002, the gap had closed significantly on such items as experiencing freedom at work, learning new things, having a say in how the job is done, and being creative. This finding is consistent with the increased level of compensation women earned in 2002 versus 1977, and with their movement into higher-level jobs.

Overall, women have gained significantly in the workplace. While they have not reached parity with men, and it may take decades before they do, they have made substantial gains in terms of income and real progress in terms of moving up the employment ladder to good, well-paying jobs, all of which bode well for them in the future.

COLLEGE GRADUATES

Levels of educational achievement always have been strongly related to income levels in the United States, and that relationship grew even stronger over the last thirty years. The "education premium" in terms of wages enjoyed by workers with college degrees over workers with high school diplomas increased from about 30 percent in the 1970s to 45 percent today.[6] For both women and men who complete their degrees, the returns are substantial in terms of annual income: 67 percent for women with four-year degrees and 37 percent for men, when compared to high school graduates.[7] In addition, college-educated workers are much less likely to be unemployed. If they are, they stay unemployed for shorter periods of time than do less-educated workers; again, a trend that has become stronger in recent decades.[8]

Compared to thirty years ago, the work itself has gotten better for individuals who have undergraduate or advanced college degrees. Data from the University of Michigan survey show that education levels are clearly related to the nature of work Americans do: the more educated we are, the more likely we are to work at home, to be creative, to learn new things on the job, to use our skills and abilities, and to have freedom in terms of how we do our work. Finally, and not surprisingly, education correlates positively with job satisfaction.

In 2006, economist Alan Blinder and other scholars noted that the inflation-adjusted incomes of college graduates in the U.S. workforce appear to have fallen in the early years of the new millennium. It remains to be seen if this change is merely a blip or the beginning of a long-term trend in which education no longer will serve as a buffer against the effects of globalization. In Part IV, we discuss how American employers, workers, and the federal government can respond most effectively to that future possibility.

BLUE-COLLAR WORKERS
IN UNIONIZED INDUSTRIES

As noted, the large decline in union membership has had a significant impact on the wages and benefits of American workers, reducing the incomes
of union and nonunion workers alike. Nonetheless, unionized workers still
earned a premium in 2003 of almost 32 percent in wages and 44 percent
in total compensation over nonunion workers.[9] But as the ability of unions
to negotiate for higher wages and lucrative benefit packages has declined,
so has the effect of the threat of unionization. Formerly, managers in
nonunion shops would raise wages to discourage or stave off organizing
drives. Today that union spillover effect often works the opposite way: for
example, in the airline industry, such start-up nonunion carriers as Jet Blue
put pressure on unions for wage concessions at larger, older, organized airlines like United and American. As noted, offshoring exerts further downward pressure on blue-collar salaries, particularly in such long-unionized
industries as airlines, steel, and autos that have large numbers of retired
workers who represent high "legacy costs" in terms of ongoing pension and
healthcare commitments.

As the decline of unionization has lowered the wages of both union and
nonunion workers, the effect has been felt primarily by high school graduates because relatively few college grads are union members or work as la-
borers in unionized industries. Hence, the decline in unions also helps
account for the growing wage differential between highly educated and
less-educated workers. This negative impact on incomes has fallen dispro-
portionately on African Americans. In the first five years of the twenty-first
century, the number of blacks in unions fell by 14.4 percent, while the
number of whites fell by 5.4 percent. In 2004, blacks accounted for 55 percent of the decline in union membership even though whites outnumber
blacks six to one in total union membership; doubtless the membership decline was a contributing factor to the relatively steeper decline in the median wages of black workers during 2004 and 2005.[10] The root of this
problem has been the loss of jobs in manufacturing, for example in the De-
troit-based auto industry, and cutbacks in government employment, both
of which historically have had relatively high percentage of African American workers.

LOW-WAGE, LOW-SKILLED WORKERS

Growing wage inequality in the United States over the last thirty years is partly the result of the inability of the bottom 10 percent of workers to make significant income gains. In every year since 1979, the income levels of the very highest-paid workers have increased; over the same time, incomes of the lowest-paid workers stagnated or slightly dropped. A number of factors have conspired to worsen the relative position of low-wage, low-skilled workers. One has been the observed declining role of unions; another has been the precipitous fall in the real value of the federal minimum wage since its high point in the 1970s. A rough estimate is that the inflation-adjusted value of the federal minimum wage in 2005 dollars has dropped from approximately $6.50 in the 1970s to $5.15 in 2005. As a result, many workers earn less today in real income than they did in the 1970s and the national poverty rate, which hit a low of 11.1 percent in 1973, increased to 12.7 percent in 2004.

Low-skilled workers are worse off today than they were thirty years ago in ways other than income. In particular, the risks associated with unemployment have increased greatly. Since the 1970s, the average length of a spell of unemployment has increased by 50 percent to nearly twenty weeks, the number of Americans who are unemployed for six months or longer has increased (the percentage doubled over just the last five years), and low-skilled workers are overrepresented in those ranks. In the1970s, jobless workers could collect up to fifteen months of unemployment compensation but, in 2004, Congress reduced that to six months. In the late 1970s and 1980s, legislation was passed to make those benefits taxable, and state requirements were tightened to make fewer workers eligible to collect benefits. In early 2005, among the 8 million American unemployed, only 2.9 million were receiving benefits.[11] At the same time, federal spending on training was reduced from roughly $27 billion to $4.4 billion.[12] And federal spending on welfare has also been reduced by about a third.

There is mounting evidence that a large number of Americans simply have dropped out of the labor market entirely and thus are not counted as unemployed. Whatever incomes they earn are not included in the national statistics, thus driving up average income statistics.[13] By some estimates, several million Americans may simply lack the skills or motivation to do any kind of work. There also is reason to believe that their numbers have risen significantly in the last few years. Doubters need only walk the streets in America's central cities to find evidence with their own eyes.

The plight of those at the bottom of the U.S. labor force cannot be explained by the argument that they have priced themselves out of work. The relative cost of low-skilled labor is lower in the United States than in almost every developed country. When Social Security contributions are added to the minimum wage, low-skilled workers can be hired in America at only 33 percent the cost of the average worker, as opposed to 54 percent in France and about 42 percent in Britain.[14]

Part of the reason why low-cost labor is in abundant supply is, of course, the growing number of undocumented workers in the country. There is no shortage of Americans who can do the work that illegal immigrants do, but there is a shortage of U.S. citizens who are willing to do it for what is offered in terms of salary and working conditions. The issue of the unattractiveness of bad jobs was fully documented in *Work in America* in 1973. If anything, the problem has grown worse. Unfortunately, there is little cause for hope that the problem will be addressed any time soon and little reason to believe that the future will be brighter for those with the fewest skills. Although services jobs that can't be exported will remain free from global downward pay pressures, the main hopes for most low-skilled Americans—if they don't go back to school or get additional training—are increasing union organization efforts and an increase in the minimum wage. And those are thin threads on which to hang one's life hopes.

THE AVERAGE AMERICAN WORKER

In 2004, the U.S. economy enjoyed its third year of continued growth: 2.2 million jobs were created during the year, corporate profits were up 35 percent from 2002 to 2004 in the wake of the recession (increasing 13.4 percent during the last quarter of 2004, the biggest bump between 1987 and 2004, which, overall, were boom years), and unemployment stood at 4.9 percent, healthy by historic standards.[15] Yet when the U.S. Census Bureau released its official data covering the entire year of 2004, it reported that average household incomes failed to increase for the fifth straight year (the first time in history that had occurred), and the median pretax household income of $44,389 was at its lowest point in real terms since 1997 (and would have fallen further had workers not worked more hours in 2004 than in the previous year).[16] The median pay of a male worker employed full time fell by more than 2 percent in 2004 to $40,800 per year, and by 1 percent to $31,200 for a female worker employed full time. In general, wages were growing at the slowest rate since the 1980s.[17]

Clearly, something unusual is going on in the American economy. Businesses are reporting higher profits while, at the same time, the take-home pay of the average American worker is declining. Productivity is up, business is growing, but companies are reluctant to hire. Some 80,000 jobs a month were created in 2003, but a study by the Economic Policy Institute found that such new jobs paid about $14.50 per hour, on average; the jobs being lost at the same time had paid on the order of $17 per hour.[18] A short-term answer to this puzzling, contradictory situation appears to be that cost-conscious companies are looking to increase their productivity through automation rather than through investments in human capital.

The long-term explanation is that a major shift has occurred in the American economy and workplaces as the result of the confluence of all the factors we have been discussing: increases in the cost of benefits, particularly healthcare; a downward pull on wages due to competition from offshore workers; increasing use of contingent workers; the substitution of capital for labor; and a wage squeeze on services-sector employees due to growth of LC competitors like Wal-Mart. Add the decline of unionization and the stagnation of the minimum wage as compounding factors, and the result is that workers can no longer expect to receive wage and benefit increases, and some may expect decreases.

There is a new reality. For American industry to remain competitive and to continue to create enough good jobs for all Americans, each of these issues must be addressed—with clear heads and without bias borne of past experience—by corporate executives, union officials, public policy makers, individual workers, and citizens alike. This new world of work requires fresh thinking about the choices we all must make.

PART IV

CHOICES AND FUTURE DIRECTIONS

As our review of three decades of change in the American workplace illustrates, the contours of the employment arena have been dramatically transformed from what they were in the 1970s, and the consequences for American workers are various, diverse, and complex. Due to changes in the nature of jobs and careers and in the conditions of employment, some workers are better off today than before—particularly educated managers, professionals, and technical workers—while others are worse off—in general, those who are less-educated and lower-skilled. But almost all workers today have greater choices with respect to their careers, jobs, benefits, and work-life balance than did their counterparts in 1973. At the same time, the failure of individuals to make wise choices has become increasingly costly in both personal and financial terms.

It is perhaps inevitable in a free society that with greater individual choice comes greater risk. Nonetheless, we believe private employers and the government have roles to play in reducing the downside to the risks American workers face—and, even, a responsibility to create a wider range of employment and public policy alternatives with more positive upsides. At a minimum, employers and government have responsibilities to help individuals make good choices by providing them with clear and accurate information about the nature and the extent of risks they face.

It is impossible to separate the choices workers make from the working conditions offered by their employers. Nothing beats having a menu of great employment opportunities to choose from; yet corporations are constrained in the range of choices they can provide workers because they must balance their responsibilities to employees with their responsibilities to shareholders. We believe those responsibilities are far less often in conflict than corporate executives commonly assume and, in chapter 15, we document how enlightened companies can create positive employment conditions for workers that also will lead to high levels of financial performance.

It also is impossible to separate the ability of American workers to make wise choices regarding their jobs, careers, education, healthcare, and retirement from the programs and policies of the United States government. For example, federal laws influence wages and working conditions; federal economic policies with regard to taxation and trade help to determine the quantity and quality of jobs; and federal health, education, and retirement programs drive numerous decisions made by corporate executives and individual workers. We turn to these issues in chapter 16.

While the actions of employers and government greatly determine the range and number of options that workers have, individual Americans nonetheless must make job and career choices that have significant personal consequences. They are most likely to make good choices when they have adequate information about how organizations function and how the job market operates, and when they understand their own work-related strengths, weaknesses, and needs. Realistically, not all workers have the same opportunity to choose from among the diverse array of employment options available in the workplace. The numbers and kinds of alternatives individuals have are determined by a variety of factors, including their education, skills, and work history, and those, in turn, are influenced by the resources available to them and their families and by the personal choices they make early in their lives. In a world of limited resources, no one has access to all the information needed to make good career and job decisions, and no one has unlimited ability to choose. Nonetheless, individuals can do a few things to increase the number of good work alternatives available to them and to increase their odds of choosing wisely. In chapter 17 we examine a few of the increasingly complex choices facing American workers and call attention to the consequences of choosing wrongly.

In general, the guiding principle of our analyses is that good corporate, public policy, and individual choices are ones that create the opportunity to have more, and better, alternatives to choose from in the future.

15

ORGANIZATIONS AND COMPETITIVENESS

The competitive challenges facing U.S. companies have increased remarkably over the last three decades. As managers have tried to respond effectively to these challenges, the face of the American workplace has been transformed. But one important thing has not changed in the years since it was documented in *Work in America* in 1973: High-Involvement (HI) work practices are, in general, the most economically productive and most likely to satisfy the basic needs of workers. The evidence we have reviewed from hundreds of studies conducted over the last thirty years supports this conclusion. Yet today, a great many companies that could benefit from adopting HI practices have not done so. In this chapter, we explore the strategic choices executives of Low-Cost (LC) and Global Competitor (GC) companies make in order to identify how they could capture some of the benefits of HI practices. Adopting these practices, even in part, would lead to better outcomes both for their companies and their employees. As prelude, let us briefly recapitulate what we have noted about the nature of work at HI companies and about their economic performance.

HIGH-INVOLVEMENT ORGANIZATIONS

HI companies are found in almost every industry. Although they tend to be small to mediumsize—like the $1.5 billion WL Gore and Associates described earlier—there are a few notables in the *Fortune* 1000, including such corporate giants as UPS and Costco. (In the past, such giants as Hewlett Packard and Xerox were also HI companies.) HI companies do a variety of things to make employees feel they are members of supportive communities: aiding workers when they have financial problems; providing health and education benefits to family members; offering flexible working arrangements, maternity/paternity leave, and child and elder care; and sponsoring social events. Most important is the way these companies structure and supervise work: employees are offered challenging and enriched jobs and a say in the management of their own tasks. Typically, they also are members of small, self-managing teams. HI companies often use elements of Deming's way, such as teaching front-line workers statistical and other analytical skills so they can monitor the quality of the products they make, learn to control costs, and assume responsibility for tasks viewed as managerial prerogatives in traditionally run businesses. In general, HI companies promote from within, offering clearly defined career paths along with extensive training and development opportunities.

HI workplaces are relatively egalitarian with few class distinctions between managers and workers. All employees tend to be salaried (as opposed to paid hourly wages), and most participate in company stock ownership and share in company profits (or in small-unit productivity gains). Finally, HI companies make a commitment to low employee turnover and to minimizing layoffs during recessions. As we have seen, research shows that the greater the number of such mutually reinforcing characteristics an HI company has, the more likely it is to generate community and commitment among its workforce and, as a result, enhanced worker-productivity and value-added performance.

On the surface, HI workplaces appear to meet the needs of both employers and employees; yet there are far fewer HI companies in America than there are LC and GC companies. There are several related explanations for why this may be the case:

☐ Executives in LC and GC companies believe the constraints of their competitive strategies and business models make it impossible for them to adopt HI practices and still be financially successful. More-over, they believe HI firms can succeed only in certain market niches.

☐ Executives in LC companies have no choice economically but to re-duce their labor costs to those of their most-efficient competitors.

☐ The costs of creating community and commitment in GC companies outweigh the benefits.

☐ The way in which social costs are accounted for discourages LC em-ployers from investing in their workers beyond the absolute mini-mum required by law and, in GC companies, beyond the requirements of the tasks workers are doing.

☐ The human resources practices of companies are matters of manage-rial choice, and the cultures of HI companies are simply inconsistent with the values of many executives today.

☐ Most executives have been trained to manage LC and GC firms and, thus, don't know how to create or to run HI-type work environments.

Here is what the research shows about these arguments:

WEIGHING THE COSTS AND BENEFITS

Extensive research on HI companies reveals they frequently (but not invari-ably) enjoy a set of performance advantages and benefits, including high lev-els of worker commitment, teamwork, trust, reciprocity, loyalty, productivity, and identity with the overall needs of the company, along with low levels of employee turnover and absenteeism. Because of the above, the need for supervision is often reduced. Hence, total labor costs at HI com-panies are lower because layers of management can be eliminated. Fre-quently (but not necessarily) there are disadvantages and costs associated with the HI approach, such as a loss of operational flexibility due to the time it takes to alter a workforce's mix of skills and capabilities; employee resis-tance to major changes in strategy, technology, and products; and the cre-ation of a sense of dependency on the organization. At worst, HI organizations can become rigid and paternalistic, even cultlike, with un-healthy pressures for conformity and a loss of individual freedom. A major problem across the board at HI companies has been with the sustainability of their cultures: since the conditions they offer typically are dependent on the values of their CEOs and senior leaders, a change of leadership frequently leads to changes in managerial philosophy and practices that, in turn, destroy the sense of trust and community on which an entire culture depends.

Behavior-oriented management professors have been studying individual HI companies for at least forty-five years, examining their performance on both financial and human measures. More recently, economists have studied the performance of entire industries on an aggregate basis to measure the financial returns on investments in the innovative human resources practices standard in HI companies. Economist Kathryn Shaw has examined this growing body of evidence and concluded that HI practices typically increase worker productivity and, in general, are sound business investments. She notes that the firms most likely to gain from these investments are ones that "produce high-quality goods or face highly complex problems, or those firms that are also making investments in new information technologies."[1] The transition costs associated with adopting such HI practices as self-managing teams and information-sharing tend to be high: workers have to be retrained, new incentive pay systems need to be introduced, and managers need to change their roles from policemen to expert consultants to their workers. As a result, new companies or new facilities are more likely to adopt HI practices than are existing firms with old practices and habits to break.

Shaw and her colleagues analyzed data from thirty-four steel mini-mills and found significant returns on investment from programs designed to enhance worker performance.[2] These returns resulted from "building the problem-solving capacity" of the firms—that is, they encouraged workers to share information with each other and to build social networks among fellow workers and supervisors who had expertise they could tap when problems arose. The researchers found that workers built complex communications links within HI mills and interacted frequently with other employees on their own and other shifts. In traditionally managed steel mills, in contrast, the researchers discovered that "workers interact with a much smaller number of their peers and managers." As a result they had lower levels of productivity, made poorer-quality products, and left more unusable scrap. It seems clear that creating a sense of community reaps economic benefits.

In the 1980s, Nucor Steel was the first U.S. mini-mill to figure out how to compete against low-cost foreign products. In the words of Ken Iverson,

Nucor's CEO at the time, "What we did was push aside the notion that managers and employees have inherently separate interests. We've joined with our employees to pursue a goal we *all* believe in: long-term survival." Iverson was able to boast that Nucor had the lowest labor costs per ton of steel and the highest-paid workers in the industry (and that, during Nucor's only bad year on his watch, he was the lowest-paid *Fortune* 500 CEO). Nucor's methods then—and today—are based on employee participation in the financial gains (and losses) that result from their efforts and ideas. To create trust, Iverson committed the company to that course, promising employees it wouldn't deviate from the path in good or bad times. As he explained in 1997: "Can we expect employees to be loyal and motivated if we lay them off at every dip in the economy, while we go on padding our own pockets?"[3]

Since research demonstrating the economic benefits of HI management comes from many industries, not just steel, the question then becomes: why don't more companies follow the lead of such HI organizations as Nucor? Shaw suggests that firms may be underinvesting in innovative human resources practices because managers don't, or don't know how to, measure the intangible benefits of such activities as training and community-building. Because they cannot measure the benefits, firms undervalue these activities and thus underinvest in their human capital. In addition, such HI practices as training, forming teams, and sharing information frequently have up-front costs; but their yields tend to accumulate slowly over a number of years, which make them unattractive to mangers faced with short-term financial pressures.

ACCOUNTING FOR SOCIAL COSTS

Perhaps the most important analytical contribution of the *Work in America* report was to demonstrate that work, health, family, and education activities do not reside in discrete compartments. In fact, those spheres of activity are complexly interrelated and mutually influential, each affecting the others in numerous positive and negative ways. The report drew on the economic concept of "externalities," a measure of the costs and benefits generated by the production of a good or service that are not accounted for in its price. For example, the cost of pollution at a coal-burning power plant may be borne unwillingly by those who live nearby the facility, *not* by those who buy the electricity it produces. As economist Milton Friedman has demonstrated, that situation is both economically inefficient *and* unfair, and warrants actions/incentives to force utilities to internalize the costs of pollution control in the price of the electricity they sell.[4] Similarly, the practices of some workplaces pass on costs that are socially inefficient. For example when employees of a company that does not offer health insurance become sick or injured, local communities and taxpayers must bear the cost of their medical care; similarly, the medical costs generated by stressful jobs are often borne by health care systems and by workers themselves.

On the positive side, creating a sense of community in the workplace has identifiable, and important, social benefits, some of which are quite unexpected. The cultures of HI companies are, in fact, *socially efficient* because they internalize or reduce negative effects on the health and family lives of employees; moreover, they actually may produce positive externalities that benefit the greater society. For example, in southern California a crazed motorist recently attempted to commit suicide by driving his SUV onto railroad tracks. At the last moment, he thought the better of it, abandoned the SUV, and ran home. Unfortunately, seconds later a full commuter train crashed into the vehicle, leading to terrible loss of life and severe injuries to hundreds of passengers. The accident occurred directly behind a Costco Warehouse store. Almost immediately, blue-collar Costco employees organized themselves into an emergency brigade and, armed with forklifts and fire extinguishers, set out to rescue trapped passengers and deliver first aid to the wounded.

The behavior of these employees raises an interesting question: Is it coincidental that Costco's culture stresses the importance of each worker, rewards all for taking initiative, and trusts them to solve problems without close supervision and detailed rules? Costco is among the leaders in the retail industry in terms of making heavy investments in workforce development. Costco seeks to create a mutually supportive community among its employees. If the train accident had to occur, were the passengers at least fortunate in that they were near a group of people whose skills and instincts were primed to spring to their aid? Of course, we cannot know what would have happened had the accident occurred outside a store owned by a retail chain that adheres to the more-prevalent human resource strategy of viewing employees as a cost that needs to be minimized. But there is good reason to speculate that employees who are told simply to obey their supervisors, and whose development is not seen as a corporate responsibility, would be less prepared to respond to an emergency as quickly, effectively, and appropriately as did the Costco employees.

Management theorist Douglas Smith recently called attention to the indirect social consequences of how workplaces are organized. He writes: "Organizations are not just places where people have jobs. They are our neighborhoods, our communities. They are where we join with other people to make a difference for ourselves and others. If we think of them only as the places where we have jobs, we not only lose the opportunity for meaning, but we endanger the planet."[5] One of the seldom-measured costs and benefits of work is its impact on the formation of character. Perhaps only the military services measure the ways in which character is formed as a result of how people are treated and trained, yet employment conditions in all workplaces can influence the course of human development.

As the recent Sarbanes-Oxley legislation acknowledges, the culture of a business organization is a prime determinant of the extent to which its employees will behave ethically. And the cultures of HI companies are designed to encourage employees to become self-policing, mutually supportive, concerned with the good of other members of the workforce and with the overall well-being of their organization. For example, for nearly two decades, the CEO of SRC Holdings, Jack Stack, has treated his blue-collar workers as peers, deserving of the same respect he would give to them if the were ivy-leaguers. Even though most only have had high school educations or less, Stack has taken the time to teach them all everything they might be taught if they were MBA students. He has taught them to read balance sheets and income and cash flow statements. He has given them the authority to use that information not only to be self-managing, but to share in the financial rewards that come from having a company full of people taking initiative. Stack believes that by treating his people with respect, they will have the chance to grow, and the company will benefit from hiring whole humans—their brains, not just their hands. One of the consequences has been a truly ethical corporate culture: would anyone try, or could they get away with, cooking the books in such an environment? As the company's chief financial officer once said, "It is like having seven hundred internal auditors out there in every function of the company." Such character traits have a positive spillover to activities outside the workplace, as exemplified by the behavior of the Costco employees.

HEEDING THE LAWS OF ECONOMICS

In general, most corporations do not measure, nor are they held accountable for, the positive or negative externalities generated by the working conditions they offer. Such incomplete accounting may contribute to the decisions of many retailers to reject the Costco approach of paying employees sufficient wages to support families, providing them with affordable health insurance, and rewarding them for participating in self-management. Instead of weighing the total social costs and benefits of the employment conditions they offer, most LC retail companies appear to consider only one factor: investing in workers is costly, and doing so may drive them out of business.

But does paying good wages and investing in employee development really *not* pay off? If it were true, UPS would have lost out to FedEx instead of having gained market share in certain areas FedEx used to dominate, such as overnight delivery. As FedEx has moved to a low-cost model for its drivers (even contracting out), UPS has stayed with its commitment to long-term employment and high pay: UPS drivers are paid 20 percent over market, their supervisors 10 percent over market, and its CEO way under market.

UPS's leaders have made the choice to pay "high" wages and invest in their employees because they believe their drivers are a key to corporate success and that having informed and committed workers is the best way to serve customers. Because most of UPS's leaders are former drivers themselves, they have empathy with their workers. Their experience tells them the lowest-level worker in their organization has much the same basic needs as they do and deserves similar opportunities for development and career mobility.

But the leaders of many large GC and LC corporations are not driven by that assumption. In recent decades, a new class of executives, raised in the suburbs and educated at leading universities where they received MBAs and advanced engineering degrees, has moved into executive suites. As we have seen, these individuals identify more with the owners of their corporations than with their hourly employees, and they are financially rewarded for doing so. More often today than before, top executives of major GC and LC companies are likely to have started their careers in other companies; they are not "homegrown." Not only have many executives not worked "on the line" in the companies they now head, they share little organizational identity with their workforce: many do not know their workers personally, and

The World's Largest HI Employer

UPS is a large company with many HI characteristics typically found only at small to midsize companies. UPS promotes from within, and most members of its top management started as drivers. The way to get to the top at UPS is through years of service in which managers are developed by being rotated through various company functions. (Drivers who choose not to pursue managerial careers have their own, separate, career development path.) Because everyone at UPS starts in the same place, there is a relatively high degree of egalitarianism among employees at all levels, and even the CEO is on first-name basis with new employees. There are no limousines for company directors; instead, regular UPS delivery drivers pick them up and take them to quarterly board meetings that local employees are invited to attend. The company spends $250 million annually on tuition reimbursement, a great deal of which goes to seasonal and part-time student employees who are rewarded for their willingness to work long hours over holidays and for serving on night shifts. After UPS employees work for twenty years, the company celebrates their contributions in a full-page ad in *USA Today* in which all their names are cited, and a banquet is held in their honor.

they live in different neighborhoods and send their kids to different schools. As Alexis de Tocqueville warned long ago, all this makes empathy unlikely. Perhaps it is this growing social gap between managers and employees that leads GC and LC executives to conclude that significant investments in employees are justified only for the highly skilled professionals at the top of the corporate hierarchy. They assume that only the talented few—people like themselves—deserve and require high pay, generous benefits, and participation in a supportive corporate community. If workers down the line do not like the conditions offered, they are free to quit and look for employment elsewhere.

Again, many executives say that corporations have "no choice" in this matter if they are to remain competitive. After all, one simply can't dictate the laws of economics. For example, when the CEO of Wal-Mart was recently asked on MSNBC about the highly visible problems his company was encountering with its hourly workers, his reply was that Wal-Mart had no choice but to remain a low-wage employer if it was to meet the needs of American consumers for low-priced goods. No doubt executives are correct when they say their human resources strategy must be consistent with their company's business model, but paying the lowest-per-capita salaries is not the only viable strategy. The accompanying box compares the competitive employment

A Tale of Two Employment Strategies

In 2004, Costco employed 68,000 workers, one-fifth of whom were unionized while Sam's Club (the division of Wal-Mart that competes most directly with Costco) employed 102,000, none of whom were union members. A Costco employee earned, on average, $33,218 per year ($15.97 per hour); while the average Sam's Club employee earned $23,962 ($11.52 per hour). When a Costco employee quits voluntarily, the full cost of replacing him or her is about $49,827; when a Sam's Club employee leaves the company, the replacement costs amount to only $35,943. At first glance, it appears that the low-wage strategy at Sam's Club yields greater savings in turnover costs. However, at Costco, employee turnover is only 6 percent per year (4,080 employees); it is 21 percent a year at Sam's Club (21,420 employees). Therefore the total cost of turnover at Costco is $203,290,000 ($49,827 times 4,080), while at Sam's Club it is $769,900,000 ($35,943 times 21,420). Costco's opportunity savings (costs not incurred as the result of keeping its turnover relatively low) exceed $566 million per year compared to Sam's Club.

Wages are not the only distinguishing characteristic between the two retailers. At Costco, 82 percent of employees are covered by a healthcare insurance plan, with the company paying an average of $5,735 per worker per year in premiums. Sam's Club's health insurance plan covers 47 percent of its workers, at an average annual company outlay of $3,500. Fully 91 percent of Costco's employees are covered by retirement plans, with the company contributing an average of $1,330 per employee per year; 64 percent of employees at Sam's Club are covered, and the company contributes an average of $747 per employee. Again, it appears that Sam's Club has a decided competitive advantage over Costco in terms of the benefits it offers.

However, Costco has one of the most productive workforces in retailing: while Sam's Club's 102,000 employees generated some $35 billion in sales in 2003, the one-third fewer employees at Costco generated sales of $34 billion. (Costco generated $13,647 in operating profit per hourly U.S. employee, compared to $11,039 at Sam's Club.) Looked at another way, labor and overhead costs at Costco were 9.8 percent of sales, versus an estimated 17 percent at Sam's Club (by comparison, these costs were 24 percent at Target Stores). Costco's motivated employees also sell more: $795 of sales per square foot versus $516 at Sam's Club (and $411 at BJ's Wholesale Club, the other primary competitor in "club" retailing). Finally, Costco has the industry's lowest rate of employee pilfering.

These figures illustrate that it is not always correct to assume that labor rates simply equal labor costs. Costco's hourly labor rates are almost 40 percent higher than those at Sam's Club ($15.97 versus $11.52), but when employee productivity is considered (sales per employee), Costco's labor costs are significantly lower (9.8 percent versus 17 percent). Costco's CEO James Sinegal concludes that "paying your employees well is not only the right thing to do, but it makes for good business." To make its high-wage strategy work, of course, Costco constantly must look for ways to increase its efficiency, such as by repackaging goods into bulk items to reduce labor costs, speeding up its just-in-time inventory and distribution system, and boosting sales per square foot by being the industry leader in innovative packaging and in merchandising mix. For example, Costco was the first wholesale club to offer fresh meat, pharmacies, photo labs (and original art masterpieces online). Costco employees have an incentive to come up with such new ideas (even labor-saving ones) and to cooperate with management when they are introduced.

In contrast, the low-wage strategy Wal-Mart uses at its Sam's Club division brings undeniable benefits to customers in terms of low prices, and it serves as a major source of employment to young workers and those who may not have other options. The company also has been a great long-term investment for shareholders, although they have not fared quite as well as Costco's in recent years. (In mid-2005, Wal-Mart's stock was selling at nineteen times earnings, compared to a multiple of twenty-three at Costco.) A fuller accounting of Wal-Mart's human resources strategy raises a variety of questions that the company doesn't address in its annual report: low-wage employment in certain geographical areas (for example, where the cost of living is high), and among certain demographic groups (for example, those attempting to support a family) may lead to the phenomenon known as working poverty. The working poor and their children are particularly vulnerable to a variety of social problems, the costs of which are borne by local communities, much as Wal-Mart's benefits policy transfers healthcare costs to local taxpayers.

—Adapted from Wayne Cascio, "The Economic Impact of Employee Behavior on Organizational Performance," a paper commissioned for this study.

strategies of Costco and Sam's Club to illustrate how working conditions can be managed in such a way that higher-paid, and better-trained, workers are made productive enough to offset the costs of their salaries and benefits.

A MATTER OF CHOICE

We cite Wal-Mart here and elsewhere not as an archvillain, but as the archetype of a growing number of companies whose executives assume their labor policies are determined by their LC business model. Contrary to the way it is often portrayed by its critics, Wal-Mart is in fact far from being the worst employer in America. It pays above the minimum wage to almost all its employees and supports increasing the federal minimum wage. Moreover, Wal-Mart probably could not be the low-price leader in its industry if it paid the same high salaries, and offered the same training and benefits package to its employees, as Costco does. In the final analysis, Costco's business model works because, unlike Wal-Mart, it sells a large quantity of higher-priced items over which it can spread its labor costs. Nonetheless, Wal-Mart might invest more in workers and raise their wages *if* it saw that those expenditures resulted in lower rates of absenteeism and turnover, better customer service and employee decision-making, fewer union organizing drives, and less negative publicity.

It must be recognized that Wal-Mart's current business model did not arrive at its Bentonville, Arkansas, headquarters etched on stone tablets. Instead, it resulted from numerous policy decisions made by Wal-Mart executives over many years. When founder Sam Walton was alive, he chose to involve his employees in a generous stock ownership program, to encourage their engagement in making the enterprise successful, to continue to live frugally in the same middle-class neighborhood where he had begun his career, and to take a relatively small salary in comparison to other CEOs at the time. Subsequent Wal-Mart executives have made different choices.

Wal-Mart has chosen to favor investors over workers, when it could have chosen to meet the needs of both, as Costco does. To be fair, Wal-Mart's executives are under constant pressure from Wall Street to make exactly the kinds of pro-shareholder choices they have made in recent years. Yet Costco executives face the same pressure. In a 2005 *New York Times* article, Emme Kozlof, a financial analyst at Sanford C. Bernstein & Company, publicly faulted Costco's CEO, James Sinegal, for being too generous to his employees: "He has been too benevolent." Specifically, Kozlof argued that Costco should stop mollycoddling its workers by paying such a large percentage of their healthcare premiums; rather, it should reduce the company's contribution and pay the savings out to investors.[6] Wal-Mart executives have chosen to accede to such pressures from the investing community; Costco's leaders have chosen to reject them. In turn, investors are free to choose which company to invest in. And, finally, workers also have a choice among employers, and Costco's HI working conditions give it an edge in competition with its rivals for the most-productive employees. Such choices are the essence of a free-market society.

Why do executives make the choices they do with regard to the conditions they offer employees? They seem to be influenced by a combination of factors: a reckoning of the immediate costs and benefits of alternatives, the dictates of a competitive labor market, the requirements of their business models, perhaps a consideration of the social costs and benefits of their actions, response to pressures from the financial community, and their personal values and experiences. It is worth noting that Costco's CEO James Sinegal is the son of a coal miner and steelworker and started his own career in the retail business unloading trucks at age eighteen.

To this complex mix of influences, Jeffrey Pfeffer adds: the effects of business school training (an Aspen Institute study shows that the values of MBA students change over the course of their education, with students coming to place more emphasis on meeting the needs of shareholders and less on meeting those of employees and customers); a "follow-the-leader" mentality that permeates American business (the practices of managers often are driven by fads, fashion, and imitation; in this "me-too" world, the values of community and commitment are not in vogue); and, finally, the subtle influence of the prevailing social zeitgeist (the ascendant American value system is consistent with a workplace ethos of everybody out for him- or herself, which is "very much contrary to the idea of organizations as communities of shared fate").[7]

Given those factors, Pfeffer says it is hardly any wonder that so few American executives think of their organizations as communities. But he concludes his analysis on a positive note: the current business climate actually leaves a competitive opportunity for companies that operate differently. As in product markets, competitive advantage in labor markets comes from offering a different—and better—value proposition. Doing what everyone else does basically produces the same results everyone else gets. Variation in performance, either positive or negative, comes from being different. So, the competitive advantage in attracting employees Costco enjoys, for example, grows to the extent its culture and communal orientation are increasingly unique and superior. And that, in turn, leads to superior operating results.

CHOICES AND CONSEQUENCES

Yet, most corporate executives believe that adopting HI practices is costly and confers benefits only to certain companies in certain industries. Moreover, many executives calculate that the benefit of gaining an advantage in recruiting employees does not warrant the extra effort and expense. However, on close analysis, the benefits of HI practices can come in many, and often unexpected, forms. For example, the U.S. airline industry has never recovered from the shock of September 11, but some airlines have fared better than others, and in many cases the difference is a function of how they treat their employees. In the aftermath of the tragedy, Delta, Northwest, US Airways, and United all filed for bankruptcy, and American narrowly avoided doing so in 2003. The initial difficulties relating to a fall in demand for air travel have been compounded not only by soaring fuel costs but also by poor people management, as the experience of United illustrates.

In the 1990s, United briefly appeared to have solved its labor problems when its employees exchanged pay for company stock and boardroom seats. But the promise of long-term labor-management cooperation was never realized, in large part because United's top executives made a series of mistaken choices. For example:

☐ The company agreed to appoint union representatives, not workers, as company directors, thus setting up an adversarial relationship in their boardroom.

☐ United executives refused to learn from the experiences of other employee-owned companies. They insisted on exercising the kinds of managerial prerogatives common in investor-owned companies, but inappropriate when labor/management cooperation is essential. Moreover, United didn't educate adequately its managers or employees about the special nature of employee-owned companies.

☐ Management agreed to the request of its flight attendants to opt-out of ownership, thus establishing two classes of workers, owners (pilots and mechanics) and employees (flight attendants).

After September 11, United CEO Jim Goodwin sent a doomsday letter to all employees saying the company was "hemorrhaging money" and *they* would have to sacrifice. But by that time relations between United's executives and employees were so strained, and trust was so absent, that workers resisted even management's sensible efforts to restructure company operations.

In contrast to United, before and after September 11 Continental's top management made a completely different set of choices with regard to their workforce, and harvested quite different outcomes. In 1994, when Gordon Bethune took over as CEO, the company had recently been in Chapter 11 bankruptcy, and its market capitalization was less than the trade-in value of its jet fleet. Its labor relations couldn't have been worse, thanks to the ham-fisted leadership of the company's former CEO, Frank Lorenzo. But Bethune, who had started out as a mechanic on navy planes and later became a pilot, identified with his employees and sought immediately to build a spirit of honesty and open communications with them and with their unions. He began by listening to them, by telling them the truth about the company's financial situation, and by rewarding them for behavior that was in their self-interest *and* in the interest of the company. For example, he gave every employee a $65 bonus check each month the company ranked in the top three of airlines in terms of ontime performance. Bethune and his team came down from the executive suite and spent time in the field and on planes getting to know Continental's employees and addressing their concerns.[8] Within hours of the September 11 attacks, Bethune sent a voice-mail message to all employees telling them everything he knew about the situation. When it later became necessary to cut back the company's flight schedule and to lay off 4 percent of the workforce, there was a broadly shared spirit of cooperation in an attempt to save the company. Thanks largely to extra efforts by its employees, Continental ended up being a survivor in the wake of September 11: it lost less than its major competitors, did not go into bankruptcy, and was able to acquire U.S. Airways.

Of course, the airline that has fared best since September 11 has been Southwest. Since it was formed in the 1970s, the company has sought to avoid adversarial relations with the nine unions representing some 90 percent of its workforce. For example, when the company decided to offer employees a flexible benefits plan, it did so without forcing the unions to negotiate for it. According to researcher Thomas Kochan, the company maintains a large employee "culture committee" that identifies problems in the workforce and then forms small teams to develop solutions. For example, one team addressed the problem of "employee burnout" among those who were on one job for long periods of time. In general, instead of governing the company by rules and formal structures, Southwest has built a consistent culture of employee involvement. After September 11, the company simply continued as before, and continues to be profitable.

THE LIMITS TO PEOPLE MANAGEMENT

If nothing else, these Southwest and Continental examples underscore a key characteristic of the leaders of HI companies: under all contingencies, they remain focused on long-term performance, recognizing that their approach to people management is an investment in the future.

But as much as the evidence supports the choice of executives to treat their people right, HI practices alone are not panaceas: they need to be tailored to the specific mission and strategy of each company, they need to be implemented fully and effectively, and there must be a long-term commitment to them. Even the best human resources practices will not compensate for a bad strategy or mismanagement; after all, Enron had some of the most progressive employee development practices in American industry.

An even more sobering example is another energy giant, AES Corporation, which from 1994 to 2002 had perhaps the most-progressive human resources policies in a large U.S. corporation. Under the leadership of its then-CEO, Dennis Bakke, the company offered almost all the best practices developed at such pathbreaking companies as Avis in the 1960s and 1970s, Herman Miller and Sweden's SAS in the 1980s and, most recently, at WL Gore and SRC Holdings, along with a judicious admixture of guru-grounded practices. When it came to treating people right, what Bakke did at AES was textbook perfect. To Bakke, creating "joy at work" didn't mean providing workers with beer busts and skittles; instead, it meant giving "people the freedom to use their talents and skills for the benefit of society, without being crushed or controlled by autocratic supervisors or staff offices." To accomplish that, he tossed out organization charts, job descriptions, and the human resources department, and gave every worker the authority and opportunity to learn, grow, and make a difference to the company's performance. He put nearly all of AES's 35,000 workers on a salary basis, organized them into self-managing teams of fifteen to twenty members, gave them access to "insider" financial data, and then left them free to find ways to improve the organization's effectiveness. He followed up by carefully measuring their performance, holding them accountable, and rewarding them based on their contributions. Everything he did was predicated on the virtuous leadership principle that if you treat people like adults, they will act like ones.[9]

After AES's share price hit its high of $70 in 2000, it fell to below $5 less than two years later. The company's board lost confidence in Bakke and, shortly thereafter, he "resigned" as CEO. What happened is complicated, and there are at least two credible sides to the story, but, in the end, the financial mess that ended his watch tarnished the admirable record of all the good things Bakke had done with and for his employees. Without doubt, he was an impressive manager of people, perhaps one of the best in America during the 1990s when too few leaders demonstrated ethical concern for their employees. But he also was an unfortunate—perhaps incompetent—business strategist. And even being the greatest people manager doesn't compensate for that when bills come due.

While the events at AES remind us of the necessity of being realistic about the limitations of good human resources management, we must emphasize that AES did not get into its financial difficulties *as a result* of treating its employees right. Nor did Enron get into hot water *because* of its innovative managerial development practices. The problems at both companies occurred *despite* their textbook HI practices. The real lesson that executives need to understand is that good people policies are not the be all and end all of management; instead, HI practices need to be well-meshed parts of an integrated approach to running an entire enterprise.

HIGH-INVOLVEMENT PRACTICES
IN LC AND GC COMPANIES

Executives at LC and GC companies can benefit by choosing among, and tailoring, HI practices to fit their various business strategies. Even without adopting the entire HI philosophy, leaders of conventionally managed GC and LC companies can creatively adopt and integrate selected HI practices into their existing business models. In doing so, they can benefit from an honest self-assessment of their current workplace practices, asking:

- ☐ To what extent is the company's existing human resources strategy consistent with its business model, and to what extent does it lead to a competitive advantage?
- ☐ To what extent is the company's human resources strategy sustainable over the long-term, and to what extent does it help or hinder its ability to change as circumstances necessitate?
- ☐ To what extent are the company's jobs and working conditions structured to capture employee value-added?
- ☐ In terms of its internal accounting, to what extent does the company measure the full costs and benefits of its human capital and management practices?

☐   To what extent does the company measure and internalize the full social costs and benefits of its human resource practices?

In light of these questions, below we ask what HI practices would enhance
the financial and human performance of companies with GC and LC business models.

BUSINESS MODELS OF GC COMPANIES

As we have seen, in rapidly changing competitive environments, where advantages go to companies offering the latest and best products, the key to
success is having the talent needed to produce the next "new thing." That is
why global manufacturing and entertainment companies—and, to a somewhat lesser extent, financial and professional services firms—must be agile
in deploying their workforces. For these GC companies, it is often cheaper
"to buy than to build" talent; thus they are constantly recruiting workers
with currently needed skills and shedding employees who are seen as redundant (or "legacy costs" in the euphemistic vernacular of the age).

The key characteristics of employment in GC corporations include
extensive use of incentive pay—often above market, and based on skills
and performance—and challenging, technically interesting work. U.S.-
based GC companies often have two classes of employees: a core of top
managers and staff people on fairly traditional career paths and a larger
body of contingent or contract professionals, who may or may not be
Americans or physically located in this country. The hierarchies of GC
companies tend to be flat and their organizational structures fluid. Their
professional workforce is more likely to be organized in teams than along
conventional functional lines, and work routines tend to be unpredictable. Supervision in these companies is loose, but performance expectations are extremely high. The ultimate measure of performance is
the wealth created for shareholders.

The business model of GC companies is sustainable as long as there is a
sufficient supply of skilled and educated workers willing to bear the risks of
unemployment and the costs of their own training and development. The
human resource strategies of GC companies are far more sophisticated than
those at LC companies, but their internal auditing processes often fail to ac-

count fully for a number of hidden management costs, including those related to constantly needing to integrate new people and the expenses entailed in having to use financial incentives to lure contingent workers.
Furthermore, costs associated with the absence of employee loyalty are hard
to measure: who knows what it costs GCs in terms of lost customer service
and productivity to have employees constantly on the lookout for their next
jobs? Also hard to reckon are the costs involved in the effort to sustain the
culture, knowledge, and core capabilities of these organizations in light of
their relatively high turnover. Finally, GC companies are vulnerable to competitors that adopt characteristics of HI companies. Indeed, that is why parts
of many GC companies use HI practices to one degree or another—but they
do so inconsistently and sporadically, and with little philosophical or long-
term commitment to doing so.

HI PRACTICES APPROPRIATE AT GC COMPANIES

It is significant that such successful GC companies as Adobe Systems,
Genentech, Microsoft, Amgen, Medtronic, and Cisco often act like HI
companies in terms of building a sense of community, encouraging worker
participation, and offering stock ownership and generous benefits. Leaders
at these companies use their strategic and moral imaginations to create
human resources policies that allow them to treat their employees better
than their competitors do, even if they can't offer all their workers a great
deal of job security. Indeed, there are numerous HI practices GC companies
can adopt if they wish to compete for employees in terms of the working
conditions they offer, and if they wish employees to demonstrate loyalty and
enthusiasm. For example:

- ☐ GC companies can reduce the social distance between corporate leaders and workers. Although their company hierarchies are increasingly
  being flattened, many bosses nonetheless interact infrequently or in-
  sufficiently with front-line people.
- ☐ They can pay more attention to the nature of work itself—for example, to how jobs are designed in terms of how much autonomy workers have and their opportunities to influence the outcomes of their
  own tasks.

□ They can design jobs to be not dead-ends but, instead, as steps in career tracks. Doing this may require the creation of a variety of career tracks within a company.

□ GC companies can avoid outsourcing jobs, particularly when all the work involved is directly related to the company's customers. Doing this prevents the creation of two separate classes of employees.

□ Workers can be salaried instead of being paid by the hour.

□ GC companies can provide employees opportunities to develop their skills by paying for their training, providing them with information about internal job openings, and rewarding their development.

□ They can adopt profit sharing and employee stock-ownership, and share financial information with employees as widely as legally feasible.

□ GC companies can calculate the full costs of employee turnover, including the hard-to-measure impact on productivity, innovation, morale, commitment, and loyalty. Companies can share those calculations with all managers and with the board of directors.

Obviously, these rules of thumb run counter to the prevailing beliefs of executives at many large GC companies who fear that instituting HI practices would cause their companies to lose their competitive edge. And when the issue is limiting outsourcing, offshoring, or downsizing, the common verdict among GC executives is, "If our competitors are doing it, then we have to do it." But experience shows that this widely held belief is not necessarily correct. For example, during the extended 2001 to 2003 recession, when hundreds of thousands of American workers were losing their jobs, most corporate leaders assumed they had no other choice but to lay off workers. Nonetheless, Wim Roelandts, CEO of Xilinx (a billion-dollar high-tech company with over two thousand U.S. employees), believed there had to be an alternative, even when company profits plummeted by 50 percent. Members of his board and some of his top executives argued that lay-offs were the only way Xilinx could stem the flow of red ink.[10]

But driven by his stated communitarian values of respect for employees—and by commitments he had made to provide for their development as workers and human beings—Roelandts charged a task force of managers with finding alternatives to layoffs. They came up with a dozen programs that subsequently were put into place, including funding educational sabbaticals for workers and paying them modest stipends for volunteering in nonprofit organizations. A year later the company came roaring back, all its employees imbued with a deep commitment to making it a financial success. Employee turnover at Xilinx is less than 4 percent per annum, close to, if not the, lowest in the computer industry.

Similarly, Palo Alto's Genencor, a billion-dollar biotech innovator employing over 600 people, has an annual employee turnover of less than 4 percent, roughly a quarter the average for its industry, and an average job tenure of 7.4 years, also extremely long for a GC company with a highly skilled professional workforce. Since the cost of recruiting and training a replacement employee at Genencor is on the order of $70,000, such low turnover gives it a competitive advantage. To keep turnover low, the company invests heavily in its workers. For example, Genecor gives them a voice in developing its unique benefits package (which includes such extras as free loaner cars and an on-site drycleaner), which adds about $700 a year to the cost of fringe benefits for each employee. Genencor involves its employees in all manner of decisions, even in the recent design of its headquarters building, and gives them the freedom to innovate because it sees employee creativity as its core competence. Not surprisingly, the company had the highest employee job satisfaction rating in a recent survey of northern California employers.[11]

We believe that the lessons from Xilinx and Genencor can be transferred to other high-tech and biotech GC companies that compete for talent: since the cost of turnover in these industries is often equal to, or greater than, an employee's annual salary, it makes sense to invest in workers so they won't be tempted to leave for greener pastures. Although some large, sophisticated employers pay close attention to the costs of turnover, the internal cost accounting at many GC companies is much more likely to capture the savings from an employee layoff than it is to capture those from an employee retention.

In the manufacturing sector, worker productivity is a key to success among exporters of finished goods. In this regard, GC manufacturers might borrow a page profitably from the HI practices of motorcycle manufacturer Harley-Davidson. Nearly defunct when Richard Teerlink became its CEO in 1989, Harley was resuscitated largely as a result of adopting such HI practices as organizing its 5,000 employees at the time into teams and rewarding them for their ideas and efforts to improve product quality and customer service.[12] Current CEO James Ziemer—who started with the company while in high school and who sometimes still wears blue-collar overalls to work—has negotiated imaginative contracts with the unions representing

Harley's workers, agreeing to keep production in the United States in exchange for constantly reducing total labor costs by automating tasks and changing work rules. Because Harley regularly reassigns workers whose tasks are automated to other parts of the company rather than laying them off, its total workforce has grown to over 9,500, even while its productivity has greatly improved.

Harley's results are in striking contrast to those at Ford and General Motors, where labor costs are up, sales down, and total employment is constantly shrinking. Significantly, in the 1970s, U.S. automakers and the United Auto Workers (UAW) turned their backs on promising efforts to adopt the kinds of HI practices found today at Harley. The UAW, Ford, General Motors (and its spin-off, Delphi) are paying a heavy price today for that mistake. We draw the conclusion that almost all managers of GC companies have some choice when it comes to organizing their workplaces to engage employees in increasing performance—and prudent executives adopt HI practices before it is too late for them to benefit from doing so.

BUSINESS MODELS OF LC OPERATORS

At least as customers, all Americans are familiar with companies that compete in terms of the price of the goods and services they offer: gas stations, fast-food and retail outlets, cleaning and maintenance companies. The business strategies in these price-sensitive industries are predicated on a basic tenet of capitalist economics: *the consumer is king*. On the theory that customers will buy from the vendor offering the lowest price, the business model of LC companies requires them to keep their costs—in particular, their labor costs—as low as possible. Managers of these companies are able to keep labor costs down because the jobs they offer are low-value-added (in politically incorrect terms, that means anyone can do them with little or no skills or training), and the supply of people willing to do them is plentiful: LC companies draw on the pool of the 50 percent of Americans who lack college educations, among whom the rate of unemployment is typically 2 percent above the rate of the more-educated.[13] They often are the only major employers who will hire non–high school graduates.

As we have noted, the key employment characteristics of LC companies include low wages, few benefits, simple tasks, close supervision, and high variability of hours and days worked. These companies make heavy use of part-time, seasonal, and temporary employees who often are in school or have "second jobs." Employee turnover tends to be extremely high (over 100 percent annually is not unusual), but replacement costs are not high because they invest so little in employee recruiting and training. The vast majority of their front-line workers are not on career tracks, and they have little opportunity for upward mobility. However, these companies also have a second category of employees: a core of managers and functional experts whose technical capabilities hold the company together and represent its "knowledge capital." These upper-level employees enjoy formal career tracks, receive extensive training, have good benefits, and are well paid. Indeed, the top tiers of LC companies look very much like those of GC companies, with whom they compete for managerial and technical talent.

The business model of LC companies is sustainable for as long as (1) the products or services they provide cannot be offshored; (2) there is an adequate supply of cheap labor; (3) society is willing to bear the employment costs these companies don't internalize, including costs related to worker education, health, and retirement; and (4) the indirect costs of their management model remain low. Indeed, the sustainability of many LC companies comes into particular question when their hidden, indirect costs are taken into full account: few of them fully cost-out the expenditures they make in terms of turnover, the extra supervision required to control poorly trained and unmotivated workers, and the effects on customer satisfaction of poor service and low-quality products.

HI PRACTICES APPROPRIATE AT LC COMPANIES

There is relatively little that LC companies can do to improve the way they treat employees *if they have defined their competitive comparative advantage solely in terms of low per-capita labor costs.* We say "per-capita labor costs" advisedly, to distinguish them from "total labor costs." Although HI companies incur high per-capita labor costs, typically their total labor costs are relatively low because they need fewer employees to do tasks. Higher-paid, better-trained, self-managing HI workers are not only more productive than lower-paid, undertrained, and heavily supervised LC workers, they produce higher-quality goods and services. Hence, more sophisticated use of human resource metrics—such as accounting for the full costs of turnover and the negative impact on customers of dealing with poorly trained "service" person-nel—might demonstrate to LC employers that it is worth rethinking some of their human resources practices. Indeed, we believe it is almost always cost-ef-fective for services companies to reduce employee turnover and to provide in-centives that motivate and engage their workforces. (The exception may be such purely transactional activities as ticket-taking in movie theaters.)

It is discouraging to report so little change in human capital management practices. As early as the 1960s, the benefits of HI practices were well known, and experts assumed it was just a matter of time before all companies would adopt the practices of the best-managed firms. Prior to the publication of *Work in America,* Peter Drucker had written that "I have come to the con-clusion that the decisive change which underlies the rise of organizations is the shift from viewing the worker as a cost center to viewing him as a 're-source.'" His declaration of victory in this regard turned out to be extremely premature. Even today, too few managers treat their workers as resources, and too many treat them mainly as a cost, particularly among LC operators.

But even if managers at LC companies conclude they cannot justify the added expenses entailed in HI activities, it always makes sense for them to lis-ten to their employees because the simple truth is that employees in most LC companies lack an effective voice. That is apparently why the Wal-Mart Work-ers Association was formed in Florida in 2005. Sponsored by labor unions and supported by foundation grants, the association is petitioning Wal-Mart and the state of Florida to improve working conditions and wages on behalf of the company's nonorganized workforce. The association argues that it is not hostile to Wal-Mart but rather is calling attention to the fact that the company does-n't listen effectively to its employee concerns. One member of the association, a cashier earning $7.40 an hour, said she joined because her work hours had been reduced from full- to part-time and her requests for more hours weren't heeded: "I'm a single mother trying to raise my son, so not having that money makes it hard," she told a reporter, "sometimes I have to decide, am I paying the rent, or will I have food on the table?" She added, "I like Wal-Mart, I enjoy working for them, but what they are doing is wrong. They need to fix it."[14]

Although they don't have the resources GC companies have to pay their employees as well or to train them as fully, every large LC company has suf-ficient resources to tell them the truth about the jobs they offer. We believe there is no shame in offering minimum-wage jobs with few benefits or op-portunities for promotion—particularly when the company is recruiting young people who are living at home and covered by their parents' health insurance. But such companies should be honest with adult workers trying to support families. The pay and benefits of most LC jobs are insufficient for a single breadwinner, and often even for a working couple, to care for children adequately. And that is the first thing a responsible LC employer should tell prospective hires.

Southwest Airlines goes beyond merely being honest with its workers; it has created a business model that affords flexibility to both the company and its employees and gives hardworking ones the opportunity to earn decent wages by any standard. Southwest's human resources strategy didn't just happen by accident: former CEO Herb Kelleher used his imagination to create a business model that was simultaneously good for customers, owners, and employees. Southwest is worker-friendly, but its practices also "pay." For example, through employee cross-training and multitasking, the company has the fastest plane turnarounds, lowest employee headcount per number of flights, and the best on-time record in the industry. Given such manifest benefits to all parties, it is remarkable that so few LC executives see it as their task to do something similar at their own companies.

For example, in the services sector, even though expenditures on employee training can almost always be justified in terms of increased customer satisfaction, too few LC companies make a real commitment to training. Providing non-job-related educational opportunities to workers is viewed as a costly and unnecessary frill; for that reason it is nearly unheard of in the low-cost services sector. Yet almost all LC companies, their employees, and their customers, could benefit from company-sponsored English as a second language programs. Fetzer Vineyards extends education benefits to all its employees—including Spanish-speaking immigrant field workers—and the company's president argues that doing so is cost-effective: "The more educated the workforce, the better decisions they make. Our education programs allow us to push decision-making down to where it should be—to the fields or the bottling plant or the sales force. That allows us to respond quickly to the needs of the marketplace."[15]

HI PRACTICES ALL COMPANIES SHOULD ADOPT

Compensation Practices

Many LC and GC companies could benefit from adopting HI compensation practices. For example, at HI-company Whole Foods, 85 percent of stock options are held by nonexecutives, a rate of participation unheard of in most retail companies. Indeed, there seems to be inherent injustice across-the-board in corporate America in terms of the distribution of stock options: in the typical company 75 percent go to CEOs, 15 percent to the next fifty highest-compensated executives, and only 10 percent to all other employees.[16]

And most GC and LC corporate boards commonly assume they have "no choice" but to pay their CEOs as much as those at other large companies and to pay their front-line workers as little as their competitors pay. But corporate officers and directors could start from another place, basing the pay of all employees on a reckoning of their relative contribution. They could ask, *is the CEO's proportionate contribution to the organization ten, one hundred, one thousand times greater than that of a store manager, human resources officer, or front-line worker?* Asking such questions is practically unheard of in the boardrooms of giant companies, but boards in a few small and medium-size HI companies—such as Whole Foods—have done so, and then established ratios as low as 20 to 1 between the compensations of their highest-paid executive and average worker. That ratio may sound unrealistic, but it makes some sense when the numbers are run. If the average worker makes $20 an hour, the CEO in even a "low-paying" company can make $1 million. The ratio seems out of the question only because the current ratio in *Fortune* 500 companies approaches 500 to1.

The goal is not necessarily to limit the pay of CEOs—although the most egregious executive pay practices should be curtailed: for example, granting executives big bonuses and raises for conducting major layoffs or for winning wage and benefit concessions not only rewards past managerial failures, it amounts to a gratuitous slap in the faces of employees. The real goal should be to find ways to push up the salaries of productive workers down the line who add value to the company. Doing this is not an act of charity. The dictates of the labor market must be heeded. An LC company would price itself out of business if it paid its clerks as much as it pays its managers; however, executives can increase opportunities for even first-line employees to raise their own standards of living. For example, boards can distribute stock and stock options more broadly. The late Sam Walton couldn't pay his Wal-Mart service workers much more than the minimum wage, but he had the moral imagination to cut them into the upside by making many of them equity owners. CEOs and boards tend to forget there are a number of well-tested methods—all consistent with the rules of the mar-

---

Choosing to be Paid Less

In most American companies, the salaries of top executives are set with refer-ence to surveys of compensation of executives in comparable positions in other firms. Boards say they have "no choice" but to pay their executives salaries at least equal to those paid by competitor companies. But there is evidence that boards actually have some choice in the matter; in fact, they may be able to get off the executive compensation escalator if they have the moral courage to do so. Ethan Berman, CEO of the financial consultancy RiskMetrics, shocked Wall Street in late 2005 when it was revealed that he had asked the chairman of his board's compensation committee to pay him less. Although his company's rev-enues of $100 million increased by over 40 percent, Berman wanted no raise or stock options, and to participate in profit sharing only to the same extent as all his 270 employees. In making his case, Berman quoted the legendary banker J. P. Morgan who said he would never lend money to any company where the highest-paid executive was paid more than twenty times that of the lowest-paid employee. Berman said that much of RiskMetrics' success was the result not of what he did as a CEO but by the contributions of many employees, and it was their efforts that would "create value in the long run" for the company.[17]

---

ket—for objectively and fairly linking rewards to the relative contribution of employees: profit sharing, gain sharing, ESOPs, and the like.[18]

Internalizing Social Costs

One of the fundamental requirements for efficient markets is that all costs re-lated to a transaction need to be internalized in the price of a product. As we have seen, one of the main areas where employers produce inefficient external-ities is with regard to employee health, where society and employees are often forced to bear the costs. We believe that all employers have an economic re-sponsibility to create healthier work environments. To do this, they ought to recognize that the costs of poor employee health extend far beyond increased insurance premiums, as if those rising costs weren't reason enough to act. In ad-dition, the indirect costs of physical stress and mental depression are enormous when measured in terms of lost worker productivity, poor customer service and work quality, turnover, and workplace conflict. Clearly, employers do not pay the full cost of the stress produced on the job: workers and society bear the rest. From an economic point of view, this is both inefficient and unfair. Again, the failure of business organizations to internalize the full costs of their operations amounts to an involuntary subsidy that others are forced to pay. The result is a misallocation of resources and market inefficiencies benefiting those producers most adept at pushing their costs on to others. Hence, healthier workplaces are in the public interest. Here are some potentially cost-effective HI actions employers can take to make their workplaces healthier:

1. Encourage exercise and weight control

All companies can and should make an effort to educate workers about their responsibilities for limiting their own health-risk factors. Numerous well-tested programs are available to help employees understand the need for proper diet, exercise, and healthy lifestyles (for example, not smoking). Some companies also offer programs in stress-management, helping individuals with personality characteristics that put them at high risk for cardiovascular disease to avoid or cope with conflict and other anxiety-producing work situations. Rayona Sharpnack, founder of the Institute for Women's Leadership, offers good advice to people who are suffering stress: "Consider the possibility that you are colluding in your own demise. Suffering is optional."

Increasing numbers of employers are introducing "wellness" programs (41 percent according to Hewitt Associates, up from 34 percent a decade ago).[19] Most such programs consist of relatively passive activities: distributing pamphlets to workers about diet, nutrition, and the risks of smoking, and the voluntary testing of blood pressure at health fairs. But more employers are providing exercise rooms at workplaces (with incentives to use them), and weight reduction programs; some offer memberships in health clubs.

It is neither necessary nor ethical to force employees to participate in such programs—for example, the CEO of Weyco who recently fired workers who smoked clearly transgressed on their individual liberties. But providing information, education, resources, and incentives to exercise and lead healthy lives are legitimate employer initiatives that benefit workers, their families, society, and the company itself (such programs may even pay for themselves in the long run, although the jury is still out on that score). Nonetheless, responsible employers are honest with employees about why they offer such programs: they are in everyone's self-interest and thus are *not* employee "benefits."

2. Manage people right

In general, as we have seen, stress occurs when workers don't know what is expected of them, when they are told to do one thing and then punished for not doing another, and when they lack adequate resources to do their as-

Employee Safety and Health
Best Practices in Companies Big and Small

BIG COMPANY

In 1986, Alcoa's then CEO, Paul O'Neil, surprised the business world when he declared that worker safety was "the company's most important internal priority" and established the goal of zero days lost to injuries, zero fatalities, and zero work-related illnesses. That was remarkable for three reasons: (1) the company had not been forced by the government or unions to make this commitment, (2) the company was in a line of businesses known for having high accident and injury rates, and (3) the commitment—which still stands today—came from a giant global company with 131,000 employees at 436 locations in 43 countries.

While O'Neil was CEO, the company changed its entire corporate culture to meet the incredibly high standards he had set. It had to change its relationships to workers and unions, change how and what it measured, and change who and what it rewarded. For example, reporting safety and health problems became the norm at all levels; in the past, managers would try to cover them up. Education programs were put in place to heighten employee health and safety awareness and, over the years, thousands of local initiatives were started and sustained to meet O'Neil's unattainable goal of perfection. To that end, the company constantly reports in real-time on its website to its employees, customers, and investors data relating to injuries and days lost.

AND SMALL

American Cast Iron Pipe Company (ACIPCO) is an anomaly no matter how one looks at it: the company is the only old-line heavy manufacturer to have made *Fortune*'s list of "100 Best Companies to Work For" every year since the feature's inception in 1988. The work done in the company is hot, hard, and unglamorous. Nobody ever said that casting molten iron into 5,000-pound pipes is fun, yet the company's annual turnover rate is only 2.3 percent, one of the lowest in the nation in any industry (half of its 2,554 workers have been on the job twenty years or more). The company has been owned since 1924 by a trust operating it on behalf of the employees, nearly a third of whom are African Americans.

The average annual salary for hourly workers is $41,831. In addition, the company spends $3,450 annually for single employees and $8,940 for those with families to cover the cost of its on-site medical center where twenty doctors and nurses, eleven dentists and hygienists, and four pharmacists provide healthcare for the entire staff, their dependents, and 1,200 retirees. No one pays health insurance premiums, but all pay $10 for a doctor visit and 25 percent of prescription costs. If employees choose to go to a private physician, the company pays a fixed percentage of the cost.

ACIPCO also spends about $266 per employee for an on-site gym and for bonuses for those workers who strive to stay healthy. Nearly 70 percent of the workforce participates in its WellBody Club in which they can earn annual bonuses ranging from $10 to $200 based on their scores on a variety of risk factors, including blood pressure, body fat percentage, cholesterol levels, days of exercise per week, and not smoking. ACIPCO says it spends about $600,000 on its wellness program but reckons it saves about $1.2 million in productivity and healthcare costs that would have been lost through illness to workers.

Many experts conclude that the working conditions companies offer are solely a reflection of the businesses they are in and the business strategies they are pursuing. Yet on closer inspection, it is clear that even companies in the same industry, and located in the same city, often have quite different ideas about what employees want, need, and what will motivate them. For example, the other major manufacturer of cast iron pipe in Birmingham, McWare, Inc., made the news when it was revealed that it had been cited for around eight hundred safety and environmental violations over the last eight years, including numerous cases in which employees had been maimed, burned, made ill, and even killed. Among other issues, workers at McWare had not been trained to handle the flammable materials in the plant. In contrast, at ACIPCO the training of blue-collar workers is a priority, and workers serve on committees that set and monitor plant safety and work rules. Since both of these companies make money, it would seem that corporate executives have some choice when it comes to the working conditions they provide.

signed jobs. Most such stress is caused by mismanagement. Hence, good managers do three basic things:

☐ They clearly communicate the overall task of the organization and how each worker's job contributes to doing that task.
☐ They clearly state how the performance of each job is measured and then closely tie worker rewards to those measures.
☐ They provide the resources workers need to perform their jobs successfully, including adequate information, training, authority, staff, tools, technology, budget, and time.

Good managers thus create the conditions under which the people who report to them can carry out their assigned tasks. Although creating these conditions is often difficult, there is something elegant about being a good manager: the healthy workplace that results also turns out to be a productive one.

3. Make supervision supportive

If recent workplace research is clear about anything, it is the importance of supportive supervision. Yet one need only visit a fast-food franchise or a retail shop in a mall to witness evidence of supervisors "missing in action." Some symptoms of poor supervision include: front-line workers who don't know what to do, who fail to serve customers, who make mistakes and don't learn from them, and who don't apologize when they do. Worse, of course, is when supervisors berate or abuse employees who make mistakes. When workers perform poorly, it is almost always the fault of management, and the first step in correcting that is to train supervisors. Indeed, almost every organization can benefit from more, and improved, supervisor training, and not just at lower levels. By definition, managers at all levels supervise others; hence, supervision is the essence of management. Yet few companies pay adequate attention to what it really means for managers to provide a supportive environment for workers. Alas, as the late Peter Drucker wrote, "So much of what we call management consists of making it difficult for people to work." A study of best practices at HI companies quickly reveals that they spend a great deal of time and attention on training managers to improve their communication skills and to help them reduce conflict, encourage teamwork, and create environments in which workers have confidence they will get help when they need it.

4. Encourage work/family balance
Experience at HI workplaces shows that well-designed employer efforts to provide child care, elder care, flexible scheduling, job sharing, and the like can help to reduce role conflict and increase organizational support of workers in ways that make for healthier and more productive workplaces. The challenge here is for managers to creatively tailor such programs to fit situations where too clearly "they won't work." For example, while the average number of hours worked at the Big Four accounting firms has risen greatly as the result of increased demand for CPA services created by the passage of the Sarbanes-Oxley act, 30 percent of the two thousand accountants at Jefferson Wells International have reduced or flexible workweeks. Some 10 percent are on a flexible schedule and receive benefits (a thirty-hour week is typical), and others work fewer hours on a contract basis and receive no benefits. As the result of the way work is organized, many of the 70 percent of Jefferson Wells accountants who are full-timers work fewer hours than do their Big Four counterparts.

5. Create a sense of community
The controversial practices of HI-company Patagonia—a $240 million firm with nine hundred employees, most located in California—might not seem

at all applicable at most companies. For example, Patagonia offers maternity/paternity leave, subsidized on-site child care, and family-friendly flexible working hours. (Actually, the CEO says the work environment is more "task-oriented than time-oriented," and workers can be seen taking off for a bike ride in the middle of the day or heading to the beach when the surf is up.) The company also gives 1 percent of its profits to grassroots environmental organizations and plays a leading role in an organization that insures that the employees in plants in the developing world that supply fabrics to American companies like Patagonia are paid fair wages and have adequate working conditions.

But there is another reason why there are hundreds of applications for every job that opens up at Patagonia: its employees can receive full pay while working for two months in a nonprofit agency. Similarly, Timberland gives its employees a paid week off once a year to volunteer in local nonprofits and offers a limited number of six-month sabbaticals to workers who want to work for community organizations. The company also closes down for a full day once a year so that all five thousand employees can take part in a company-sponsored community project.

Although such community-oriented programs are not all that expensive to operate, workers often view them as valuable psychic benefits, particularly those workers whose jobs are not intrinsically challenging. As University of California, Berkeley, professor David Vogel documents in *The Market for Virtue,* enthusiasts tend to over-ballyhoo, and critics tend to over-disparage, corporate philanthropy and company-sponsored employee participation in community activities—which go under the general rubric of corporate social responsibility. While their contributions to the welfare of communities and society may be marginal, such programs often contribute tremendously to employee morale and build the sponsoring companies' reputations as "enlightened employers." People want to work for a company they can be proud of; they want to be part of something "bigger than themselves." For example, after Merck made headlines by giving away a drug to cure river-blindness in the developing world, Roy Vagelos, the company's CEO at the time, said, "We could hire almost anybody we wanted for ten years."[20]

Just being employed by Apple or Genentech—working on the next electronic gizmo or wonder drug—is often a sufficient source of pride. But for workers at a supermarket or a chemical plant, having a paid day off once or twice a year to volunteer in the community can be a great morale booster.

Ethicist Kirk Hansen documented the effects in a GE plastics plant in San Diego at which employees were given a few days off from work to completely rehabilitate a school in a disadvantaged neighborhood, ripping it down to its studs and then totally remodeling it.[21] Every employee in the plant participated. The rebuilt school was a beauty to behold, but the employees gained the most in terms of community-building and a boost to their collective pride.

What seems to work best with regard to employee community involvement is a practice introduced at Levi-Strauss in the 1980s where employee committees were empowered to make decisions about which local organizations would receive corporate contributions, usually ones in which the employees themselves were willing to volunteer their time. Importantly, this is an area where large companies are not at a comparative disadvantage to smaller ones in terms of creating a sense of community. Financial giant Washington Mutual gives all its employees eighty hours off each year to volunteer in their local communities and contributes 2 percent of company profits to community causes. Executive Daryl David says, "Pride in the company has a lot to do with 'what my team did when we built a playground at the local school.'"

Evaluating the degree of virtue involved in such community activities is an extremely complex matter. After Hurricane Katrina devastated the Gulf states, Wal-Mart made generous contributions to help local communities deal with the immediate crisis and to help them get back on their collective feet. This was an example of virtuous corporate social responsibility. But such admirable community-spirited corporate activities should not be seen as substitutes for treating employees right.

THE "OTHER" AMERICAN WORKFORCE

Small cultural dissimilarities not withstanding, research shows that good work is good work, whether it is in Silicon Valley or Saigon. Yet in the manufacturing sector, managers of American-owned businesses often assume that employees in their factories in less-developed countries have different basic needs than do their U.S. employees. Managers often insist that workplace customs and worker aspirations are "different" in the United States from those in underdeveloped countries and, therefore, employment standards applied at home are by necessity different from those applicable abroad. In sum, they say they have "no choice" but to conform to local laws and customs.

That is true, but only up to a point. In the international marketplace, local economies and laws dictate how much workers are paid and what their basic working conditions will be, but those constraints do not absolve American managers of their ethical responsibilities to employees. That people are paid less in countries with lower standards of living is an economic fact that is not going to change, but the ethics governing the treatment of human beings are the same everywhere. Workers are entitled to respect in whatever setting, and that respect begins with such courtesies as listening to their needs, informing them in advance of decisions that affect their well-being, and telling them the truth about their prospects for continuing employment and economic and career advancement.

In particular, young children should not be employed when they should be at school, and employees should not be required to work long hours, and weeks on end, without rest, or to labor in unsafe or unhealthy conditions. If it was morally reprehensible that girls and young women worked twelve-hour days in American textile mills in the nineteenth century, it is morally reprehensible in 2006 that young Chinese women put in sixteen-hour days in American-owned factories, and factories that supply U.S. firms. American managers cannot hide behind the convenient argument that the Chinese government blinks at transgressions of its own labor laws. At a minimum, as U.S. companies offshore jobs, they must continually emphasize the need for foreign suppliers, contractors, and governments to enforce all international environmental, labor, and human rights standards.

By necessity our focus has been on work in America, but we would be remiss in not recognizing the fact that U.S. companies are increasingly becoming major employers and purchasers of goods from subcontractors in underdeveloped nations. We accept that fact as a given. But even if American corporations are free to offshore jobs, they cannot offshore their moral responsibilities to employees.

16

PUBLIC POLICY

The actions of private corporations will be the most powerful determinants of the future of the American workplace, but corporate executives do not hold all the cards. If the United States is to maintain its largely free-trade policies and, at the same time, succeed with its de facto national competitive strategy of being the world's leader in high technology and high value-added goods and services, the federal government will have to realign or revise many of its current policies and programs. The U.S. government needs to enact a set of supportive policies that increase the ability of corporate executives and individual workers to choose wisely and effectively in matters relating to the workplace. In particular, the government must:

☐ Thoroughly reform K–12 public education, with the goal of greatly improving performance in basic skills

☐ Increase the number of American college graduates and university postgraduates, especially in mathematics, science, and other technical disciplines

☐ Use community colleges more effectively as the prime providers of skills training and retraining

☐   Increase national support for research and development to public and private universities and through incentives to private industry

☐   Clarify post–September 11 immigration policies, particularly with regard to foreign students and skilled workers

☐   Encourage entrepreneurial activities as a major source of innovation and job creation

☐   Analyze the effects of federal laws and policies, including the minimum wage and Social Security, on job creation and worker mobility

☐   Decouple health insurance from employment status—which is the most important action the government must take in the short run.

EDUCATION

In America today, education is increasingly the key to individual success in the workplace. Even as the economy struggled after the 2002 to 2003 recession, there was a strong 2.2 percent growth in employment among workers with college degrees and a 1.3 percent *decline* in employment opportunities of those with less than high school educations.[1] Today, workers with high school educations earn $15.07 per hour, compared to $26.23 per hour for four-year college graduates.[2] These aggregate figures can be somewhat misleading, because they are compounded by effects of race and gender, with whites making more than blacks, and men more than women, at every level of educational attainment. But breaking the numbers down demographically reveals that education is often a more important factor than race or gender for every group. In California, Asian women who were born in the United States earned $19.30 per hour in 2001 on average; U.S-born Latinas earned $15.10. The prime determining factor seems to be educational attainment, not race: some 55 percent of California's Asian women have college degrees in contrast to only 14 percent of Hispanic women.[3] Further evidence of the importance of education: foreign-born Latinas, among whom the percentage with college degrees is negligible, earned only $10.40 per hour on average. Education-based income and status gaps promise to grow in the future: according to the U.S. Bureau of Labor Statistics, between 2000 and 2010, employment in occupations requiring at least a bachelor's degree is expected to grow by nearly 22 percent, and all but two of the fifty high-paying jobs will require a college degree.[4]

If the future belongs to the best-educated country and to the best-educated workers, then the effects of current U.S. educational policies and priorities at almost every level of instruction take America and Americans in exactly the wrong direction. While the country does an admirable job with K–12 education in its small, elite, private schools, and in some well-funded suburban public schools, urban public schools fail miserably to prepare boys and girls for work, job training, or further education. And, in general, American schools do poor jobs with math and science at all grades and in all locations in comparison to other developed, and even some developing, nations. America's top colleges and universities are the best in the world but, in general, higher education turns out far too few graduates in math, science, and engineering, and, in particular, far too few American citizens in those fields.

Hence, we add our voices to the growing chorus of critics of the nation's educational system—or, more precisely, nonsystem—calling particular attention to the critical relationship of individual educational attainment to success in the workplace, and the relationship of American economic competitiveness to the overall skill level of our workforce. Few of the recommendations we make to employers about using High-Involvement management practices can be successfully implemented without better-educated workers, and the nation's competitive strategy cannot succeed unless America has the world's *best-educated* workforce. But the nation is far from being there; in fact, we are slipping farther behind where we need to be. More students are dropping out of high school, and too many of those who do graduate are ill-equipped for either work or further education. Whereas the United States recently led the world in terms of providing access to higher education to its citizenry, many European nations now nearly match us in terms of bachelor's degrees, and some Asian countries are catching or surpassing us in terms of the quantity and quality of their graduates in technical fields.

Even if there were no workplace consequences to the deteriorating quality of the nation's schools, the situation still would be a national disgrace because basic education is a requirement for a healthy democracy (for example, high school dropouts are less likely to vote than are graduates) and a necessity for men and women to manage their economic affairs and lead good lives (for example, families of high school dropouts are more likely to live in poverty).

The problems in higher education, while nowhere near as serious as those in the public schools, still require attention because access to the best educational institutions is being increasingly restricted by cost. In addition,

Education and the Biotechnology Industry

If the driving force in innovation and job creation in the latter half of the twentieth century was the global diffusion of information technology, many are predicting the twenty-first century will be the "Age of Biology." Advances in biotechnology are likely to have profound impacts on health, agriculture, the environment, and industry, affecting as much as 50 percent of global gross domestic product in the coming decades. A quick look at the evolution of this heavily knowledge-intensive industry illustrates some emerging challenges and opportunities for the American education system.

The United States created the world's first biotechnology companies in the late 1970s—Cetus, Genentech, Biogen, Amgen—and dominated the industry for the first twenty-five years of its existence. A set of interrelated factors, sometimes referred to as a "high-skill ecosystem" or the "Silicon Valley model," has helped America to develop clusters of successful bioenterprises that other countries have had difficulty emulating. These factors include: cutting-edge innovations and highly skilled graduates produced by top U.S. universities and research institutes; strong legal protection for intellectual property; the Bayh-Dole Act of 1980, which gave universities strong incentives to patent and commercialize the results of their research through spin-off companies or licensing agreements; access to the large amounts of capital needed to develop highly risky technologies; and the world's largest and most profitable market for biomedical and bioagricultural products.

Although American companies still have a dominant position in the global bioscience market, all the major developed and newly industrialized nations are seeking to close the gap and build their own strong presence in the industry. The island-nation of Singapore, for example, has invested billions of dollars to create a biotech cluster that seeks to combine many of the elements of the high-skill ecosystem found in the United States. The number of American biotech firms has remained relatively stagnant at about 1,500 over the last fifteen years; Europe and Asia have seen an explosion in bioscience start-ups and now surpass this county in their total number of biotech companies. With the entry of India and China into the World Trade Organization, and adoption of the TRIPS agreement (for intellectual property protection) in 2005, those countries are likely to emerge as the most powerful new global competitors. India alone has over four hundred bioscience companies, most created in the last decade. Even though many of these firms are likely to fail, it is clear that the United States will face growing competition in this most knowledge-intensive of all industries. (It employs more PhDs as a percentage of the workforce than any other sector.)

At a time when the competition for bioscience leadership is increasing, it is not clear whether the U.S. education system is up to meeting the challenge. Most Americans have low levels of scientific literacy—for example, most don't know that tomatoes have DNA. Thus, as a nation we are ill-equipped for the coming world of genetics-based medicine and biology-driven industry. While some states are experimenting with programs to improve science education, others are considering changing their biology and geology curricula in ways that will hinder the teaching of established scientific facts.

At the other extreme of the educational spectrum, the number of years required in university training to complete a biomedical PhD (6 to 7 years on average), followed by multiple postdoctorates, and relatively low-paying research positions, make this career track unappealing to students entering top universities. As a consequence, scientific leadership, and the accompanying employment opportunities in biotechnology that underpin other key sectors of the economy, may gradually migrate from the United States to Asia, where a pool of scientific talent is available and growing.

—Adapted from David Finegold, "Is Education the Answer?" a paper commissioned for this study.

not nearly enough Americans are enrolled in the disciplines needed to maintain the levels of innovation and entrepreneurial activity that once created a predictably steady stream of social and material progress. To put the total education issue in a nutshell, we are in trouble as a nation—and not just in the workplace—when only one in three of us know that DNA is a key to heredity, when only one in ten know what radiation is, and when one in five think the sun revolves around the earth. And the problem isn't confined to "the ignorant masses": a 1999 Princeton study of college seniors in elite institutions found that only 22 percent knew that the Gettysburg Address was the source of the words "government of the people, by the people, for the people," and 25 percent believed the Magna Carta was signed by the Pilgrims on the *Mayflower*.[5]

The Nation's Schools

We cannot address here the numerous and complex political, financial, and social problems plaguing the nation's public schools. Thus we confine ourselves to calling attention to the important linkages between education and work, in particular the long-festering problem of an insufficient supply of well-educated workers. As early as 1983, American policy makers recognized that our educational system was failing to prepare the majority of America's young people for the challenges of an increasingly global, knowledge-based economy. The landmark report *A Nation at Risk* used inflammatory cold war rhetoric to frame the problem:

Our once unchallenged preeminence in commerce, industry, science, and technological innovation is being overtaken by competitors throughout the world. . . . If an unfriendly foreign power had attempted to impose on America the mediocre educational performance that exists today, we might have viewed it as an act of war. As it stands, we have allowed this to happen to ourselves. . . . We have, in effect, been committing an act of unthinking, unilateral educational disarmament.[6]

In the two decades following the report, a nearly continuous series of educational reforms have taken place, ranging from the introduction of more rigorous standards for high school graduation, to a variety of experiments introducing market mechanisms into K–12 education, including school choice (charter schools, vouchers) and hiring for-profit companies to manage failing school districts (the Edison Project). Despite these reform efforts, a high percentage of young people in the United States still remain educationally at risk.

In international comparisons of math, science, and reading proficiency, American students consistently trail behind their main European and Asian competitors. In the most recent comparison, conducted by the Organization for Economic Cooperation and Development's Program for International Students Assessment in 2003, American tenth graders' scores were average in reading, below the OECD average in science, and very poor in practical math and problem-solving, ranking twenty-fourth out of twenty-nine nations. Over one-quarter of the American high school students tested failed to reach even the most basic standard of math proficiency.[7]

The problem is particularly acute among the most rapidly growing segments of the U.S. population, Latinos and African Americans in inner-city public schools; and it is compounded by the more than 1 million illegal immigrants in our schools, most of whom are not native English speakers and who place a large, unfunded burden on many already overcrowded, financially strapped urban schools. In California, which has the largest number of illegal immigrants, the public school system is in dire shape: only 60 percent of Latinos and 57 percent of African Americans graduate from high school in four years, compared to 84 percent of Asian Americans, and 78 percent of whites.[8] The situation is worse in Los Angeles Unified School District, where only 39 percent of Latinos and 47 percent of African Americans graduate with their age cohort.[9]

Indeed, a large part of the growing stratification of the workforce cited earlier has its genesis in the classroom. The Bill and Melinda Gates Foundation has taken the lead in addressing this issue, calling attention to some unsettling facts:[10]

- ☐ On average, high school dropouts earn $9,245 less per annum than do those with diplomas.
- ☐ High school dropouts are more likely to be unemployed (and in prison) than graduates.
- ☐ The families of dropouts have twice the likelihood of living in poverty than the families of graduates.

These problems are correlated with race: Only half of all black, Latino, and Native American teens earn a regular high school diploma in four years, and only about half of those who do graduate are able to read at a college level.[11] There are now more young African American men in prison than in college. Indeed, the number of African Americans in prison has increased fivefold since 1980, when young black men were three times more likely to be in college than incarcerated. The problem starts with the very young—only 15 percent of low-income fourth graders can read.

There is some good news: in July 2005, the National Assessment of Education Progress found that the nation's nine-year-olds have made significant progress in recent years in terms of their reading and math scores, and that the biggest gains were made among minority youths.[12] Thus, there is some reason to hope that the recent educational reforms aimed at minority children in early grades, which stress tougher standards and clearer expectations, might be paying off. If these young people continue to progress as they move through school, the overall effect on American society and economy could be profound. Indeed, in the arena of international economic competition, America's greatest underutilized resource may be the untapped human capital in its African American inner cities, Hispanic barrios, and Native American reservations. Among those many million Americans who currently lack equal education opportunity, the odds are that a black Bill Gates is washing cars, a brown Meg Whitman is a common laborer, and a Native American Jack Welch is unemployed.

The results of the National Assessment of Education Progress tests are hard evidence that low expectations have been at the heart of the poor performance of minority public schoolchildren. A mounting body of anecdotal experience and case studies support that conclusion. For example, thirteen years ago a northern California businessman, David Guggenhime, pledged to provide tutoring and other forms of educational assistance to a class of twenty-nine underprivileged minority first graders in a school with historically high dropout rates and incidents of antisocial behavior.[13] By 2005, all the students in the program were enrolled in four-year colleges. Similar efforts in New York and elsewhere have been successful *when there has been disciplined, loving support and high expectations for success on the part of parents, teachers, and those volunteering tutoring time and scholarship money.* It is increasingly clear that minority students are capable of much higher performance in school and, when they underperform, what they typically are missing are things that privileged students have ready access to: small classrooms, support and high expectations at home and in the community, exacting college-oriented curricula and standards, and the real prospect of college attendance. In the words of educator Robert Maynard Hutchins, "The best education for some is the best education for all."[14]

What is too often overlooked in discussions of educational reform is that the college-oriented curriculum at the best prep schools is increasingly the appropriate curriculum for success at work. *Every* young person needs to acquire the tools of learning—competence in the use of language and in dealing with computers, calculators, and scientific instruments. And the skills that need to be acquired with those tools are the basic linguistic, mathematical, and scientific skills of reading, writing, speaking, listening, observing, measuring, estimating, and calculating that are necessary for success in the classroom and at work. Students and workers both need to acquire subject matter knowledge in language, literature, fine arts, mathematics, natural sciences, history, geography, and social studies. Finally, they both need an enlarged understanding of ideas and values and to have their creativity, imagination, intellect, and powers of critical thinking stimulated by discussing important questions that do not have right or wrong answers.

In sum, "the goal at which any phase of education, true to itself, should aim is more education," as John Dewey observed. "Other objectives may surround that goal, but it is central."[15] Dewey wrote those words in the early part of the twentieth century, but in today's working world, in which continuing employability is contingent upon the ability to continually learn new skills, his observation has become an imperative. Or, as Hutchins later advised students: "Get ready for everything, because that is what is coming."[16] Learning how to continue learning throughout one's life is the prime vocational skill every student needs to acquire today. That is what high schools should be focusing on teaching, *not* specific job skills that quickly become obsolete.

Meeting lofty educational targets requires not only major improvements and radical innovation in the public education system, but also focusing investments where they can yield the greatest return. As economist Kathryn Shaw notes in a paper written for this report, those returns are highest (on the order of 17 to 20 percent) at the earliest stages of life when individuals have the greatest learning capacity and when foundational knowledge and interpersonal skills are formed. Based on a large body of research on education, learning, and work, some specific reform options the nation should consider with regard to public schools, and readiness for school, include:

❑ Provide support for pregnant women to insure their nutritional and health needs are met and that they provide stimulation for their infant starting in the womb and continuing throughout childhood.

❑ Use a combination of public and private resources to provide high-quality universal preschool education for three- to five-year-olds. (Currently only 38 percent of children whose mothers dropped out of high school take part in preschool, compared to 70 percent of children of college graduates.)

❑ Create smaller schools, or schools within schools, with a focused mission and intimate environment where teachers are aware of the progress of all learners.

❑ Extend such programs as Teach America, America Reads, and America Counts to put more new college graduates and volunteers and well-qualified teachers into the classroom to help provide at-risk students with more individualized attention. Programs could be expanded to include growing numbers of baby boomers who are retiring but are interested in working and contributing to society. Often they have a wealth of subject expertise—particularly in math and science—that public school teachers often lack.

❑ Create targeted programs to encourage the most rapidly growing segments of the future labor force—women, Latinos, and African Americans—to pursue science and engineering careers. This means reaching them early in their schooling (no later than middle school, but ideally earlier) to get them excited about technical careers and to ensure they take courses necessary for them to qualify for science and engineering degree courses. Programs that provide guaranteed college admission and scholarships for students who meet the necessary standards have been shown to have a strong motivating effect.

☐ Raise the status of the teaching profession by creating awards, financial bonuses, and mentoring opportunities for the best-performing teachers, while making it easier for principals to remove teachers who do not meet reasonable performance standards.

Colleges and Universities

One of America's greatest national assets is its higher education infrastructure. Unfortunately, it does little good to have the world's best universities and colleges if our high school students are ill-equipped to matriculate or, if they are qualified, cannot afford to attend. As the costs of tuition have skyrocketed at the nation's leading private universities, and increased substantially at financially hard-pressed state systems, higher education has increasingly become the province of the wealthy and a few poor top-notch students who qualify for full scholarships. The median annual income of families with children enrolled at Harvard is $150,000. Between 1976 and 1995, the percentage of students from the upper quartile of families enrolled in elite colleges rose from 39 to 50 percent, even as the incomes of those families grew much faster than incomes in the other three quartiles.[17]

Four years at a top private college now costs on the order of $160,000, and out-of-state charges at state universities have climbed to well over $110,000. Middle-class students have felt the squeeze particularly, as have sons and daughters of hourly workers, who decreasingly are enrolled in top-tier colleges and universities. A child growing up in a family earning over $90,000 has a one in two chance of getting a college degree by age twenty-four; one from a family making less than $35,00 has only a one in seventeen chance. Put another way, 8.6 percent of students from the poorest quartile get college degrees, while nearly 75 percent of those from the richest quartile do.

Over the years, America's higher-education system successfully compensated for the relatively poor educational preparation of high school graduates. Throughout the latter half of the twentieth century, the system generated a larger supply of college graduates than did the systems of competitor nations. This helped to fill the growing number of managerial, professional, and other white-collar jobs that were created as the U.S. economy underwent its long-term shift away from agriculture and manufacturing to services. In the last two decades, however, other nations have closed the gap, dramatically increasing their output of college graduates, while the overall percentage of the U.S. population obtaining a bachelor's degree has grown at a slower rate, from 23 percent of the twenty-five- to twenty-nine-year-old age group in 1980 to 28 percent in 2003. The shift in relative educational advantage is illustrated by comparing the United States with South Korea. At the end of the Korean War, South Korea had virtually no higher-education infrastructure, and the majority of its population was illiterate; today, South Korea has almost universal literacy, and over 80 percent of its young people go on to higher education, compared to 59 percent of their American peers (where there is an alarming attrition rate of 42 percent among those seeking bachelor's degrees).[18]

As we have seen, the United States' relative loss of comparative advantage in higher education is most pronounced in the fields of science and engineering. Graduates in those fields have been a key resource fueling the growth of high-tech industries; however, since the publication of *Work in America,* there has been a dramatic decline in the relative strength of the nation's technical workforce. In 1975, the United States ranked third internationally in the percentage of its twenty-four-year olds completing science and engineering degrees, trailing only Finland and Japan; in 2000, the United States had fallen to seventeenth place.[19] Today, fewer than 4 percent of young Americans graduate from college with science or engineering degrees, while in Finland, France, Taiwan, and South Korea over 10 percent of college graduates are in technical fields.[20] The leading Asian nations, in total, now produce eight times as many science and engineering graduates as the United States and the trends in this regard are alarming: China now has 17 million students in technical schools and universities (a threefold increase in five years), the majority of whom are in science and engineering programs. China graduated 325,000 engineers in 2004 (five times the number in the United States), and increased its output of technical PhD's by 14 percent.[21]

Not only has the number of engineering graduates been declining in America since the 1980s, demographic trends suggest the problem is likely to get worse. The most rapidly growing segments of the U.S. higher-education population—including girls and women, who are now a majority of those going on to college—historically have been underrepresented in science and engineering. Many women and minority group members graduate from high school without the math and science foundations needed to pursue technical courses at a university. A clear sign of inadequate preparation in science and math is the high attrition rate of those who enter universities hoping to pursue technical degrees: fewer than half of the 120,000 U.S. college students who enroll each year for an engineering degree complete their studies. Contributing to the declining appeal of science and engineering is the fact that careers in law and finance often offer higher salaries and require fewer years of higher education to become qualified.

The most recent trends are alarming: the number of doctorates in science and engineering awarded to U.S. citizens since 1997 has declined by 16 percent, including a 25 percent drop in computer science and mathematics PhDs.[22] The reason this has not amounted to a full-blown crisis is because foreign nationals have picked up the slack. The United States has historically supplemented its own supply of technical graduates by attracting the best and the brightest workers from other countries, but recently there has been a sharp increase in the educational qualifications of the legal immigrant workforce: in 1990, one-quarter of all PhD scientists working in America were foreign born, as were some 50 percent of graduate students currently being trained in U.S. science and engineering graduate programs. The percentage of foreign-born people with new doctorates working in the United States grew an astounding 760 percent between 1973 and 1997, over twice the growth rate of American-born PhDs.[23] By the 1990s, the odds on an infant receiving an engineering PhD from a U.S. university were greater if the child was born in Taiwan than in America. Significantly, immigrant scientists outperform their American-born counterparts on a range of measures of research productivity, from publication of the most influential articles, to membership in the prestigious National Academy of Sciences. They also play a key role in creating new high-tech enterprises, with Indian and Chinese immigrants alone accounting for over 25 percent of new start-ups formed in Silicon Valley.

The post–September 11 environment has threatened the vital supply of foreign technical workers: concerns about terrorism have led to immigration restrictions, making it significantly harder for foreign-born students to come to the United States and to remain here to work when they have completed their studies. The annual quota of visas for highly skilled immigrants to obtain long-term jobs has been cut in half. These policy changes, along with harder to quantify shifts in American attitudes toward immigrants, have had a chilling effect on the demand of foreign students for U.S. educations: in 2003 and 2004, American universities experienced the first decline in international student *enrollment* in thirty-five years. The overall decline was a relatively small 2.4 percent—with a more significant 8 percent drop among students from the Middle East—but the decline in foreign student *applications* was an incredibly high 28 percent, with an even sharper drop of 45 percent among Chinese applicants.[24] At the same time, a growing number of other countries, notably Australia, Singapore, Canada, Great Britain, and India, are competing aggressively to attract international students and to keep their own brightest students at home. And they are succeeding: in 1990, significantly more students from Taiwan, South Korea, and China came to the United States to pursue doctorates than studied at home; by 2000, the situation had been reversed. The most dramatic change occurred among the Chinese, with over 8,000 students earning doctorates in China as compared to just over 2,000 in the United States.

In sum, between 1970 and 2000, American universities did an unsung job of successfully recruiting and training foreign students, particularly in engineering and the sciences. Their efforts made a positive contribution to the balance of payments and, to put it crudely, saved the nation's posterior by providing American industry with a steady supply of highly qualified technology workers. According to David Heenan's 2005 book *Flight Capital*, "Half of the Americans who shared Nobel Prizes in physics and chemistry in the past seven years were born elsewhere. Nearly 40 percent of MIT graduates are from abroad. More than half of all Ph.D.'s working here are foreign-born, as are 45 percent of physicists, computer scientists, and mathematicians. One-third of all current physics teachers and one-fourth of all women doctors immigrated to this country."[25]

But, as Heenan illustrates, foreign-born, American-educated technicians and professionals now are returning in droves to their native lands. We are now exporting the intellectual capital on which the future of the economy depends, and a class of entrepreneurs who create good jobs for Americans, and are failing to replenish the supply domestically. As a nation, we face a choice: either recruit and maintain greater numbers of foreign-born technology workers, or develop our own home-grown supply. To do neither amounts to throwing in the towel in the international competitive arena. The choice, of course, is not either/or. It makes the most sense for the nation to commit scarce resources to educating our own people first, particularly since we have such a deep reserve of untapped human potential, while welcoming foreign nationals who can contribute to the economy. The worst possible scenario is where we are today: not adequately educating our own people, while educating bright foreigners and then encouraging them to leave.

Make no doubt about it, the immigration side of this issue is tricky: for example, American universities currently are granting on the order of 25 percent of their engineering and science doctorates to Chinese nationals, many of whom then return to China to create the next generation of high-tech industries designed to overtake the United States in the very areas where we need to maintain our comparative competitive advantage. At a minimum, it seems both fair and sensible to adopt venture capitalist John Doerr's suggestion that all international students who successfully complete U.S. graduate programs should be granted "green cards" to work permanently in this country, if they so desire.

The nation faces many complex choices with regard to what work should be done by Americans and what should be done by foreigners, and what should be done in this country and what should be done abroad. For example, in 2005, much was made in the popular press of the possibility of sending MRI data to Asia to be diagnosed by medical specialists in countries where that technical work can be done more cheaply than in the United States. The example is instructive because it highlights the many factors that must be considered in such decisions: in addition to short-term financial reasons to export knowledge work, it is also important to consider such factors as the value of having patients close to doctors, the cost of mistakes, and the difficulties involved in keeping foreign workers up to speed with the latest scientific developments. It also is necessary to consider all the alternatives. If healthcare cost-cutting is the goal, then there are other options besides exporting the jobs of American MDs. For example, greatly increasing the supply of doctors in this country by expanding medical schools would create good careers for more Americans and perhaps reduce the fees that medical specialists in the United States currently command. The point is that America is not a helpless economic giant without options.

Whatever the nation does to insure an adequate supply of highly educated workers will require additional spending on both public schools and on higher education. To develop home-grown math, science, and engineering talent, America will have to greatly improve primary and high school education and provide more scholarships and research support to higher-education institutions. Ironically, the nation will have to do the very same thing even if it chooses to attract foreign nationals—as Heenan points out, among the main reasons given for the flight of foreign-born techies is that American primary and secondary schools are not up to educating their children and the U.S. government and American industry are cutting back on the research and development funding that is the main attraction keeping them in this country.[26]

The nation needs to take several steps to expand higher-education enrollment among Americans. First, it must address the decline in funding of state colleges and universities. In 1977 about 6.7 percent of state revenues went to higher education; in 2000 that figure was down to 4.5 percent. Between 1991 and 2004, the share of public university revenues coming from state and local governments fell from 74 percent to 64 percent.[27] At the same time, tuitions in public institutions rose faster than inflation. Second, the nation should insure that those double-digit annual increases in tuition do not deter qualified men and women from attending college. This can be done by increasing existing federal student loans and private scholarships and targeting resources to those institutions that do the best job of controlling costs and reducing dropout rates. The United States also could replace the current student loan system with a "graduate tax," as in England and Australia; these programs cover most college costs and graduates then pay back what they have been advanced through the income tax system once they begin earning above a minimum threshold. Since the lifetime earnings of a college graduate are, on average, over $1 million greater than those of a high school graduate, there should be a high rate of return on this national investment.

Community Colleges:
The Best Bet for Training and Retraining

Almost all growing technical occupations—from computer repair to medical technology—are best learned in community colleges. In fact, the Bureau of Labor Statistics estimates there will be a 35 percent increase in the number of jobs requiring associate degrees between 2000 and 2010.[28] Because occupational training is the unique strength of two-year colleges, high schools and four-year colleges should get out of that business, leaving it to the institution that does it best. Even accounting education might better be left to community colleges, given the unfortunate reluctance of most four-year colleges to require their accounting students to pursue a broad range of liberal arts courses.

Private employers and government program-officers who support occupational training should work closely with community colleges to build
solid programs at those institutions. At the same time, they should provide
counseling to workers about the well-documented value of the community
college programs relative to those offered by private for-profit job-training
institutes. At a minimum, counselors should help potential students to distinguish between legitimate private training programs and those that too
often deliver too little and, in some cases, even exploit highly vulnerable
people. Fine private training programs do exist, but the quality of the instruction they offer and their job placement rates need to be independently
documented before they are endorsed by public agencies and receive public
funds. In most cases, training in a community college is the most-reliable
and cost-effective choice.

Workers whose jobs have been exported should have priority for government-sponsored retraining. To be effective, such retraining also should
entail close coordination between local employers and community colleges.
A major negative side effect of the nation's current competitive strategy and
free-trade policy is that hardworking and loyal employees often are left behind as factories and other workplaces are automated, closed, and jobs exported—and retraining either is unavailable or too expensive for displaced
workers to pay for themselves. The issue then becomes who should pay for
it. *Work in America* offered an innovative proposal for funding worker retaining and others have advanced alternative plans, many of which appear
promising. At a minimum, the Trade Adjustment Assistance Act, a $1 bil-
lion federal program that underwrites the retraining of 75,000 manufacturing workers per year, should be expanded to include displaced service-sector
employees.

Here, the changing realities of the workplace cause us to register a note
of sober realism. Although we favor increasing the retraining efforts undertaken by employers and through the community colleges, we are realistic
about the limits to such efforts. It is extremely difficult to retrain a displaced,
middle-age, blue-collar worker who wishes to move to an equally well-paying white-collar job. Odds are, such individuals will have to go to college—
which is expensive, time-consuming, and not necessarily on their
agendas—or they may have to settle for a lower-paying service job. At a minimum, one thing the nation can do for them is to make certain that they and
their families are not left without health insurance or without a social safety

net in their old age. This should begin with increasing federal safeguards of private pensions and resisting temptations to reform Social Security in ways that increase the risks of the most vulnerable seniors.

RESEARCH AND DEVELOPMENT

All told, the United States spent $282 billion on research and development in 2003, compared to Japan's national expenditure of $104 billion, and China's $60 billion.[29] The U.S. figures may look impressive but they are somewhat deceiving: because Chinese scientists and engineers make only a fraction of what their American counterparts earn, China's outlay supports 1.3 million researchers to America's 743,000. Moreover, China greatly increases its R&D expenditures every year; the trend in both the public and private sectors in this country has been to reduce expenditures. The National Science Foundation's budget was cut by $100 million in fiscal year 2005 to 2006, as were the R&D budgets of almost all federal agencies, including Defense. In contrast, the European Union has proposed increasing government R&D spending by one-third between 2007 and 2013.

Likewise, American private-sector R&D expenditures are declining, and U.S. corporations are moving more of their development dollars overseas, exporting even some higher-level research projects. Motorola has nineteen R&D labs operating in China, and GE recently established an industrial research center in Shanghai employing twelve hundred people. GE also pays for scholarships in engineering and applied sciences at Chinese technical universities. Some of the benefits of U.S.-sponsored research in China may trickle back to this country, but so far the benefits seem to have been largely one-way: toward China. While we leave it to those more qualified in matters of national security to assess the wisdom of R&D investments in a totalitarian nation, we wonder why such investments—arguably ones that create the best jobs in industry—are not being made in America, particularly if corporations fund them in any part by using U.S. tax credits or write-offs. Are American corporations going overseas because of the perceived quality of American university science and engineering programs? If so, U.S.-owned corporations could invest more in improving those programs.

Corporations and the government have made conscious choices to spend less in this country on research. Granted, some federal R&D money is wasted, and corporations often have a hard time justifying research that does not have immediate commercial application; but cutting back on research investments amounts to eating our national seed corn. If America chooses to ride the crest of the technological wave, it must increase domestic R&D funding—even if those expenditures cannot be justified using the same short-term metrics that apply to other investments. In the long term, scientific and technical leadership creates industrial breakthroughs and new products—and new and better jobs for Americans. This country needs a coherent national competitive strategy that leads to the creation of new good jobs, and increased spending on R&D is a necessary complement to improving university engineering and science programs.

CREATING "GOOD JOBS"

For decades, the U.S. economy has created enough jobs to meet the monthly increases in the number of individuals entering the labor force, including young Americans taking their first jobs, parents and older Americans returning to paid employment, and job-seeking immigrants, documented and not. However, technology is constantly changing the nature and mix of the jobs available, and therein lies the challenge. The application of information technology (IT) has led to a change in the nature of jobs, usually upgrading them. But recently, as productivity increases resulting from IT have continued to multiply, the economy has not been able to create enough new good jobs and to upgrade enough existing ones to keep pace with the demand from Americans for good employment. While the numbers are somewhat suspect, low-wage employers were recently creating 44 percent of new jobs, and high-wage employers only 29 percent of the remainder.[30] By observation, it appears that the United States is creating more bad jobs in Low-Cost companies—in restaurants, hotels, hospitals, retail, and personal services—that frequently go to immigrants, often undocumented, than it is creating jobs in High-Involvement and Global Competitor companies. In particular, outside of construction, which is a cyclical industry, few well-paying jobs are being created for the middle class. In the so-called jobless recovery of 2002 to 2004, American companies actually did create some new good jobs—overseas. And the expected productivity dividend to workers resulting from the introduction of IT never materialized: in that period, productivity rose by 12 percent, but median household incomes stagnated in real terms.[31]

The United States faces the unprecedented situation in which productivity is increasing but good job creation and average worker incomes are not. Economists say the country must choose among three basic policy alternatives:

☐ Option 1: Try to stop job losses by protecting American industry from foreign competition and by regulating employers' ability to hire at will and to export jobs.

☐ Option 2: Do nothing to discourage the forces of globalization or to limit employer flexibility—in the confidence that eventually American industry will find its comparative competitive advantage in the international marketplace.

☐ Option 3: Patiently wait while increased productivity generates economic growth and new jobs in the long term. In the meantime, make efforts to increase job creation in the short term, and provide a safety net for those American workers who fall through the cracks during the transition.

We believe the first option would not work; rather, it actually would harm American workers in the long term. One of the great strengths of the American economy over the last fifty years has been the flexibility and mobility of its workforce and the "creative destruction" of obsolete companies. Historically, when recessions have hit Europe, and when industries have declined, laws on the Continent designed to protect workers made it extremely costly for employers to lay them off. Moreover, European laws requiring high severance pay discouraged the hiring of new workers, which has led to historically higher rates and longer periods of unemployment—and lower rates of job creation and upward social mobility—than in the United States. The lesson to be drawn is that to restrict employer flexibility here would hamstring the efforts of American companies to create viable new businesses and good jobs.

However, we should be careful not to overgeneralize with regard to national differences. Americans tend to think of Europe in the singular, assuming all its nations have higher rates of taxation than in the United States, tighter regulation of industry in terms of its ability to lay off workers, and more generous benefits to the jobless. In fact, those three characteristics are found together mainly in Germany and France. The social policies in Britain and Ireland are probably closer to those in the United States than to the two largest continental countries and, in Spain and Italy where taxes and the standard of living are relatively lower, workers on the dole receive little in the way of government support (although there are tight restrictions on laying them off). The Netherlands and Scandinavia have yet a fourth model: employers are pretty much free to lay off workers at will, but those workers then receive generous benefits. Significantly, the average periods of joblessness in the Netherlands and Scandinavia are the lowest in Europe because workers are required to participate in well-funded retraining programs and are helped to find jobs. Those countries also have the lowest rates of poverty, the highest standards of living, and the most economic equality in the world. And they are the most like the United States in terms of being high-tech economies attempting to compete in world manufacturing markets increasingly dominated by countries with low-cost labor.

It is important to acknowledge that the negative effects of globalization on manufacturing jobs are not confined to the United States: work is being exported from almost all developed countries and technology is causing most of them to lose jobs. In fact, since the 1970s, the sharpest percentage decline in manufacturing employment in the world has been in Britain, from 35 percent of the workforce to 14 percent. The real issue is how countries cope with the challenge. The United States has two particular comparative advantages: its labor mobility and industrial flexibility. In most of the rest of the industrialized world, workers are less likely than Americans to move great distances to find work, and governments are more likely to restrict the ability of employers to engage in lay-offs. But workers in those nations have significant advantages relative to those in the United States: their governments are more likely to provide the national health insurance, social safety nets, and retraining programs that take some of the sting out of industrial dislocations and create a greater sense of national unity among employers, unions, and government.

There is clearly no one right way to configure national employment policies. But, at a minimum, it would seem prudent for all developed nations to learn from the experiences of others. Yet, the ingrained belief in "American exceptionalism" all too often causes even thoughtful people in this country to believe things are so different here that we can't possibly benefit from foreign experience. To the contrary, we believe that the United States can learn from the successes and failures of other nations as we wrestle with the very same employment challenges others face. Countries from Denmark to New Zealand are experimenting with various policy alternatives that are worth studying. Some European countries are experimenting with innovative ways to become more competitive and, at the same time, to provide a social safety net for workers suffering job dislocations. For example, in Austria employers pay a tax into the individual training accounts of all workers that they can draw on when unemployed; if a worker stays on a job for a number of years, the money starts to go into a pension fund. Current efforts to "invent" such personal reemployment accounts in this country apparently are being undertaken without benefit of learning from the Austrian experience.

Americans also might learn something from the experiences of countries that made the transformation from manufacturing to services before we did. Years before the United States started exporting jobs, most native-born Swedish citizens had long since ceased working in factories. Yet through a judicious partnership among employers, unions, and government, Swedes have maintained their high standard of living through entrepreneurial innovation and by creating a national competitive niche in design, as those who have visited an IKEA store will appreciate.

The approach has been different in Japan. There the Ministry of Economy, Trade, and Industry has encouraged Japanese corporations to manage their relationships with the companies in China that now do their low-cost manufacturing by keeping core technology and R&D at home, and insisting on supplying internally the high-quality components that China cannot produce as effectively. Japan's brains are constantly at work figuring out how to use China's muscle more efficiently, and Japanese business leaders are more willing in this regard to drive hard bargains with China than are many of their American counterparts. Japan also makes more efficient use of IT and other technology than the United States does in order to keep high-paying manufacturing at home; for example it employs 57 percent of all the world's industrial robots. Thus, even as Japan increased the total number of *jobs* it exported to China, in 2003 its export of *products* to China grew by 68 percent, thus creating a number of new good jobs at home. Toyota and other Japanese manufacturers also reinvest in their business to a greater extent than do American companies, and Japan's growing foreign reserves and positive balance of payments reflect that fact. In sum, the experiences of other nations show that there are better alternatives than opting out of the global economy, and those include creativity in public policy and innovation in industry.

In light of these examples, it seems clear to us that the second employment policy option open to the United States—to simply let the market sort things out in the long term—would not work any better than the first. That's because national issues related to research, education, training, retirement, and health need to be resolved in order for the nation's global businesses to succeed. As in other nations, American businesses require an effective and appropriate contribution from their government. The market can, and should, be allowed full rein to work its magic in the arena of job and wealth creation. That is why we believe the third option is the best: the most effective long-term approach to creating good jobs in America is for the country to grow them through a combination of government and private actions.

Realistically, America cannot look to its large, global corporations to provide enough new, good jobs. While the *Fortune* 500 play important supporting roles in creating a growing economy, most of the largest and oldest corporations in the United States—Ford, General Motors, Sears, and AT&T—have many fewer employees today than they did a decade ago, and many giant companies that appear to have grown—such as Exxon-Mobil—have done so by mergers and acquisitions in which thousands of jobs were lost at the companies they absorbed, for a net total job loss. In general, such young companies as Google and eBay grow through internal reinvestment. However, at a certain stage, they either stop increasing employment or do so only by acquisition or foreign expansion. Instead of creating new jobs, large corporations often create the *best* jobs and perhaps create some new jobs indirectly through subcontracting, purchasing, and R&D.

It is entrepreneurs who actually create the most new jobs, but they do it under the radar screen. If all the current start-up businesses in America were combined into one giant company, the astonishing number of jobs they are creating would make headlines. But the media fail to notice the tens of thousands of small businesses creating hundreds of thousands of new jobs—until one of those companies grows into a Microsoft. Every day scores of new businesses are being started all over the country; most will fail or stay small. But with proper nourishment, every now and then a start-up will grow into a generator of a large number of good jobs. In essence, jobs in America are created on the foundation of four virtuous and complementary activities:

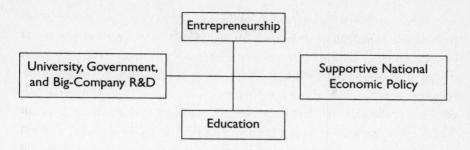

For example, in 1996 four managers at Mobil Oil wanted to commercialize a product that had been developed in that giant corporation's R&D lab. Since big companies are often poor at starting new businesses in fields not directly related to their core missions, the managers bought the idea from Mobil and started their own company: Trex (not to be confused with Trek, the HI bicycle manufacturers). This northern Virginia–based company recycles plastic and wood, turning the reclaimed materials into durable decking and railings for home construction. The company now buys over half the recycled grocery bags in America to supply the hundreds of millions of pounds of raw materials its three factories require. Trex employs over six hundred people, providing good salaries and generous benefits to blue-collar workers and their families. The keys to their success are that Trex makes and sells a high value-added, high-tech product that requires educated and skilled managers to bring to market, and, of course, their access to capital.

A similar story, but at an earlier stage of development, is unfolding in southern California where FiskerCoachbuild recently announced that it will produce up to three hundred cars a year in its Orange County workshop. CEO Henrik Fisker, who until recently was head of Ford's advanced design studio, plans to customize car bodies and interiors on the frames of Mercedes-Benz and BMW sports cars. After Fisker's ultra-modern designs were watered down at Ford, he says "I just thought that I could do better design on my own than in a big company."[32] He has ten investors in a company that will sell high value-added products for over $200,000. Will he succeed? Who knows? If he does he will create good, high-paying manufacturing jobs for Americans. Multiply Trex and Fisker by a factor of thousands, and one starts to appreciate the power of America's hidden job creation engine.

Instead of trying to protect U.S. jobs in declining industries, we believe the nation should choose to support entrepreneurial efforts to create *new* jobs in *new* industries. Based on our reading of the research, we conclude the most important thing that can be done to encourage American entrepreneurs is to get out of their way. Starting a business in the United States needs to be simple and free of bureaucratic paperwork. And the nation needs to honor successful entrepreneurs as much as, if not more than, it does celebrity CEOs of large corporations (who take relatively less personal risk and seldom create as much wealth or as many jobs). It is a positive sign that, in recent decades, women, often in middle age, have turned in increasing numbers to entrepreneurial activities as alternatives to working for corporations, finding greater opportunity for innovation and freedom to create their own lifestyles. Finally, Americans should support efforts to encourage entrepreneurialism among the young through such established programs as Junior Achievement and the innovative organization Independent Means, which focuses mainly on girls. Another underrated source of good work in America is self-employment, which often is the first step in the creation of a small business.

In addition to finding access to capital, one of the biggest obstacles entrepreneurs and self-employed people face in starting a business is paying for health insurance. Even if they are eligible (thanks to COBRA, the Consolidated Omnibus Budget Reconciliation Act) for short-term coverage under a former employer's plan, they still have to pay a steep monthly premium. And when entrepreneurs hire their first employees they are faced with the incredibly tough decision of either attempting to provide them with health coverage or telling them they have to go uncovered, at least until sometime in the future when the company is profitable. There is mounting evidence that one of the greatest deterrents to the creation of jobs in small businesses is the reluctance of entrepreneurs to take on the burden of providing health insurance to employees.

While we believe entrepreneurial activity is the key to growing good jobs in the future, as it has been in the past, we must note that the effects of globalization and technology have changed the operating environment in ways that require unprecedented cooperation among business, government, foundations, universities, and unions. Most labor-force projections indicate that virtually all of the roughly 20 million new jobs likely to be created in the United States between now and 2014 will demand at least some college education, with the majority requiring a BA or higher. In addition, we also believe bold investments will be needed in science and technology to stimulate the creation of whole new industries and high-end jobs in the United States, while simultaneously tackling many of the most pressing problems facing the world. In California, for example, despite a budget deficit larger than those facing the other forty-nine states combined, a large majority of voters decided in 2004 to spend $3 billion over the next decade on stem cell research, a promising yet controversial area of biotechnology. Voter initiatives may not be the most rational way to make public policy, but it does signal America's continued willingness to make major public investments in scientific research when it shows promise of long-term economic and social benefits.[33]

In the end, for the United States to grow its supply of good jobs, American students will have to study harder, corporate managers will have to create more-effective organizations, government officials will have to create wiser policies, researchers in the nation's labs will have to be better supported, entrepreneurs will have to be more innovative, and the nation will have to invest more in education. There is no alternative.

HEALTH INSURANCE

The numbers are depressingly familiar. To add a few to those cited earlier: U.S. spending on healthcare was $1.7 trillion in 2003, amounting to more than 15 percent of total gross domestic product, and six times the amount the country spent in 1980. If current trends continue, Stanford's Allen Enthoven estimates healthcare expenditures will constitute some 28 percent of U.S. GDP in 2030.[34] Increases in spending for medical care far outpace the overall annual rate of inflation, and the amount paid by employers for health insurance rose 11.2 percent from 2003 to 2004, the fourth straight year of double-digit growth during an era of relatively low inflation. In total, medical costs covered by employers rose 59 percent between 2000 and 2005. In 2003, private employers paid an average of nearly $1.50 per hour per worker for health care, a figure that is grossly understated for companies that provide health benefits because it includes workers in all companies, even those that don't provide health insurance.[35]

In late 2005, the Kaiser Family Foundation released its annual report on healthcare coverage. The findings would have been shocking if it were not an extension of years of bad news.[36] The average cost of health insurance for a family of four—$10,800 per annum—now exceeds the *entire* annual income of a minimum-wage worker. Between 2000 and 2005, health insurance premiums rose by 73 percent while wages grew by 15 percent. As the

Kaiser report was released, Starbucks chairman Howard Schultz announced that the company would spend more in 2005 on health insurance than on all the raw materials it buys to brew coffee.

The number of Americans without any health insurance reached 45 million in 2005. Moreover, it was estimated that, during 2002 and 2003, some 82 million Americans were without health insurance for at least some period of time. Even for the 60 million American workers and their families with employer-provided health insurance, recent trends are anything but comforting. Ten years ago, well over 60 percent of workers in private industry were covered by a company health plan; the latest figure is around 45 percent.[37] While almost all large employers still offer coverage to at least some employees, only about 65 percent of midsize, and less than 50 percent of small companies, do. The likelihood that someone is covered by health insurance rises significantly with income level: among people in households making less than $25,000 in 2004, 73.7 percent had insurance, compared to 91.6 percent of those in households with incomes of over $75,000. And one recent study showed that 43 percent of low-income, and 31 percent of middle-income workers, would be unable to afford coverage if they lost their employer-provided benefits.[38] Even those still fortunate to have insurance are paying more in premiums and getting less in services and coverage. In 2002 and 2003, some 75 percent of U.S. employers changed the design of their healthcare plans, 67 percent of those who did so increased employee copayments or coinsurance, 65 percent increased employee premiums, and 68 percent decreased prescription drug benefits.[39]

The negative consequences of maintaining the current healthcare system are enormous for American society and individual workers: Expenditures on healthcare are gradually driving out other public investments, such as education and infrastructure improvement; real wages are stagnating as employers pump profits into health insurance instead of increasing worker compensation; and healthcare expenditures are creating the need to raise taxes at all levels of government, with negative implications for economic growth and job creation. Moreover, the escalating cost of health insurance is becoming untenable for American employers for a number of reasons:

☐ In an effort to reduce costs, companies are spending more and more unproductive time and energy designing and redesigning healthcare programs, negotiating with insurance providers and HMOs, processing claims, and dealing with employee complaints.

☐ Healthcare benefits have become the major sticking issue in union/management relations, leading to constant disagreements, conflicts, and even strikes.

☐ Rising costs are creating ethical dilemmas for executives forced to reduce coverage or to eliminate employee medical insurance, and even for those who find themselves driven to use healthcare benefits as recruiting chips: "Do we want to allow competition based on the exploitation of the workforce?" asks Craig Cole of Brown & Cole stores, a supermarket chain that offers health insurance to about 95 percent of its employees.

☐ Executives are making major decisions about creating and eliminating jobs, outsourcing, and offshoring based on analyses of healthcare costs of the alternatives. Former economic advisor to the president, Laura Tyson, concludes: "We're losing jobs in high-wage, high-benefits sectors like manufacturing, where employers are responding to this surge in healthcare costs."

☐ American exports are at a competitive disadvantage to those produced by companies from countries with national health insurance systems (which is to say almost all the developed world).

☐ Older companies with large numbers of retirees covered by company-provided healthcare plans are being forced into bankruptcy.

Our health insurance system clearly has become the tail wagging the dog, driving business decisions, determining which companies will succeed and which will fail, increasing the costs of U.S.-made goods, and hampering the creation of new domestic jobs. These problems are peculiar to this country because the United States is the only developed nation that ties most of its health insurance directly to employment status. As Ford Motor Company CEO William Clay Ford concludes, "I just think that as a country, if we have a model that isn't working and a model that is driving jobs overseas, then we had better take another look at it." Ford is part of a growing number of employers who are calling for a total overhaul of the way healthcare is financed in the nation. There is increasing recognition that American industry needs a level playing field, both domestically and internationally, and to achieve that it has to get out of the business of offering health insurance.

We believe that America has no choice but to decouple health insurance from employment if it wishes to: (1) Have a large number of Low-Cost corporations that keep the cost of goods low to consumers, (2) Pursue the strategy of competing internationally by giving GC corporations the flexibility to quickly, and without penalty, hire and dismiss employs, (3) Continue to provide good work and good benefits to workers in HI companies, and (4) Encourage entrepreneurs to create new jobs.

The good news is that there are a variety of promising ideas for uncoupling health insurance from employment status while at the same time preserving freedom of choice and the private provision of healthcare. An analysis undertaken for The Century Foundation illustrates one way the nation can get its medical costs under control, free employers of the burden of providing health insurance, and cover every American in the process.[40] This proposal, similar to one developed by the Nixon administration in 1973, would "keep intact the existing relationship between doctors, insurers, patients and preserve U.S. leadership in medical innovation," according to its author, Leif Wellington Haase. The proposal would replace the current employer-funded system with one in which the federal government would subsidize the purchase of private health insurance. Based on individual need, everyone would receive such a subsidy, and everyone would be required to purchase health insurance. Medicare and Medicaid, which continue to grow and currently cover 27.7 percent of the population, would be phased out; the government would negotiate with private insurers over premiums and rules; and an independent board would evaluate the cost effectiveness of medical procedures. "The system would offer a basic and decent health care plan—a 'floor'—to all Americans while encouraging those who want more comprehensive coverage to join higher-end insurance plans." To pay for the system, current federal tax subsidies for employer-based insurance would be eliminated, and a payroll tax and a dedicated corporate tax would be instituted. Among other things, the proposal would eliminate the advantage employers who don't offer health insurance have over those who do.

It is not our place to endorse any proposal; nor do we pretend to have expertise in the economics of healthcare. But it is clear to us that, unless the health insurance issue is dealt with effectively and soon, it will be nearly impossible for the nation to maintain its precarious lead in the emerging global economy, even if our corporations do everything else right. Therefore, we urge our public and private leaders to make this issue their highest priority on the national domestic agenda.

RETIREMENT

Decisions relating to retirement will loom larger with every year as the baby boomers begin to turn sixty in 2006. For personal and financial reasons, the majority of boomers probably still will be at work, at least part-time, until they are well into their seventies. Indeed, a recent Rutgers study shows that only 13 percent of American workers expect ever to stop working entirely.[41] And, as the longevity of Americans continues to increase, there is no reason to put productive men and women out to pasture just because they reach a traditional retirement age. To ensure that the retirement choices individuals make are voluntary, the government will need to be as diligent with regard to age discrimination as it has been with regard to race and gender bias in the workplace. It should also make sure that federal laws do not discourage people from taking jobs after they have "retired" by penalizing or preventing them from drawing on their private or Social Security retirement funds while still working. In addition, federal regulations of defined-contribution pension plans should insure that all the money in individual accounts is fully portable, that employer contributions are fully vested at the end of one year of service, that the accounts are protected from fraud, and that it is easy for individuals to enroll in them. In the case of defined-benefit plans, the government needs to insure that they are fully funded and insured.

Some men and women, particularly those who are in menial or hard-labor jobs, will want to take, and will have earned, retirement at sixty-five, if not earlier. The problem, of course, is that eligibility for Medicare does not begin until age sixty-five, so individuals deciding to retire before that age often face the prospect of going without health coverage. The benefits provided by Social Security are, by themselves, clearly insufficient to support people in comfort in their old age. Yet millions of Americans have no other significant savings; therefore, either they must do without many necessary goods and services, or find part-time work. They also must pray that they remain in good health.

It is essential that the federal government not place such vulnerable people at even greater risk than they now face through radical changes of the Social Security system. A major theme of our research has been the incredible increase in both the choices and risks Americans now have with respect to their work lives, and we have applauded the increases in choices, particularly as they apply to young and to well-educated workers. But older and less-educated workers may not benefit from more choices than they already have, and cannot bear more risk when it comes to their healthcare and retirement income. Therefore, at a minimum, we believe nothing should be done to reduce the social safety net they now enjoy.

17

INDIVIDUALS

The *Work in America* report focused almost exclusively on the responsibilities of private employers and government policy makers to provide decent working conditions; it paid little or no attention to the important consequences of the choices individuals make with regard to their own careers and jobs. It is indicative of the nature of the changes that have occurred in workplaces and society over the last three decades that issues of personal choice are now front-and-center whenever questions about employment policy are raised. Part of the change is ideological; there has been a pronounced shift in national values with regard to personal responsibility in recent decades, perhaps most clearly illustrated in the decision to end welfare as it was known in the 1970s. Moreover, today most American workers are no longer seen as passive recipients of benefits bestowed by paternalistic employers or the largesse of a benevolent government; instead, they are said to have responsibilities to make decisions for themselves. In fact, many more Americans today have both the freedom and the resources to make important decisions. Yet with every increment of personal freedom to choose has come an element of additional risk.

THE NECESSITY OF CHOICE

As we have noted, the actions of employers and the policies of government greatly influence the range and numbers of options workers and citizens have. Nevertheless individuals increasingly are required to make personal job and career choices that have significant consequences for their own long-term well-being. Given the alarming rise in the costs of choosing poorly, it behooves workers to do everything in their power to increase the number of good alternatives available to them and to increase their odds of choosing wisely. Some of those things are obvious: studying hard in school and getting as many years of education as possible is the first and perhaps the single most important thing Americans can do to improve their chances of finding rewarding employment. Choosing to stay in school creates opportunities to make a wider variety of choices later concerning what to study, what career to pursue, what company to work for, when to change jobs and careers, and when (and if) to retire. Below we briefly examine a few of the increasingly complex choices facing American workers and the associated risks involved.

What to Study?

A growing challenge for college undergraduates today is the choice of a major. Increasingly, young Americans are told to major in business or in computer science, because graduates in those fields are most-immediately employable. True, but over-specialization presents its own risks, whether one's major is accounting, information technology (IT), dentistry, or English. The world simply changes so fast that it is risky for students to narrow prematurely their field of study, even if their chosen major is preparation for whatever career counselors at the time are calling the "fastest-growing occupation." For example, in 2005, some 3.5 million Americans were employed as "information technology professionals." If any recent career choice seemed like a safe bet in the 1990s, it was preparation in IT.[1] Yet, surprisingly, the total number of such jobs has stagnated over the last half decade: there turns out to be a limit to even the number of programmers needed in a high-tech economy. Moreover, as it has become evident that pure programming jobs are the easiest to export, the number of American college students majoring in computer science has declined correspondingly, by 39 percent since 2000. What just yesterday looked like a winning major now looks like another career with an uncertain future.

In practice, it is difficult to get the job prospect information needed to make effective career choices and extremely complicated to draw useful personal inferences from the information that is available. For example, at the same time job opportunities in computer sciences have been stagnating, there has been a growing demand for individuals skilled in IT *applications* in such diverse fields as engineering, business, and biology. Indeed, the University of California at Berkeley now offers a graduate course in "services science" to teach its students how to apply IT to improve productivity in the services sector. The lesson for students is this: graduates with the best job prospects often have majors in physics, psychology, biology, anthropology, or some other academic discipline, *and* minors (or a lot of course work) related to IT. Similarly, while undergraduate English majors have a hard time finding jobs, many employers find English majors who *also* have taken courses in economics, along with introductory courses in accounting, statistics, IT, and marketing as highly desirable job applicants. In general, the more versatile, flexible, balanced, and broadly educated graduates are, the more valuable they are to employers in the long run because they have demonstrated their ability, and willingness, to learn.

Young people entering college, who have burning desires to be dentists, doctors, lawyers, engineers, teachers, or whatever, are members of an extremely fortunate minority. Relatively few people their age have strong inclinations about what professions they want to pursue. In our late teens or early twenties, it is hard for most of us to know if we will be happy ten years later in an operating room, a courtroom, a classroom, or an office designing a new machine. Hence, it is risky for young people to choose a college major solely because it seems a safe bet to pay off in a good first job. Such short-term thinking is a dangerous way to begin a long career and a longer life. Not only are forecasts of future demand for workers in specific occupations notoriously unreliable, it is risky to choose a field without some real knowledge of what it is like to work in it or without a true desire to do that work. To major in accounting, for example, because there is a shortage of accountants is seldom a good idea—unless one is excited about the work CPAs do all day.

Economists draw the useful distinction between "investment goods" and "consumption goods," making no moral judgments about the relative value of each. In the eyes of most economists, education is an investment good: one pays tuition and goes to college to get skills and a credential that will pay off down the line in a good job. But education is also a consumption good—it is fun to go to college, and it is a pleasure to learn—and it is also an investment in a way economists seldom use the term: by going to college, students invest in their growth and development as human beings, even under circumstances when that investment earns no real direct financial return. As important as work is, it is only one part of life, and an undergraduate education is too valuable a thing to waste on simply getting a credential in a narrow field one doesn't love.

Indeed, it is worth noting a growing trend among doctors, lawyers, and other highly and narrowly trained professionals to quit practicing their chosen occupations in mid-career because they have become dissatisfied. We wish we had better data on this, but the sheer number of anecdotes about unhappy lawyers and dissatisfied doctors may be indicative of a deep problem. For example, shortly after *Work in America* was published, a young man in his late twenties described for us how, when he was eighteen, he had wanted nothing more than to become a dentist. He thus enrolled in a predental undergraduate program at a prestigious university, took only bioscience courses, and then entered dental school at the end of his sophomore year. After several more years of exacting—and expensive—professional education, he borrowed money to purchase the practice of an older dentist who wanted to retire. Sadly, as the young dentist recalled, within months of beginning his career, "I began to realize I disliked dentistry; yet I saw I had no choice but to continue unhappily on the career path I had prematurely chosen."

For many undergraduates the best advice is "to keep your options open," recognizing that, if they do well in college, they can go back to graduate school for professional training later when they have a clearer notion about what they want to do for "the rest of their lives." Counselors in professional schools often advise young people that one of the best ways of informing their decisions about what educational course to pursue is to try working in a profession—as volunteers, if no other way is available—to get a sense if the work is "right" for them. The good news, of course, is that fewer Americans today need to be, or will accept, being trapped in jobs and careers that turn out to be wrong for them. And the lesson is that the more-educated—and more-broadly educated—they are, the more options they have throughout life when it comes to choosing and changing careers. Particularly in an age when most people will have multiple careers, the most useful skill is to know how to learn.

What Career to Choose, and How to Choose It?

In the past, choosing a career was like buying a one-way train ticket from Rome to Copenhagen on a local train that made all the stops along the way. The train schedule was fixed, the stops at each station were lengthy, and detours and side trips were not permitted. Today choosing a career is more like buying a lifelong Eurailpass, with no set final destination, no fixed travel agenda, and no timetable. These days, at least for the well-educated, people are free to go pretty much wherever they please, whenever they please—getting off the main track wherever they like and staying in any one place for as long as they are welcome (of course, they aren't in complete control of their schedules; they might get fired or laid-off). But if they so choose, they can transfer to the career equivalent of a plane, bus, or ferry—or perhaps even drive themselves (a.k.a. self-employment).

Young, educated Americans have an awful lot more career (and life) freedom than their parents enjoyed a generation ago, which on balance is a good thing. But the availability of numerous alternatives can lead to choice overload: because there are more careers to choose from, there is more information to process. How does one choose whether to be an acrobat, actor, airplane pilot, animal trainer, artist, and so on down through the z's? In the end, decisions about career choice often come down to identifying one's needs, desires, aspirations, and skills. Perhaps the best advice to a young person choosing a career is to "know thyself." To begin that process, there are four general kinds of questions that experts in careers say one should ask:

1. *What do I really like doing?*
2. *What am I good at?*
3. *What is it that I enjoy doing, and I am good at, that someone will pay me to do?*
4. *And if no one will pay me to do what I want to do, is it possible to start my own business?*

It is important to identify a few "must-knows," including one's personal preferences and aptitudes, information about the educational requirements of candidate professions, and the nature of the tasks people in those professions do. Fortunately, research on career choice has become quite so-phisticated. Batteries of tests and college career counselors to help young people make better choices—for example, to identify their interests and then to match those with the skill demands of various professions—are available through school.

The reality, of course, is that most people will change their work prefer-ences as they grow older, as their life circumstances change, and as they gain in experience. Consequently, the ideal is to have good options available as one progresses throughout the stages of one's career. As we have noted, ca-reer switching has become increasingly possible, and the stigma once at-tached to doing it has all but disappeared; at the same time, the resources needed to enter a new career—often entailing significant retraining and per-haps an additional college degree—also are growing. For that reason, choos-ing an employer who offers substantial, and flexible, education and training benefits is often a good decision.

In thinking about careers, it is necessary to keep in mind the incredible diversity of the American workplace. For example, it would be a mistake to overlook the fact that many people still have quite traditional careers with large companies—even at a Global Competitor company as much as half the workforce might be engaged in inching their way up the hierarchy dur-ing a twenty- (or more) year career. And, as we have noted, a fundamental problem with careers is that too few people have them. For many Americans, the challenge is simply to get on a career track. There are probably more op-tions than commonly recognized. For example, Wal-Mart offers significant career opportunities to its hardworking and motivated employees, even those who lack college educations. As the company's CEO recently ex-plained to *BusinessWeek:* "At Wal-Mart you can, without a high school de-gree, start as a cart pusher in the parking lot and end up being a regional vice-president."[2] Indeed, most Low-Cost companies offer opportunities for those in apparent dead-end jobs to become shift and department managers, then store managers, and, perhaps, to move beyond. Clearly, it is not as easy today as it was when Sam Walton started the company for workers without college degrees to climb to the highest rungs of the Wal-Mart hierarchy— there is now a glass ceiling above which one needs technical training—but employees who move up the organization can choose to go to college to gain the credentials they lack, and the company probably will facilitate their doing so.

Where to Work and What to Do?

Although in practice not every American has a true *career* choice, almost all have *job* alternatives to choose among, each with a unique set of consequences. Identifying those consequences should be the first step every job applicant takes. Paradoxically, it is both easier and harder today to gain an understanding of what it means to work for an employer in a specific job. While almost every large and midsize company has a Web site where potential employees can find at least basic information about the terms of the employment contract it offers, many of those sites don't provide much detail about the nature of the work itself, and some are mere puff pieces with respect to benefits and promotion opportunities. (More objective information often is available at independent Web sites.) Because every company's total employment package is comprised of multiple elements—including such soft, but crucially important, factors as corporate culture, training opportunities, and the degree to which employees are respected—it is helpful, if not essential, for prospective hires to talk with current and past employees about their experiences before committing to a job.

Because LC, GC, and High-Involvement companies offer quite different working conditions, the first step for aspiring workers is to identify which type of employer offers conditions that fit their needs. In general, the benefits of working for an LC employer include: relative availability of jobs; low requirements in terms of experience and education; short waiting periods for hiring decisions; and minimal demands in terms of attitude, attention, and commitment. As noted, these employers offer jobs that are worth considering if one is young and/or undereducated, or if all that is needed is a paycheck to support one's surfing habit. The downsides of working for an LC company are as obvious, but worth repeating: relatively low pay; unchallenging tasks; and few if any benefits or opportunities to learn, grow, or develop a career. But, as at Wal-Mart, even LC companies may offer some good jobs, and they may offer the best available employment opportunity for those lacking an education. However, poorly managed LC companies are vulnerable to downsizing, acquisition, and even bankruptcy, all of which create the risk of unemployment.

The benefits of working for a GC company are far greater: high pay, excellent benefits, interesting work, and further opportunities for learning and advancement, either at the current employer or at a subsequent one. For people who are ambitious and assertive, GC companies tend to be great employers; for those who are truly competitive and aggressive, they are ideal. They are especially good places to work for risk takers and for those looking for flexible, nonconventional working arrangements, such as contingent and part-time employment. Since job security doesn't exist at GC companies, they turn their potential weaknesses into virtues and congratulate themselves for the flexibility, choice, and excitement they offer employees. GC companies offer those recruits who have skills that are in high demand the opportunity to negotiate pay, benefits, and conditions of employment, including what tasks they do, where and when they will do them, and to whom they will report.

HI companies offer employees the choice of quite different working environments, ones more oriented toward employee participation and development. As we have documented, employees at HI companies almost all have careers, not just jobs, and are treated with equal respect as members of a supportive community. The benefits of employment tend to be generous for workers and their families, but there also are risks associated with employment at HI companies, the most pronounced of which is sustainability. Over the last twenty years, even HI companies with solid records of providing steady employment have been susceptible to layoffs when technology changes—as at Polaroid and Digital—when competition stiffens—as at Herman Miller and Levi-Strauss—and some companies abandon, or de-emphasize, HI practices when there is a change in their leadership—as at Xerox, Hewlett-Packard (HP), Malden Mills, Dayton-Hudson, and Weyerhaeuser. Finally, working at an HI company can be quite demanding: off-the-job training and development can be time consuming, and it may not be possible to leave job concerns in the workplace.

What Tasks to Do?

One of the greatest dangers at work today is getting comfortable in one's job. Particularly in GC companies where the constant is change, employees who become complacent and quit learning put their futures at great risk. Increasingly there is no hiding from risk in the workplace—but there are strategies to lessen the impact of the unexpected, and choices to make about the nature of the risks one assumes. For example, almost everything workers do to hone their skills—and, in particular, to learn new and broader skills—can reduce their risk of unemployment. The good news is that most large companies now increasingly offer opportunities to do just that. Most now use one form or another of ad hoc task forces to solve business and organizational problems, and employees who choose to volunteer to participate on such teams gain practical experience in both new functional and discipline areas and on higher-level tasks. Moreover, as work rules are gradually loosening and narrow job descriptions are beginning to broaden—particularly in GC and HI companies—enterprising workers now have greater opportunities to choose to take on additional tasks that can help them to develop new skills.

Join a Union?

In general, work in America has entered an era of free-agency in which old notions of loyalty have been largely replaced by self-interest on the part of both private sector employers and their employees. As in professional sports, free agency typically brings out the worst behavior among both "owners and players," but it does provide greater freedom of choice for all and, especially, a greatly enhanced financial upside for the best performers. But marginal players—who are easily replaced—are at considerable risk in a world of free agency. Since the fundamental purpose of a union is to reduce the risk of the most vulnerable workers, it is no coincidence that some of the strongest unions today are found in professional sports.

Historically, American workers have looked to unions to reduce the risks associated with employers making arbitrary decisions with regard to their security, pay, benefits, and working conditions. But, as noted, today unions representing American manufacturing workers are less and less effective at reducing those risks because industrial corporations are free to move their operations offshore. In contrast, professional sports are domestic monopolies; team owners can't run away from unions. Moreover, for the most part, sports unions have been relatively more flexible than traditional unions in dealing with owners, recognizing that ultimately they are both passengers in the same boat, and they have been considerably more responsive to the changing needs and wishes of their members. The NFL players' union was the first to move in this direction, and the results have been positive for both athletes and owners.

In most HI companies, unions are irrelevant because employers have chosen to reduce the key elements of employee risk and to provide benefits unions offer without the costs. While large numbers of employees in GC companies are at risk, in most cases unions have failed to address the specific needs of those workers. For example, unions have not chosen to bargain for guarantees from companies to make good on the promises in their "new employment contracts" to provide training and development opportunities. One exception is the formation of several embryonic Hollywood-type unions in Silicon Valley that are providing group insurance plans, job Web sites, and other services to contract professionals.

In global LC companies, unions simply encourage offshoring or outsourcing and, as a result, have gained no traction among employees. The situation is quite different in LC industries that are by nature domestic in their operations; workers here have a meaningful choice with regard to joining a union. However, currently, employers in those industries appear to be doing a better job demonstrating to workers the downsides of organizing than unions are doing communicating the upsides. Healthcare is a major factor that could alter that equation; if the health insurance situation in America continues to worsen, it will make increasing sense for unorganized workers in services industries to choose to join unions. Less likely, but possible, unions might change their stance and advocate practices associated with HI management, thus becoming attractive to workers in both LC and GC industries.

Self-Employment?

The Census Bureau reports that 17.6 million Americans work for, and by, themselves, a number that increased by 3.9 percent in 2002, with the largest increase occurring in northern California.[3] Enterprising Americans can create good jobs for themselves, even if they do not have college degrees. There are numerous opportunities for individuals to learn skills at community colleges and then to go to work on their own or for small businesses. As those who have recently tried to find a worker to repair their roofs, resurface their floors, or add a room to their homes can attest, certain kinds of skilled labor are in short supply. There is a continuing need for people who can repair appliances, televisions, computers, and cars, and many communities need electricians, plumbers, and tailors. Apparently there is a shortage of shoemakers: customers in eastern and midwestern states send their worn-out shoes to be resoled by a repairman in San Francisco who advertises his services on the Internet.

When the dot-com bubble burst and the 2001 to 2003 recession hit Silicon Valley, instead of reporting in as "unemployed," tens of thousands of laid-off tech workers went to work for themselves as consultants and as solo operators in the construction, real estate, and landscaping industries. This explains the mystery of why the unemployment rate in northern California did not rise appreciably even as tech firms there were laying off tens of thousands of educated workers. Apparently, when technical, managerial, and professional workers are laid-off today, they often choose self-employment over retirement and/or unemployment. Part of this response is entrepreneurial, part self-defense, and part face-saving (for the sake of one's self-esteem, it is far better to be an "independent consultant" than it is to be out of a job and on the dole). There is nothing really new here: traditionally, when lawyers have failed to make partnership in law firms they have hung out their shingles and become solo practitioners. Now, the ranks of the self-employed are being swollen by computer technicians, engineers, managers, and financial and human-resource "consultants," solo practitioners in their own fields who market their wares on the Internet, through networking, and through temping.

And the self-employment option once enjoyed mainly by highly educated professionals is now opening up to individuals with all levels of education and skills. Redundant office and factory workers are becoming self-employed repair people, gardeners, window-washers, and limo drivers. During the recent recession, there was an observed increase in the number of people formerly employed in corporations entering the real estate and construction fields. Those individuals may no longer be working full-time, and most probably are not making as much as they earned working for someone else, and close to none of them enjoys benefits. However, they are earning a living. Some doubtless have more freedom and flexibility than they had working in corporate settings, and if media reports are at all accurate, some truly enjoy running their own businesses, making and selling things, providing services, and being their own bosses. Yet by all traditional measures, former corporate managers who now work twenty hours a week as consultants, technicians who work full time but earn half what they did before they were laid off, and former executives who are now freelance tour guides are all "underemployed." Economist Henry Farber finds that college graduates who were laid off in the 1980s experienced a 10 percent decline in their income once they were back to work; in 2004, laid-off college grads earned 30 percent less in their next jobs.[4]

Yet if "work/life balance" and "the quality of life" are not meaningless phrases, many of these individuals are happier and healthier now that they are out of "the rat race." And not a few of them are starting businesses that will grow in the future and create jobs for others. Almost all are providing an alternative source of goods and services to American businesses and consumers. They are contributing to the gross domestic product, paying taxes (at least some of them, some of the time), and, clearly, staying off the unemployment and welfare rolls. Hence, they help make U.S. unemployment figures look good in comparison to those in other advanced countries (where they would be counted as out of work if they applied for job-seeking help from their respective governments). So, on balance, the mixed-blessing of growing self-employment is better than the alternatives of unemployment or quitting the labor force.

What is problematic is that self-employment may add to the observed social isolation of American workers. By definition, the self-employed do not have workplaces, do not have coworkers, and probably do not experience as much a feeling of being part of a shared community as do those working for organizations. In this, the self-employed are quintessential examples of the new American worker: independent, flexible, entrepreneurial, risk-assuming, and alone. As corporations move even further in the direction of outsourcing, virtual work, part-timing, contracting, hoteling, and the like, these workers may be the unwitting vanguard of tomorrow's workforce.

Ironically, as the traditional workplace was disappearing in many sectors of the economy, a popular, and sophisticated, cartoon strip about old-fashioned work made its appearance in newspapers across America. "Dilbert" accurately depicts the disappearing nine-to-five workplace dominated by the water-cooler and an old-fashioned hierarchy. In fact, there is a growing shortage of such workplaces. Working with others in traditional offices, factories, stores, and warehouses is being replaced by working alone, on a cell phone or computer, in homes, cars, hotel rooms, libraries, wifi cafés, and at Kinko's, MailBoxes Etc, and Starbucks. While that freedom is a good thing, it is hard to put a happy face on the growing social isolation of the American worker. The latter is clearly an important factor to be weighed before choosing self-employment.

TO RETIRE, OR NOT TO RETIRE?

As retirement increasingly becomes more a privilege to be earned rather than a right, it is incumbent on younger workers to make good, early choices about savings and investments if they hope to have options when they grow older. Indeed, failure to make the right personal financial choices early in their careers severely limits workers' later options regarding both their retirement and the financing of their children's educations. The good news about the shift to defined-contribution plans is that it is now possible for workers to forecast the amounts needed to save in order to retire, even when they change jobs and careers.

Since few workers have sufficient knowledge to make wise decisions on their own regarding such choices as how to invest the money in their retirement accounts, whether to invest in their employer's stock, and when to exercise stock options, it seems to make sense, in general, for them to seek independent financial advice with regard to the management of their retirement funds.

The consequences of the financial choices made when one is young reverberate throughout one's life. For example, the Employee Benefit Research Institute reports that "only 25 percent of the workforce are very confident that they'll have enough money to live comfortably in retirement," yet *Essence* magazine runs a regular feature profiling women, some as young as in their forties, who have "retired." One of the main reasons why these women have options that the majority do not is that they made conscious efforts to save when they were young, and they made wise investments. The decisions those women made early in their careers left them able to choose later whether to do volunteer work, go back to school, engage in hobbies, or take on new careers more fulfilling than their first ones. As one such "retiree" explained, "Retirement doesn't mean you've got a ton of money and can now buy yourself out of a life of misery into a life of bliss. Retirement means having freedom to live the life you choose."

CHOICES, CHOICES, CHOICES:
GOOD, BAD, AND UGLY

Many employers have succeeded in giving workers more choice in terms of when and how they will work, what kinds of jobs and tasks they do, and what benefits they receive, all of which afford a wider range of alternatives affecting workers' careers and lifestyles than they have enjoyed in any time or place. All these choices make some Americans feel like kids in a candy

The "Retirement" of the Boomer Generation

January 1, 2006 was a red-letter day for America's 75 million baby boomers. That's when the oldest members of the age cohort officially turned sixty, with the rest of their peers queued up to follow them into seniordom at the rate of one every 7.7 seconds over the next eighteen years. Unlike their parents—who were busy planning for retirement well before they reached the dawn of their seventh decades—the vast majority of boomers are not so inclined. In fact, recent surveys show less than a third say they contemplate traditional retirement.

If nothing else, boomers are the most surveyed, probed, and analyzed generation in history, so we don't have to speculate about either their actions or motivations. Modal boomers report plans to continue working, at least part-time, for as long as their health allows, doing so both for financial reasons and "to keep busy and involved." Some have no choice in the matter: roughly a third say they expect "never to be able to afford to retire." With the cost of living outpacing the returns on their savings, health care costs skyrocketing, and defined-benefit pensions on the road to extinction, these grandmas and grandpas are likely to be working as Wal-Mart greeters for years to come—and age discrimination promises to be a continuing, contentious workplace issue for the next two decades. Predicted labor shortages as the result of boomer retirements ignore the law of supply and demand and the willingness of employers to provide phased-retirement and part-time jobs to deal with what at worst will be short-term shortages. Economist Peter Cappelli has presented data demonstrating that concerns about growing labor shortages are exaggerated at best.[5]

At the other end of the income spectrum, about a third of the boomer population—managers, professionals, and those lucky enough to have had employers who provided generous and secure pensions—have accumulated nest eggs sufficient to support them in comfort at Leisure World. But what is remarkable is that the R word is taboo among these relatively affluent boomers: they are betting on living at least until they are ninety, and intent on making the most out of those many remaining years—and rocking chairs and day-time television don't figure in their projected personal scenarios.

There is evidence that many boomers resist even considering the possibility that they might someday retire. While popular magazines devote entire issues to retirement "financial planning," offering advice on how middle-aged Americans should calculate their future income, expenses, and investments so they can afford to spend their golden years on well-manicured golf courses, boomers tell researchers they are more interested in finding the meaning and happiness that eluded them in the conflict-ridden 1960s and 1970s, in the self-indulgent Reagan 1980s, and in the careerist and materialist 1990s, all rather inglorious eras they had a major hand in shaping. But now they swear they are committed, finally, to "getting it right" in their sixties, and in the years beyond. [6]

The key question on the minds of these boomers is *"What's next?"* For these men and women, life planning involves making tough decisions about how to allocate the remaining time of their lives among work, family, education, leisure, and community activities. For example, they see they must make difficult choices between seeking personal fulfillment by continuing their professional and business careers, on one hand, or devoting more time to social, political, and charitable causes, on the other. And they must make conscious tradeoffs between making more money versus spending more time learning, and doing, new things. Although each individual will make different choices in these regards, making the right personal choice depends on the willingness to explore such difficult personal questions as "What does it mean to lead a good life?" "How much money do I really need?" "How do I balance my personal needs for fulfillment with the needs of others in my life?" and "What can I pass on to the next generation?"

Resolving the tensions around such questions turns out to be a difficult philosophical process but, when boomers put their minds to it, they often make imaginative choices that allow them to learn and develop as individuals while, at the same time, contributing positively to the lives of others. Given the boomers' reputation as the "me-generation," and "the generation that taught the world how to shop," it is extremely encouraging to monitor the diverse choices that fifty-somethings have been making: a lawyer leaves his firm to work to improve the life chances of kids in an impoverished South African township; a newspaper editor goes back to college to get her BA and later, in her sixties, enrolls in a doctoral program; an entrepreneurial English professor creates an online art gallery to introduce Australian Aboriginal painting to Americans; a Protestant minister, in response to the Enron scandal, becomes a teacher of business ethics; more than one business executive takes an enormous pay cut to head a nonprofit institution; a dentist leaves her practice to run a free inner-city clinic; a burnt-out math teacher becomes a business advisor to experience-deprived dot-comers; and a financial advisor commits to a twelve year project to make sure an entire class of disadvantaged first graders all stay in school and eventually attend college. [7]

Apparently, many boomers are exploring what's next for themselves and, by extension, for others. Much as the past actions of their generation had profound consequences, for good and ill, on the ethos of the entire nation, the sum of the decisions they now make may change American society in the future, as well.

store. Alas, the fun of going to a candy store is a function of the size of one's allowance: in terms of workplace options, increased choice has most benefited those who have the most resources.

At the same time choices have increased, many employers have succeeded in shifting the burden of risk relating to job security, training, career development, and health and retirement benefits from their own shoulders onto those of employees. While this presents an opportunity to craft a satis-fying work situation for those who have the ability and resources to choose, the results can be devastating when workers make unwise decisions. And for those who have relatively few or no resources, the additional risks they bear can be catastrophic.

Too few young Americans appreciate the implications for their futures of the employment-related choices they increasingly are required to make. We believe they need to be taught about the risks of "unsafe career prac-tices." Beginning in high school, they need to be shown that the decisions they make then and over the next few years will greatly determine their fu-ture life options and lifestyles. At a minimum, they need to understand the long-term financial and career consequences of not doing well in school and of not pursuing higher education, and what their peers in Asia are doing to prepare for their futures. In the 1970s, "career education" was all the rage in the nation's high schools. If that concept has any meaning left today, it should be to prepare young people to better make the difficult choices they will face with regard to work and education, choices that will determine the quality of their lives.

PART V

CONCLUSIONS

18

FUTURE OF THE AMERICAN WORKPLACE

We began our analysis with the strategic metaphor of Uncle Sam precariously balanced on the crest of a giant wave of global competition, attempting neither to fall behind in terms of economic competitiveness nor to outrun the nation's public policy infrastructure and social expectations. The research we have reviewed leads us to conclude that surfing this global tsunami successfully is a doable task, but it is far from being an easy one.

On one hand, there is the ever-present risk that the United States will be left behind in the new global competition and become trapped in the doldrums of economic decline. That situation will occur if the nation loses its technological, educational, and business leadership and fails to create sufficient numbers of vital new industries and good jobs. But a virtuous circle of actions can prevent that from happening: entrepreneurial initiatives, sound corporate management practices, supportive government investments in education and research, and the collective efforts of the American workforce. We believe the right policies and practices can preserve, and perhaps enhance, the nation's economic and technological preeminence in the future.

On the other hand, there is the risk that the United States may be too slow in providing the social and educational infrastructure needed to support fast-moving, high-tech industries. In this scenario, a substantial portion of the workforce will be left out of the process of globalization and not receive the considerable rewards that accrue to those who succeed in the new global economy. If large numbers of workers don't have the skills and knowledge needed to do the work required to keep U.S. businesses in a leadership position, American society may become seriously divided between haves and have-nots. Although there is evidence of growing income stratification in America and of increasing numbers of individuals trapped in low-paying work and unemployment, this scenario is not inevitable. Indeed, we have identified numerous policies and practices—especially changes in government policy with regard to healthcare and education—that will lead to both a more productive economy *and* a more just society.

In the most-desirable scenario, the United States neither falls off the back of the wave nor is it crushed beneath its break; instead, the country masters the emerging art of global competition. The good news is that the key actions needed to realize this goal are identifiable and within reach. We believe the *sine qua non* of this positive future is the creation of more of what we have called "good work." As we have shown, good work satisfies the financial, psychological, and social needs of employees.

In those American workplaces currently providing good jobs and careers, employees make productive contributions, add value to the goods they produce and services they provide, and thus enhance the performance and long-term sustainability of their companies. In the future, those "extra efforts" of employees—their innovative ideas, willingness to serve customers, and engagement in work tasks—will be a competitive necessity in a nation that has carved out knowledge-related activities as the source of its competitive advantage. We believe that securing a positive future for the American economy depends on more fully realizing the untapped and profound potential of the nation's human capital. If the United States is to succeed as the global leader in technology and high value-added goods and services, more corporations must adopt the High-Involvement approach to structuring jobs and employment, individual employees must plan their lives and careers more effectively, and the government must develop new policies, especially with regard to health and education. If all those things are done, we are convinced America can, and will, continue to maintain its commanding economic position.

A COLD SHOWER OF REALISM

We are not Pollyannas. We realize that even if individuals, organizations, and the government all do the right things, and at the right pace, further and continued disruptions in American industry are likely. There is good reason to believe the ongoing process of "creative destruction" of companies and jobs will continue, and perhaps accelerate, in years to come. Realistically, in the future more workers in more companies are likely to lose jobs as their tasks are moved offshore or automated. Entire industries may either disappear or shrink significantly. In other industries, some work may be retained in the United States, but only if the wages and benefits of American workers are reduced—or if the work can be redesigned to produce sufficient added-value to justify wages that are relatively high by international standards. What is inevitable is that an increasing number of American workers, in an increasing number of industries, will need to be able to give the "right" answers to three questions:

1. *How do my wages compare to those of workers overseas?*
2. *What can I do better than workers elsewhere in the world?*
3. *What are the advantages of doing my work in the United States?*

For the foreseeable future, American workers will need to justify high wages by having exceptional skills and by being able to do things that can't be done as well or at all elsewhere. If their wages are out-of-line with global competitive realities, U. S. workers may have to accept lower wages and benefits or see their jobs disappear. The airline industry is an instructive example of the challenges American companies and workers face. This services industry would appear immune to the pressures of offshoring: not only does it operate domestically, it is protected by law from foreign competition. Indeed, many tasks done by U.S. airline workers are, by necessity, domestic, and those will stay in the United States, and continue to be relatively well paid. But all airline jobs currently done by Americans do not need to be U.S.-based in the future: aircraft maintenance often can be done outside the

United States, cabin crews on international flights do not have to be based here, software can be written in India and Russia, and call centers can be located wherever English-speaking employees can be found. The reality is that American workers currently doing those tasks may be forced to accept lower wages and reduced benefits and to clock longer hours. Or they simply may lose their jobs. The same is true in other domestic services industries ranging from insurance, to banking, to project engineering.

In the manufacturing sector, steel offers a dramatic illustration of an industry once dominated by U.S. companies that underwent tremendous workplace change to survive and in which additional, significant future changes are likely. Globally, more steel is produced today than ever before, and imports to the United States reached a new high in 2004. But the number of steelworkers employed in America has been in constant decline for the last forty years, from over 500,000 in the early 1970s, to about 100,000 today. And there has been incredible consolidation in the industry: more than forty American steel companies went bankrupt between 1997 and 2004 alone, and many of the survivors are now parts of three new mega-companies: Mittal, Nucor, and U.S. Steel.

Despite the increase in imports, the loss of American jobs, and the consolidation of the industry, American companies continue to provide about half the steel consumed in this country; the domestic industry even was profitable in 2004 for the first time in many years. Steel is still produced here because it is increasingly made by automated technologies requiring small numbers of employees in newer companies that don't have the legacy labor costs that reduced the competitiveness of old-line steel companies.

But lower legacy costs are only part of the story. Equally, if not more important, almost all American steel companies with globally competitive levels of productivity link High-Involvement management practices to their use of new technology. At those companies, there are few layers of management, production workers often have autonomy and challenging jobs, and all employees share in profits and receive other forms of performance-linked compensation. In sum, there are fewer American steel workers today, and their pay is at risk because they are paid for performance, but those who remain have relatively good jobs, are well paid, and are likely to remain so for as long as their companies are successful.

Although the American steel industry is in better shape than it has been in decades, it still faces numerous challenges. Because developing countries are constantly building new mills and developed countries are introducing new technologies and production processes, even the most-productive American steel companies must continuously improve to stay atop the competitive wave. Employees at American mills constantly must focus on how they can do their work better, and companies continually must look for new ways to improve how they are managed—and the U.S. government needs to provide better support in terms of employee retraining and healthcare. Thus, in many respects, the steel industry illustrates the changes that have occurred in general in U.S. manufacturing and highlights the ongoing challenges all American companies face in the global economy.

The steel industry also offers an important lesson applicable to all industries: those American steel companies that have survived have had leaders who were willing and able to move beyond the comforting assumptions of their industry peers. Beginning in the 1980s, Nucor's CEO Kenneth Iverson and a few other steel executives discarded the outmoded industrial model that once worked in their industry, but had since become a major cause of the decline of American steel in the global economy. These far-sighted CEOs rethought the basic assumptions that drove the actions of most other steel industry executives—for example, that big mills are more productive than smaller ones, that short-term profits must take precedence over long-term investments, that successful companies must offer a full-range of products rather than be niche players, that unions are by nature adversaries rather than partners, that the efforts of workers count for little in a capital-intensive industry, and that executives constitute a special class of employee entitled to greater privileges and benefits than those down the line. Because they discarded such widely held—and dysfunctional—assumptions, the steel executives became open to considering new strategies, new business models, and new workplace practices more appropriate to meeting the emerging challenges of globalism.

At about the same time the steel industry was changing, Southwest Airline's Herb Kelleher and Continental's Gordon Bethune challenged similar assumptions that had come to cripple most of the U.S. airline industry. They too chose to adopt new practices that were good both for shareholders and for employees. Indeed, the competitive strategies and workplace practices at all companies are ultimately the product of choices their managers make. And it is our conclusion that too many American executives— like the old-line managers who once dominated the steel and airline industries—unnecessarily limit the range of choices they consider with regard to how they utilize and develop human capital in their businesses. As we have seen, many promising workplace practices are not being implemented because executives believe they have "no alternative" but to conform to the traditions of their industry.

THE CHOICES MANAGERS MAKE

In the final analysis, management is about making choices, about strategically deciding to do one thing and not another. The first managerial choice concerns what business to be in: what product to make or service to deliver. The second choice is whom the customer should be: Will the product be low-cost for the mass market, or high-quality for top-end consumers? Third, managers must choose where and how their company will add value: Should they make the product, or buy it? Should they sell it to retailers, or market it directly to customers? Then they must decide how the strategy will be implemented: What technology should be employed and how should business processes be organized to give the company a competitive advantage? What kind of sales and marketing strategy should be used, and should that work be done by the company itself or by outside contractors? Last, but not least, should the business be financed through borrowing or equity? The sum of these decisions informs a company's business model, determining whether it will compete in terms of cost, quality, timeliness, or technology.

All these decisions have implications for a company's organizational and human capital requirements; yet, as we have mentioned, some managers conclude that once a company's strategic direction and business model are established, they have "no choice" concerning the approach they adopt to managing their people: if the business strategy of a Global-Competitor corporation is to compete against the fastest-moving, most technologically advanced foreign and domestic companies, managers say they have "no choice" but to offer contingent employment to a great many workers to preserve the flexibility to respond to unpredictable changes in the operating environment; or, if the business strategy at a Low-Cost operator is to offer customers the cheapest goods on the market, then managers say they have "no choice" but to offer low-wage, low-benefit jobs to most employees, or to offshore most work.

We believe that too many executives believe they are prisoners of iron economic laws and, thus, have "no choice" but to match the working conditions offered by their lowest-cost competitors. Especially when making decisions relating to downsizing, outsourcing, and offshoring, many managers say they have no alternative but to do what everyone else in their industry is doing. In 2003, when IBM announced plans to offshore the jobs of thousands of its American white-collar employees, the company's director for global employee relations explained, "Our competitors are doing it, and we have to do it." In 2005, when Boeing announced that it would offshore 60 to 70 percent of the components of its new 787 commercial jet, a leading aviation consultant explained, "Companies don't have a choice. If a company can go to China and get a widget for 10 cents an hour, and it costs $1 an hour in the United States, what's a company to do?" And when the Delphi Corp. called on the United Auto Workers (UAW) to renegotiate the contract with its thirty thousand hourly workers—requesting wage and benefit give-backs on the order of 50 to 60 percent—the company's CEO said that it had no choice but to do so: the alternative was bankruptcy, the loss of U.S. jobs, and the forfeiture of pension commitments. (Indeed, when the concessions weren't forthcoming, Delphi's CEO followed through and declared bankruptcy.)

Unfortunately, increasing numbers of American managers today do find themselves in positions where they have no choice but to make decisions that have negative consequences for their employees. When managers strategically paint themselves into corners, they eventually run out of options: when their labor costs exceed the value their product commands in the market, there is little choice but to downsize, outsource, or offshore. At companies like Delphi, decades of accumulated, poor strategic choices eventually make it "too late" for managers to pursue positive employment practices that, if adopted earlier, might have led to better organizational performance.

But corporate downsizing, offshoring, and bankruptcy are not predetermined fates. There is still time for managers of most American companies to adopt workplace practices that will have positive future consequences for their companies and employees. As Peter Drucker advocated half a century ago, instead of treating their workforces mainly as labor costs, most employers can profit from capturing the productive benefits of trained and engaged workers. Most managers have enough strategic maneuvering room to structure their organizations so that employees can become competitive assets—adding value in terms of productivity, quality, ideas, and customer service—and thus justifying higher wages and better benefits. While not every company is able to adopt them, we nonetheless believe that such High-Involvement practices as employee participation in decision-making, profit sharing, stock ownership, and, especially, continuous skill development can benefit many more companies than currently employ them.

American executives have more room to choose the type and form of working conditions their companies offer than they commonly assume. For example, it once was widely believed that no company in the airline industry could trust its employees to decide how best to serve customers . . . until Southwest did so. It once was assumed that no company in the discount retail industry could succeed while paying its employees decent salaries and offering them full benefits . . . until Costco did so. It was assumed that poorly educated blue-collar workers in old-line manufacturing firms could not be taught managerial accounting and then left to be self-managing . . . until SRC Holdings did so. Once the conventional wisdom in American industry was that employees have to be closely supervised and governed by rules . . . until WL Gore proved otherwise. And, it commonly was assumed that the first thing a company must do in a financial crisis is to lay off workers . . . until Xilinx found other ways.

Here we must add another astringent dose of realism: there is no free lunch. To one degree or another, executives who decide to adopt new and unconventional management practices often place their jobs and careers at risk. In going against the conventional "wisdom" in their industries, executives risk alienating their boards, investors, and fellow managers. Often they are mocked in the business press for their "naïveté" and "misplaced idealism." And, in trusting their employees to make their organizations more effective, they risk challenging some of the dominant ideas that drive managerial decision-making in America (even some that are taught in business schools). Doubtless, economic analyses and hard-headed strategic thinking about their business models played major parts in the decisions pathbreaking executives made to adopt human resources policies that are unusual in their industries. But it is also true that the choices they made were influenced by their personal values and by rigorous examinations of their own assumptions about what their workers want and need.

ASSUMPTIONS MANAGERS MAKE

The decisions we all make are driven by our values and assumptions. For example, executives in Low-Cost companies often assume that the needs and aspirations of their workers are entirely different from their own ("They are just working for a paycheck"). These managers assume that what the vast majority of Americans want is cheap goods, and not good work. As cited earlier, the CEO of Wal-Mart articulated his belief on this matter in an extensive MSNBC interview. His conclusion: *the consumer is king.* Or, as economist Arthur Laffer recently put it, every time Wal-Mart lowers the price of a product that amounts to "a raise" for the American consumer. Such assumptions have profound consequences: if people are basically consumers, then the way jobs and workplaces are organized will be quite different than if people are basically workers. If all that Americans want is cheap goods, then the working conditions currently found in LC companies are appropriate, and the executives at those companies do have no choice when it comes to offering low-pay, low-benefit, and low-level jobs.

But, in fact, are humans more workers, or are they more consumers? The issue is not an easy one to decide, but it is profoundly important. For nearly 2,500 years, philosophers, religious leaders, and economists have noted that humans use their God-given gift of reason for two main activities: working and consuming. Thus, humans are called *homo faber* on one hand, and *homo economicus* on the other. From the time of Adam Smith's 1776 *Wealth of Nations,* through the Industrial Revolution, the dominant assumption was that economic considerations ruled the lives of workers. (Even trade unionists shared the assumption. When Samuel Gompers was asked what workers want from their labor, he answered with one word: "More.")

It was only after World War II that social scientists, drawing on early Christian theory and Freudian psychology, advanced the notion that humans are, at base, more worker than consumer. In the 1950s, Abraham Maslow and Douglas McGregor argued that healthy humans achieve self-realization and social integration through good work. By the early 1970s, a growing body of social-science literature indicated that humans are workers with social and psychological needs, in addition to being consumers with economic wants. Since then, the evidence has been accumulating: in order to have dignity, all adults need to earn salaries on which they can support themselves and their families. And almost all workers want some security, predictable benefits, intrinsically rewarding work, opportunities for growth and development on the job, and to be part of a supportive workplace community. Indeed, that knowledge about basic human needs was a prime justification for the national decision to end welfare dependency.

Of course, humans are *both* workers and consumers, so the issue isn't simply either/or; rather, it is about where the emphasis is placed. It is our conclusion that American managers are currently in danger of overbalancing their workplace practices and policies on the economic side of the equation, concentrating on maximizing corporate flexibility and efficiency to benefit consumers and shareholders, while neglecting workers' needs for financial security, development, and involvement in their tasks and workplace communities. The evidence we have reviewed indicates that an effective *and just* labor market would provide balance among the characteristics of flexibility and efficiency on one hand, and security and involvement on the other. The challenge facing public and private decision makers is to create organizations that meet the needs of customers, investors, *and* employees.

The examples of Xilinx, Nucor, American Cast Iron Pipe, WL Gore, SRC Holdings, Alcoa, Costco, Southwest Airlines, Harley-Davidson, and UPS illustrate that executives have more choices than commonly assumed when it comes to creating workplace practices that serve the multiple needs of their various constituencies. These examples show that *homo faber* can be served along with *homo economicus*. These companies are as profitable as their competitors, and that profitability is in great part the result of addressing the three deepest needs of workers: for financial resources and security, for meaningful work that offers the opportunity for human development, and for supportive social relationships. An enormous body of evidence supports the fact that those are the things workers need, even if many American executives assume otherwise.

Although the range of options companies have with regard to salaries, benefits, and working conditions is far from unlimited, there are unrealized opportunities for imaginative managers willing to explore the potential benefits of a fuller-range of alternatives than they now consider. In our experience, it is the strategic options *not* considered that come back to haunt managers. When companies get into serious trouble, it is seldom because they have mistakenly chosen course A over course B but rather because they failed to consider option C. It is almost always the factor left out of the decision-making process—the stakeholder or long-term consequence not considered, the program not on the table, the nonquantifiable ethical or human factor not deemed important enough to weigh—that leads to strategic errors with severe financial repercussions.

The examples we have cited illustrate that some bad jobs can be turned into good ones with a little imagination, appropriate business models, and, most important, the executive will to do so. As Delphi downsized and offshored thousands of jobs, and reduced the pay and benefits of its surviving American workforce, Harley-Davidson increased its U.S. manufacturing business and operated profitably because it turned similar rust-belt manufacturing jobs into "good work" for its nearly ten thousand blue-collar employees. The company now competes successfully in the global export market against companies from low-wage countries. It is able to do so, in large part, because its leaders were willing to create a viable business model based on HI practices.

As Wal-Mart replaced bad jobs in Main Street variety stores with bad jobs in suburban malls, Starbucks replaced bad jobs behind the counter in urban greasy spoons with good jobs in espresso parlors. It took strategic acumen and management expertise for Starbucks' executives to create a business model in which even their part-timers can benefit: "health coverage, stock options and discounted stock purchase plans, retirement savings plan, extensive training, a fun, team-oriented work environment . . . and tuition reimbursement for eligible employees with one or more years of service." Starbucks' investors and employees have both been rewarded because its management created an imaginative business model that benefits all the company's stakeholders. We don't believe the executives at Harley-Davidson or Starbucks should be seen as exceptions; instead, they should be regarded as role models.

There also is an essential part for government to play in creating a robust economic future for America. In the past, geography and natural resources were keys to the wealth of nations; in the emerging global economy, countries will have to create, and earn, their comparative competitive advantages. Ideally, the U.S. government will take the lead and craft a coherent, national competitive strategy in support of American industry and American workers. As we have argued, prime elements of that strategy should include investment in the skills and education of the workforce and the creation of a "level playing field" for American employers in world markets by removing the burden of providing health insurance from their shoulders. At a minimum, the government has a special responsibility to alleviate some of the risks that those left behind in the competitive global arena are forced to bear, including the costs of their retraining, unemployment, and healthcare. If the government does not take such actions, we fear the nation faces a future of economic decline, increasing social stratification, and the end of the American dream of social and economic mobility.

The final question in policy analysis is the most difficult: How much of the burden of change is the responsibility of employers, how much is the responsibility of individuals, and how much is the responsibility of government? Objectively grounding policy analysis in data is an important step in finding the answer to that question, but even the clearest understanding of the facts will not absolve Americans of the necessity of making what are, in essence, normative judgments. In the end, what we do with the knowledge created by social science research comes down to a matter of choice based on our collective beliefs and values about the kind of workplaces and nation we want in the future. And, in a market economy, the preponderance of the responsibility to choose falls upon those who manage private enterprises. More than any other players, these men and women will make the key choices that determine the future of the American workplace.

The statement "I have no alternative" is one of the surest indicators of leadership failure in government, business, or any institution. Great leaders use their strategic and moral imaginations to create viable options where others see none. When there appears to be no choice but to take an action that is negative for a key constituent, imaginative leaders look for alternatives that haven't been tried or for ones that others assume "won't work." In business, such leaders take the extra step and search for actions that serve all their stakeholders.

If American companies are to meet the challenges of the new global economy, their leaders must begin to imagine what is required to build greater community and commitment in their respective workplaces, and then to create those conditions. In acting to meet the needs of their employees for good work, corporate leaders not only seize an opportunity to improve the long-term performance of their businesses, they also fulfill their responsibility to all their stakeholders—owners, workers, and nation alike.

AUTHORS OF PAPERS COMMISSIONED FOR THIS STUDY

The papers listed below are being published in a separate volume: Edward E. Lawler III and James O'Toole (eds.), *America at Work,* Palgrave Macmillan, 2006.

Stephen Barley, Stanford University, and Gideon Kunda, Tel Aviv University, "Itinerant Professionals: Technical Contractors in a Knowledge Economy."

Joseph Blasi, Rutgers University, Douglas Kruse, Rutgers University, and Richard Freeman, Harvard University, "Shared Capitalism at Work: Impacts and Policy Options."

Peter Cappelli, University of Pennsylvania, "Changing Career Paths and Their Implications."

Wayne Cascio, University of Colorado, "The Economic Impact of Employee Behaviors on Organizational Performance."

Elizabeth F. Craig, Boston University, and Douglas T. Hall, Boston University, "Bringing Careers Back In . . . The Changing Landscape of Careers in American Corporations Today."

David Finegold, Keck Graduate Institute, "Is Education the Answer? Trends in the Supply and Demand for Skills in the U.S. Workforce."

Fred Foulkes, Boston University, Sushil Vachani, Boston University, and Jennifer Zaslow, Boston University, "Global Sourcing of Talent: Implications for the U.S. Workforce."

Michael J. Handel, University of Wisconsin, and David Levine, University of California, "The Effects of New Work Practices on Workers."

Thomas Kochan, Massachusetts Institute of Technology, "Restoring Voice at Work and in Society."

Ellen Kossek, Michigan State University, "Work and Family In America: Growing Tensions Between Employment Policy and a Transformed Workforce."

Alec Levenson, University of Southern California, "Trends in Jobs and Wages in the U.S. Economy."

Paul Osterman, MIT Sloan School, "The Changing Employment Circumstances of Managers."

Jeffrey Pfeffer, Stanford University, "Working Alone: Whatever Happened to the Idea of Organizations as Communities?"

Richard Price, University of Michigan, "The Transformation of Work in America: New Health Vulnerabilities for American Workers."

Denise Rousseau, Carnegie Mellon University, "The Shifting Risk to the American Worker in the Contemporary Employment Contract."

Kathryn Shaw, Stanford University, "The Value of Innovative Human Resource Management Practices."

NOTES

PART II

1. Paul Osterman, "The Changing Employment Circumstances of Managers," in *America at Work,* eds. Edward E. Lawler III and James O'Toole (New York: Palgrave Macmillan, 2006).
2. Edward E. Lawler III and Christopher Worley, *Built to Change,* (San Francisco: Jossey-Bass 2006).
3. Small business statistics from United States Small Business Administration, http://www.sba.gov/aboutsba/sbastats.html.
4. U.S. Census Bureau. *Compendium of Public Employment: 2002.* 2000 Census of governments, vol. 3, *Public Employment,* Report CC02(3)–2. (Washington, DC: Government Printing Office, 2004).

CHAPTER 2

1. Louis Uchitelle, "If You Can Make It Here . . . ." *New York Times,* September 4, 2005, Section 3, pp. 1–4.
2. John O'Dell, "Big Three May be Shrinking but U.S. Auto Business Isn't," *Los Angeles Times,* December 18, 2005, p. C1.
3. Bureau of Economic Affairs, United States Department of Commerce, "Summary Estimates for Multinational Companies: Employment, Sales, and Capital Expenditures for 2003," April 19, 2005, http://www.bea.gov/bea/newsrelarchive/2005/mnc2003.htm.
4. McKinsey Global Institute. *The Emerging Global Market: Parts I–III* (San Francisco: McKinsey & Company, 2005), http://www.mckinsey.com/mgi/publications/emerginggloballabormarket/index.asp.
5. Ibid.
6. M. J. Slaughter, "Insourcing Jobs: Making the Global Economy Work for America," Organization for International Investment study, 2004, http://www.ofii.org/insourcing/insourcing_study.pdf.
7. John O'Dell, "Big Three May be Shrinking but U.S. Auto Business Isn't," *Los Angeles Times,* December 18, 2005, p. C1.
8. M. J. Slaughter, "Insourcing Jobs: Making the Global Economy Work for America," Organization for International Investment study, 2004, http://www.ofii.org/insourcing/insourcing_study.pdf.
9. Ed Michaels, Helen Handfield-Jones, and Beth Axelrod, *The War for Talent* (Boston: Harvard Business School Press, 2001).
10. Christina B. Gibson and Susan G. Cohen, *Virtual Teams that Work: Creating Conditions for Virtual Team Effectiveness* (San Francisco: Jossey-Bass, 2003).
11. Jay Galbraith, *Designing the Customer-Centric Organization: A Guide to Strategy, Structure and Process* (San Francisco: Jossey-Bass, 2005); Raghuram G. Rajan and Julie Wulf, "The Flattening Firm: Evidence from Panel Data on the Changing Nature of Corporate Hierarchies," NBER Working Paper 9633, National Bureau of Economic Research, Cambridge, Massachusetts, April 2003.
12. Paul Osterman, "The Changing Employment Circumstances of Managers," in *America at Work,* eds. Edward E. Lawler III and James O'Toole (New York: Palgrave Macmillan, 2006).

13. Lawrence Mishel, Jared Bernstein, and Sylvia Allegretto, *The State of Working America 2004/2005: An Economic Policy Institute Book* (Ithaca, NY: ILR Press, 2005).
14. Thomas W. Malone, *The Future of Work: How the New Order of Business will Shape Your Organization, Your Management Style, and Your Life* (Boston: Harvard Business School Press, 2004); Thomas W. Malone, Robert Laubacher, and Michael S. Scott Morton, eds., *Inventing the Organizations of the 21st Century* (Cambridge, MA: MIT Press, 2003).
15. Mishel, Ibid.
16. Ibid.

CHAPTER 3

1. Edward E. Lawler III, *High Involvement Management* (San Francisco: Jossey-Bass, 1986).
2. Gary Rivlin, "Who's Afraid of China?" *New York Times,* December 19, 2004, Sec. 3, pp. 1–4.
3. C. Shepard and D. Carroll, eds., *Working in the Twenty-First Century* (New York: Wiley-Interscience, 1980).
4. Christina B. Gibson and Susan G. Cohen, *Virtual Teams that Work: Creating Conditions for Virtual Team Effectiveness* (San Francisco: Jossey-Bass, 2003).
5. Edward E. Lawler III, John Boudreau, and S. A. Mohrman, *Achieving Strategic Excellence* (Palo Alto, CA: Stanford Press, 2006).
6. J. Richard Hackman and Greg R. Oldham, *Work Redesign* (Reading, MA: Addison-Wesley, 1980).
7. Edward E. Lawler III, *Rewarding Excellence: Pay Strategies for the New Economy* (San Francisco: Jossey-Bass, 2000).
8. Edward E. Lawler III, Susan A. Mohrman, and George S. Benson, *Organizing for High Performance: The CEO Report on Employee Involvement, TQM, Reengineering, and Knowledge Management in Fortune 1000 Companies* (San Francisco: Jossey-Bass, 2001).
9. Robert E. Cole, *Managing Quality Fads: How American Business Learned to Play the Quality Game* (New York: Oxford University Press, 1999); W. E. Deming, *Out of the Crisis* (Cambridge, MA: MIT Press, 1986); J. Richard Hackman and Ruth Wageman, "Total Quality Management: Empirical, Conceptual, and Practical Issues," *Administrative Science Quarterly* 40 (1995): 309–342.
10. Michael Hammer and James Champy, *Reengineering the Corporation* (New York: HarperBusiness, 1993).
11. Edward E. Lawler III, S. A. Mohrman, and G. S. Benson, Organizing for High Performance: The CEO Report on Employee Involvement, TQM, Reengineering, and Knowledge Management in Fortune 1000 Companies (San Francisco: Jossey-Bass, 2001); Raghuram G. Rajan and Julie Wulf, "The Flattening Firm: Evidence from Panel Data on the Changing Nature of Corporate Hierarchies," NBER Working Paper 9633, National Bureau of Economic Research, Cambridge, Massachusetts, April 2003.
12. Edward E. Lawler III, *Treat People Right!* (San Francisco: Jossey-Bass, 2003); Edward E. Lawler III and Chris Worley, *Built to Change* (San Francisco: Jossey-Bass, 2006).

CHAPTER 4

1. Denise M. Rousseau, *Psychological Contract in Organizations: Understanding Written and Unwritten Agreements* (Newbury Park, CA: Sage, 1995).
2. Bruce R. Ellig, *The Evolution of Employee Pay and Benefits in the United States* (Arlington, VA: Kirby Lithographic Company, 2005).
3. Ibid.
4. Edward E. Lawler III, *Pay and Organizational Effectiveness* (San Francisco: Jossey-Bass, 1980).
5. Lawrence Mishel, Jared Bernstein, and Sylvia Allegretto, *The State of Working America 2004/2005: An Economic Policy Institute Book* (Ithaca, NY: ILR Press, 2005).
6. Ibid.
7. Ibid.
8. Ibid.
9. Mary Elizabeth Burke, "2005 Benefits: Survey Report," Society for Human Resource Management, June 2005, http://www.shrm.org/hrresources/surveys_published/2005%20Benefits%20Survey%20Report.pdf.

10. Mary Elizabeth Burke, "2005 Benefits: Survey Report," Society for Human Resource Management, June 2005, http://www.shrm.org/hrresources/surveys_published/2005%20Benefits%20Survey%20Report.pdf.

11. Bureau of Labor Statistics, "Contingent and Alternative Employment Arrangements, February 2005," United States Department of Labor press release 05–1433, July 27, 2005.

12. Alec Levenson, "Trends in Jobs and Wages in the U.S. Economy," in *America at Work,* eds. Edward E. Lawler III and James O'Toole (New York: Palgrave Macmillan, 2006).

13. "Part-Time Workers," OECD data reported in the *Economist,* July 2, 2005, p. 88.

14. Stephen Barley, "Itinerant Professionals: Technical Contractors in a Knowledge Economy," in *America at Work,* eds. Edward E. Lawler III and James O'Toole (New York: Palgrave Macmillan, 2006).

15. Ibid.

PART III

1. Joi Preciphs, "Moving Ahead . . . but Slowly," *Wall Street Journal,* November 14, 2005 p. R3.

CHAPTER 5

1. American Enterprise Institute for Public Policy Research, "The State of the American Worker 2005: Attitudes About Work, Chores, and Leisure in America," August 30, 2005, http://www.aei.org/publicopinion17.

2. D. T. Hall, *Careers In and Out of Organizations* (Thousand Oaks, CA: Sage Publications, 2002).

3. Scott Reynolds, Neil Ridley, and Carl E. Van Horn, Ph.D., "A Work-Filled Retirement: Workers' Changing Views on Employment and Leisure," *WorkTrends Survey* 8.1 (August, 2005): 1–39, http://www.heldrich.rutgers.edu/Resources/Publication/191/WT16.pdf.

4. D. T. Hall, "The Protean Career: A Quarter-Century Journey," *Journal of Vocational Behavior* 65, no. 1 (2004): 1; D. T. Hall and J. E. Moss, "The New Protean Career Contract: Helping Organizations and Employees Adapt," *Organizational Dynamics* 26, no. 3 (1998): 22–37.

5. Tim Hall and Elizabeth Craig, "Bringing Careers Back in: The Changing Landscape of Careers in American Corporations Today," in *America at Work,* eds. Edward E. Lawler III and James O'Toole (New York: Palgrave Macmillan, 2006).

6. U.S. Census Bureau, *America's Families and Living Arrangements: 2003* (Washington, DC: Government Printing Office, 2004).

7. *Wall Street Journal Online,* "Many Americans Lack Confidence in Ability to Retire Comfortably," September 26, 2005, http://online.wsj.com/article_print/SB112769981032951772.html.

8. Pension Benefit Guaranty Corporation, 2004 Pension Insurance Data Book, Tables S–46 and M–13, http://www.pbgc.gov/publications/databook/databook04.pdf and Pension benefit Guaranty Corporation, 2002 Pension Insurance Data Book, Tables S–27 and M–12, http:///www.pbgc.gov/publications/databook02.pdf.

9. Scott Reynolds, Neil Ridley, and Carl E. Van Horn, Ph.D., "A Work-Filled Retirement: Workers' Changing Views on Employment and Leisure," *WorkTrends Survey 8.1* (August, 2005): 1–39, http://www.heldrich.rutgers.edu/Resources/Publication/191/WT16.pdf.

CHAPTER 6

1. Quoted in Garrison Keillor, *Good Poems for Hard Times* (New York: Penguin, 2005).

2. Ellen Kossek, "Work and Family in America: Growing Mismatch Between Employment Policy and a Transformed Workforce," in *America at Work,* eds. Edward E. Lawler III and James O'Toole (New York: Palgrave Macmillan, 2006).

3. Bureau of Labor Statistics, "Tables 5 and 6: Percent of Workers With Access to Selected Benefits, by Selected Characteristics, Private Industry," National Compensation Survey, Survey of Employee Benefits, 2003, http://www.bls.org.

4. Kossek, Ibid.

5. J. Bond, C. Thompson, E. Galinsky, and D. Prottas, *Highlights of the National Study of the Changing Workforce (*New York: Families and Work Institute, 2002).

6. U.S. Department of Labor, "Women in the Labor Force: A Databook," Report 973, Table 6, 2004, http://www.bls.gov/cps/wlf-databook.pdf.

7. Bond, Ibid.
8. U.S. Department of Labor, "Women in the Labor Force: A Databook," Report 973, Table 6, 2004, http://www.bls.gov/cps/wlf-databook.pdf.
9. Mary Elizabeth Burke, "2005 Benefits: Survey Report," Society for Human Resource Management, June 2005, http://www.shrm.org/hrresources/surveys_published/2005%20Benefits%20Survey%20 Report.pdf.
10. Kossek, Ibid.
11. Quoted in Warren Bennis and Robert Thomas, *Geeks and Geezers* (Boston: Harvard Business School Press, 2002).
12. Jack Welch and Suzy Welch, *Winning* (New York: HarperCollins, 2005).
13. Peter Cappelli, "Changing Career Paths and Their Implications," in *America at Work,* eds. Edward E. Lawler III and James O'Toole (New York: Palgrave Macmillan, 2006).
14. Kossek, Ibid.

CHAPTER 7

1. Richard Price, "The Transformation of Work in America: New Health Vulnerabilities for American Workers," in *America at Work,* eds. Edward E. Lawler III and James O'Toole (New York: Palgrave Macmillan, 2006).
2. Ibid.
3. Ibid.
4. Ibid.
5. Ibid.
6. Ibid.

CHAPTER 8

1. American Enterprise Institute for Public Policy Research, "The State of the American Worker 2005: Attitudes about Work, Chores, and Leisure in America," August 30, 2005, http://www.aei.org/pub-licopinion17.
2. Ibid.
3. Bureau of Labor Statistics, "Time-Use Survey: First Results Announced by BLS," news release, September 14, 2004, http://www.bls.gov/news.release/archives/atus_09142004.pdf.
4. Harris Interactive/Age Wave/Concours Group Survey, "Main Street vs. Wall Street," news release, March 1, 2005, http://www.globeinvestor.com/servlet/ArticleNews/print/PRNEWS/20050301/2005_03_01_12_1622_1320171.

CHAPTER 9

1. Ellen Galinsky, James T. Bond, Stacy S. Kim, Lois Backon, Erin Brownfield, and Kelly Sakai, "Overwork in America: When the Way We Work Becomes Too Much," Families and Work Institute, 2005, http://www.familiesandwork.org.
2. Bureau of Labor Statistics, "Public Use Data Dictionary: American Time Use Survey (ATUS) Survey Methodology Data. Variables about ATUS, 2003," 2005, http://www.bls.gov/tus/atussmcode-book.pdf; Bureau of Labor Statistics, "Public Use Data Dictionary: American Time Use Survey (ATUS) Interview Data. Variables collected in ATUS, 2003," 2005, http://www.bls.gov/tus/atus-intcodebook.pdf; Lawrence Mishel, Jared Bernstein, and Sylvia Allegretto, *The State of Working America 2004/2005: An Economic Policy Institute Book* (Ithaca, NY: ILR Press, 2005).
3. Simi Kedia and Thomas Philippon, "The Economics of Fraudulent Accounting" (AFA 2006 Boston Meetings Paper, January, 2005), http://ssm.com/abstract=687225.

CHAPTER 10

1. Lawrence Mishel, Jared Bernstein, and Sylvia Allegretto, *The State of Working America 2004/2005: An Economic Policy Institute Book* (Ithaca, NY: ILR Press, 2005).
2. Michelle Conlin and Aaron Bernstein, "Working Poor," *BusinessWeek,* May 31, 2004.
3. Mishel, Ibid.
4. Ibid.

5. Bruce R. Ellig, *The Evolution of Employee Pay and Benefits in the United States* (Arlington, VA: Kirby Lithographic Company, 2005).
6. James Krohe, Jr., "The Revolution that Never Was," *Across the Board* 42, no. 5 (2005): 28–35.
7. Arthur Okun, *Equality and Efficiency: The Big Tradeoff* (Washington, DC: Brookings Institution, 1975).
8. J. Blasi, D. Kruse, and A. Bernstein, *In the Company of Owners: The Truth about Stock Options (and Why Every Employee Should Have Them)* (New York: Perseus Books, 2003); Corey Rosen, John Case, and Martin Staubus, *Equity: Why Employee Ownership is Good for Business* (Boston: Harvard Business School Press, 2005).
9. Ibid.

CHAPTER 11

1. Lawrence Mishel, Jared Bernstein, and Sylvia Allegretto, *The State of Working America 2004/2005: An Economic Policy Institute Book* (Ithaca, NY: ILR Press, 2005).
2. Richard B. Freeman and Joel Rogers, *What Workers Want* (New York and Ithaca: Cornell University Press and Russell Sage Foundation, 1999); Peter Hart and Associates, "Americans' Views on the Economy, Corporate Behavior and Union Representation" (Washington, DC: Peter Hart and Associates, 2000).

CHAPTER 12

1. Harris Poll, "Many U.S. Employees Have Negative Attitudes to Their Jobs, Employers and Top Managers," (No. 38, May 6, 2005), http://www.harrisinteractive.com/harris_poll/index.asp?PID=568.
2. "2005 Skills Gap Report—A Survey of the American Manufacturing Workforce," National Association of Manufacturers, Washington, DC, 2005.
3. Tim Hall and Elizabeth F. Craig, "Bringing Careers Back In . . . The Changing Landscape of Careers in American Corporations Today," in *America at Work*, eds. Edward E. Lawler III and James O'Toole (New York: Palgrave Macmillan, 2006).

CHAPTER 13

1. Max DePree, *Leadership is an Art* (New York: Doubleday, 1989).
2. Robert Putnam, *Bowling Alone: The Collapse and Revival of American Community* (New York: Simon & Schuster, 2000).

CHAPTER 14

1. C. Lucier, R. Schuyt, and E. Tse, "CEO Succession 2004: The World's Most Prominent Temp Workers," *strategy + business* 39 (Summer 2005): 1–16.
2. Lawrence Mishel, Jared Bernstein, and Sylvia Allegretto, *The State of Working America 2004/2005: An Economic Policy Institute Book* (Ithaca, NY: ILR Press, 2005).
3. David Finegold, "Is Education the Answer? Trends in the Supply and Demand for Skills in the U.S. Workforce," in *America at Work*, eds. Edward E. Lawler III and James O'Toole (New York: Palgrave Macmillan, 2006).
4. Mishel, Ibid.
5. Ibid.
6. Finegold, Ibid.
7. Ibid.
8. Ibid.
9. Mishel, Ibid.
10. Louis Uchitelle, "For Blacks, A Dream in Decline," *New York Times*, October 23, 2005.
11. Peter G. Gosselin, "If America is Richer, Why Are Its Families So Much Less Secure?" *Los Angeles Times*, October 10, 2004.
12. Ibid.
13. Katherine Bradbury, "Additional Slack in the Economy: The Poor Recovery in Labor Force Participation During This Business Cycle" (Public Policy Brief No. 05–2, Federal Reserve Bank of Boston, July 2005), http://www.bos.frb.org/economic/ppb/2005/ppb052.pdf.

14. OECD figure cited in the *Economist,* April 2, 2005, p. 92.

15. Marilyn Greenwax, "Worker's Pay Fails to Match Inflation," Cox News Service, May 1, 2005; Luis Urrea, "Personal Accounts," *New York* Times, October 2, 2005.

16. Paul Krugman, "The Joyless Economy," *New York Times,* December 5, 2005; David Leonhardt, "Poverty Rate Up for '04," *New York Times,* August 31, 2005.

17. Anna Bernasak, "Jobs are Back; Too Bad Wages Aren't," *Fortune,* May 3, 2004; Eduardo Porter, "How Long Can Workers Tread Water?" *New York Times,* July 14, 2005, p. C1; Steven Greenhouse, "Falling Fortunes of the Wage Earner," *New York Times,* April 12, 2005.

18. Bob Herbert, "Another Battle for Bush," *New York Times,* December 15, 2003; Stephen Roach, "The Productivity Paradox," *New York Times,* November 30, 2003, Week in Review, p. 9. Stephen Roach, "More Jobs, Worse Work," *New York Times,* July 22, 2004.

CHAPTER 15

1. Kathryn Shaw, "The Value of Innovative Human Resource Management Practices" in *America at Work,* eds. Edward E. Lawler III and James O'Toole (New York: Palgrave Macmillan, 2006).

2. Casey Ichniowski, Thomas Kochan, David I. Levine, Craig Olson, and George Strauss, "What Works at Work: A Critical Review," *Industrial Relations* 35, no. 3 (1996): 299–333; Casey Ichniowski, and Giovanna Prennushi, "The Effects of Human Resource Management Practices on Productivity," *American Economic Review* 86 (1997): 291–313; Casey Ichniowski, Kathryn Shaw, and Gabriella Prennushi, "The Effects of Human Resource Management on Productivity," *American Economic Review* 87 (1997): 291–31.

3. Quoted in James O'Toole, "Ernest Hemingway CEO: When Executives Become Authors," *Strategy+ Business* Vol. 25, Fourth Quarter (2001).

4. Milton Friedman, *Capitalism and Freedom* (Chicago: University of Chicago Press, 1962).

5. Smith quoted in Keith H. Hammonds, "We Incorporated," *Fast Company,* July 2004: 67–69.

6. Steven Greenhouse, "How Costco Became the Anti-Wal-Mart," *New York Times,* July 17, 2005. Sec. B.1.

7. Jeffrey Pfeffer, "Working Alone: What Ever Happened to the Idea of Organizations as Communities?" in *America at Work,* eds. Edward E. Lawler III and James O'Toole (New York: Palgrave Macmillan, 2006).

8. G. Bethune and S. Huler, *From Worst to First* (New York: John Wiley & Sons, 1998).

9. Dennis Bakke, *Joy at Work* (Seattle: PVG, 2005).

10. *Xilinx, Inc., (A) (B).* Harvard Business School Case 9–403–136 (37), (Boston: Harvard Business School Press, June 12, 2003).

11. "Genenco Tops List of Best Places to Look," *San Francisco Chronicle,* January 9, 2005, Sec. G–1.

12. Rich Teerlink and Lee Ozley, *More Than a Motorcycle* (Boston: Harvard Business School Press, 2000); James O'Toole, *Leadership A to Z* (San Francisco: Jossey-Bass, 1999).

13. Lawrence Mishel, Jared Bernstein, and Sylvia Allegretto, *The State of Working America 2004/2005: An Economic Policy Institute Book* (Ithaca, NY: ILR Press, 2005).

14. Steven Greenhouse, "Wal-Mart Workers are Finding a Voice without a Union," *New York Times,* September 3, 2005.

15. Miriam Schulman, "Winery with a Mission: Fetzer Vineyards Husbands to Earth's Resources," *Issues in Ethics* 7, no. 2, Spring 1996, www.ethics@scu.edu.

16. J. Blasi, D. Kruse, and A. Bernstein, *In the Company of Owners: The Truth About Stock Options (and Why Every Employee Should Have Them)* (New York: Perseus Books, 2003).

17. Gretchen Morgenson, "The Boss Actually Said This: Pay Me Less," *New York Times,* December 18, 2005, Sec. 3, p.1.

18. James O'Toole, *Creating the Good Life: Applying Aristotle's Wisdom to Find Meaning and Happiness* (New York: Rodale Press, 2005).

19. Julie Appledy, "Companies Start up Wellness Efforts," *USA Today,* August 2, 2005.

20. David Vogel, *The Market for Virtue* (Washington, DC: Brookings Institution Press, 2005).

21. Stephanie Weiss (under the supervision of Kirk O. Hansen), "GE Plastics Case (A, B & C)" (Stanford: Business Enterprise Trust, 1991).

CHAPTER 16

1. Lawrence Mishel, Jared Bernstein, and Sylvia Allegretto, *The State of Working America 2004/2005: An Economic Policy Institute Book* (Ithaca, NY: ILR Press, 2005).
2. Ibid.
3. "Asians on Top," *The Economist*, December 4, 2004: 31.
4. "Americans on Top," Ibid.
5. Cornella Dean, "Scientific Savvy? In U.S., Not Much," *New York Times*, August 30, 2005.
6. *Workplace Visions*, SHRM, No. 1, 2002: 3. Quoted in David Finegold, "Is Education the Answer? Trends in the Supply and Demand for Skills in the U.S. Workforce," in *America at Work*, eds. Edward E. Lawler III and James O'Toole (New York: Palgrave Macmillan, 2006).
7. *Workplace Visions*, SHRM, No. 3, 2005: 2–5.
8. David Finegold, "Is Education the Answer? Trends in the Supply and Demand for Skills in the U.S. Workforce," in *America at Work*, eds. Edward E. Lawler III and James O'Toole (New York: Palgrave Macmillan, 2006).
9. Ibid.
10. Bob Herbert, "Education's Collateral Damage," *New York Times*, July 21, 2005.
11. Bob Herbert, "Left Behind, Way Behind," *New York Times*, August 29, 2005.
12. David Herszenhorn, "New York Schools Narrow the Racial Gap in Test Scores," *New York Times*, December 2, 2005.
13. James O'Toole, *Creating the Good Life: Applying Aristotle's Wisdom to Find Meaning and Happiness* (New York: Rodale Press, 2005).
14. Mortimer J. Adler, *The Paideia Proposal* (New York: Macmillan, 1982).
15. Ibid.
16. James O'Toole, *Vanguard Management* (New York: Doubleday, 1985).
17. "The American Dream," *The Economist*, July 16, 2005: pp. 8–9.
18. David Finegold, "Is Education the Answer? Trends in the Supply and Demand for Skills in the U.S. Workforce," in *America at Work*, eds. Edward E. Lawler III and James O'Toole (New York: Palgrave Macmillan, 2006).
19. Ibid.
20. Ibid.
21. Ibid.
22. Ibid.
23. Ibid.
24. D. Heenan, *Flight Capital* (Mountain View, CA: Davies-Black Publishing, 2005).
25. Ibid.
26. Ibid.
27. Sam Dillon, "At Public Universities, Warnings of Privatization," *New York Times*, October 16, 2005. p. 12.
28. *Workplace Visions*, SHRM, No. 1, 2002: 2.
29. Finegold, Ibid.
30. Stephen S. Roach, "More Jobs, Worse Work," *New York Times*, July 22, 2004.
31. Stephen S. Roach, "No Productivity Parody," *New York Times*, November 30, 2003, in *America at Work*, eds. Edward E. Lawler III and James O'Toole (New York: Palgrave Macmillan, 2006).
32. John O'Dell, "Six-Figure Makeovers for Luxury Cars that aren't Enough," *Los Angeles Times*, September 21, 2005.
33. Finegold, Ibid.
34. Allen Enthoven, "Can Health Care Expenditures be Contained?" (paper presented at lecture of University of Pennsylvania, July 16, 2005).
35. Debora Vrana, "Rising Premiums Threaten Job-Based Health Coverage," *Los Angeles Times*, September 15, 2005 and Leif Wellington Haase, *A New Deal for Health*. (New York: Century Foundation Press, 2005).
36. Ibid.

37. Ibid.
38. Ibid.
39. Ibid.
40. Ibid.
41. Scott Reynolds, Neil Ridley, and Carl Van Horn, "A Work-Filled Retirement," John Heldrick Center for Workforce Development, Rutgers University, August 2005.

CHAPTER 17

1. Steve Lohr, " A Techie, Absolutely, and More," *New York Times,* August 23, 2005, C1.
2. Robert Berner, "Lee Scott on Why Wal-Mart is Playing Nicer," *Business Week,* October 3, 2005: 95.
3. 2002 data compiled by Phil Thompson of U.S. Census Bureau in 2005 cited in Tom Abate, "More Firms go it Alone," *San Francisco Chronicle,* December 1, 2004, C1.
4. Henry S. Farber, "Alternative Employment Arrangements as a Response to Job Loss," 2000, in *On the Job: Is Long-term Employment a Thing of the Past?* ed. D. Neumark, New York: Russell Sage Foundation; Henry S. Farber, "What Do We Know about Job Loss in the United States? Evidence from the Displaced Workers Survey, 1984–2004," Princeton University Industrial Relations Section Working Paper 498, 2005.
5. Peter Cappelli, "Will There *really* be a Labor Shortage?" *Organizational Dynamics* 32(3): 221–233.
6. James O'Toole, *Creating the Good Life: Applying Aristotle's Wisdom to Find Meaning and Happiness* (New York: Rodale Press, 2005).
7. Ibid.

ADDITIONAL INFORMATION

For further information, we suggest the following articles and books. An extensive bibliography is available at http://www.newamericanworkplace.com.

Adler, Paul S. 1993. The new 'learning bureaucracy': New United Motors Manufacturing, Inc. In *Research in Organizational Behavior*, eds. Barry Staw and Larry Cummings, 111–194. Greenwich CT: JAI Press.

Appelbaum, E., T. Bailey, P. Berg, and A. L. Kalleberg. 2000. *Manufacturing advantage: Why high-performance work systems pay off.* Ithaca, NY: Cornell University Press.

Appelbaum, Eileen, and Rosemary Batt. 1994. *The new American workplace.* Ithaca, N.Y.: ILR Press.

Arthur, M.B., and D. M. Rousseau. 1996. *The boundaryless career: A new employment principle for a new organizational era.* New York: Oxford.

Atkinson, R.D. 2004. *Understanding the offshoring challenge.* Washington, D.C.: Progressive Policy Institute.

Barker, Kathleen, and Kathleen Christensen. 1998. Controversy and challenges raised by contingent work arrangements. In *Contingent work: American employment in transition,* eds. Kathleen Barker and Kathleen Christensen, 1–20. Ithaca, NY: ILR Press.

Barley, Stephen R., and Gideon Kunda. 2004. *Gurus, hired guns and warm bodies: Itinerant experts in a knowledge economy.* Princeton, NJ: Princeton University Press.

Barley, Stephen R., Gideon Kunda, and James Evans. 2002. Why do contractors contract? The experience of highly skilled technical professionals in a contingent labor market. *Industrial and Labor Relations Review* 55: 234–61.

Bartlett, C. A., and S. Ghoshal. 2002. Building competitive advantage through people. *MIT Sloan Management Review* 43 (2):34–41.

Batt, Rosemary. 1999. Work organization, technology, and performance in customer services and sales. *Industrial and Labor Relations Review* 52:539–64.

Batt, Rosemary. 2004. Who benefits from teams? Comparing workers, supervisors, and managers. *Industrial Relations* 43:183–212.

Baumol, W. J., A.S. Blinder, and E.N. Wolff. 2003. *Downsizing in America: Reality, causes and consequences.* New York: Russell Sage Foundation.

Becker, B. E., and M. A. Huselid. 1998. High performance work systems and firm performance: A synthesis of research and managerial implications. In Vol. 16 of *Research in personnel and human resources management,* ed. G. Ferris, 53–101. Greenwich, CT: JAI Press.

Beehr, T.A. 1995. *Psychological stress in the workplace.* London: Routledge.

Benson G. S., D. Finegold, and S. A. Mohrman. 2004. You paid for the skills, now keep them: Tuition reimbursement and voluntary turnover. *Academy of Management Journal* 47 (3):315–331.

Berg, P., E. Appelbaum, and A. Kalleberg. 2003. Balancing work and family: The role of high commitment environments. *Industrial Relations* 42 (2):168–188.

Blair, M. M., and T. A. Kochan. 2000. *The new relationship: Human capital in the American corporation.* Washington, D.C.: Brookings Institution Press.

Blasi, J., D. Kruse, and A. Bernstein. 2003. *In the company of owners: The truth about stock options (and why every employee should have them).* New York: Perseus Books.

Bluestone, Barry, and Irving Bluestone. 1992. *Negotiating the future: A labor perspective on American business.* New York: Basic Books.

Bond, J. 2003. *The impact of job and workplace conditions on low-wage and –income employees and their employers.* New York: Families and Work Institute.

Bond, J., C. Thompson, E. Galinsky, and D. Prottas. 2002. *Highlights of the national study of the changing workforce.* New York: Families and Work Institute.

Cappelli, Peter. 1999. *The new deal at work.* Boston: Harvard Business School Press.

Cappelli, Peter. 2003. Will there *really* be a labor shortage? *Organizational Dynamics* 32(3): 221–233.

Cappelli, Peter, and David Neumark. 2001. Do "High performance" work practices improve establishment-level outcomes? *Industrial and Labor Relations Review* 54:737–775.

Cascio, W. F. 2000. *Costing human resources: The financial impact of behavior in organizations.* 4th ed. Cincinnati: South-Western.

Cascio, W. F. 2002. *Responsible restructuring: Creative and profitable alternatives to layoffs.* San Francisco: Berrett-Koehler Publishers, Inc.

Cole, Robert E. 1999. *Managing quality fads: How American business learned to play the quality game.* New York: Oxford University Press.

Collison, J. 2005. *2005 future of the U. S. labor pool: Survey report.* Alexandria, VA: Society for Human Resource Management.

Farber, Henry S. 2000. Alternative employment arrangements as a response to job loss. In *On the job: Is long-term employment a thing of the past?,* ed. D. Neumark. New York: Russell Sage Foundation.

Finegold, D. 1998. The new learning contract: Developing competencies in a turbulent environment. In *Tomorrow 's organization,* eds. S. Mohrman et al. San Francisco; Jossey-Bass.

Freeman, Richard B., and Joel Rogers. 1999. *What workers want.* New York and Ithaca: Cornell University Press and Russell Sage Foundation.

Friedman, T.L. 2005. *The world is flat: A brief history of the twenty-first century.* New York: Farrar, Straus, and Giroux.

Galbraith, J. 2005. Designing the customer-centric organization: A guide to strategy, structure and process. San Francisco: Jossey-Bass.

Galinsky, Ellen, James T. Bond, Stacy S. Kim, Lois Backon, Erin Brownfield, and Kelly Sakai. 2005. Overwork in America: When the way we work becomes too much. Families and Work Institute. http://www.familiesandwork.org/

Gerson, K. and J. Jacobs. 2004. *The time divide: Work, family, and gender inequality,* Cambridge, Mass.: Harvard University Press.

Gibson, Cristina B., and Susan G. Cohen. 2003. *Virtual teams that work: Creating conditions for virtual team effectiveness.* San Francisco: Jossey-Bass.

Gittell, Jody Hoffer. 2003. *The Southwest Airlines way: Using the power of relationships to achieve high performance.* New York: McGraw-Hill.

Hackman, J. Richard, and Greg R. Oldham. 1980. *Work redesign.* Reading, MA: Addison-Wesley.

Hall, D. T. 2002. *Careers in and out of organizations.* Thousand Oaks, CA: Sage Publications.

Hall, D. T. 2004. The protean career: A quarter-century journey. *Journal of Vocational Behavior* 65 (1):1.

Hammer, M., and J. Champy. 1993. *Reengineering the corporation.* New York: Harperbusiness.

Ichniowski, Casey, and Giovanna Prennushi. 1997. The effects of human resource management practices on productivity. *American Economic Review* 86:291–313.

Jacoby, Sanford M. 1999. Are career jobs headed for extinction? *California Management Review* 42 (Fall): 123–145.

Kahn, Robert L. 1981. *Work and health.* New York: Wiley.

Kochan, Thomas A. 2005. *Restoring the American dream: A working families' agenda for America.* Cambridge, MA: MIT Press.

Kochan, Thomas A., and Paul Osterman. 1994. *The mutual gains enterprise.* Boston: Harvard Business School Press.

Kompier, M. A. J., and T.S. Kristensen. 2000. Organizational work stress interventions in a theoretical, methodological and practical context. In *Stress in the workplace: past, present, and future,* ed. Jack Dunham. London and Philadelphia: Whurr Publishers.

Kossek, E., B. Lautsch, and S. Eaton. 2005. Flexibility enactment theory: Relationships between type, boundaries, control and work-family effectiveness. In *Work And Life Integration: Organizational, Cultural and Psychological Perspective,* eds. E. E. Kossek and S. Lambert, 243–262. Mahwah, N.J.: Lawrence Erlbaum Associates.

Lawler, E. E., III. 2003. *Treat people right!* San Francisco: Jossey-Bass.

Lawler, E. E., III, and James O'Toole. 2006. *America at work.* New York: Palgrave-Macmillan.

Lawler, E. E., III, and Chris Worley. 2006. *Built to change.* San Francisco: Jossey-Bass.

Lev, B. 2001. *Intangibles: Management, measurement and reporting.* Washington, D.C.: The Brookings Institution Press.

Levy, Frank, and Richard J. Murnane. 2004. *The new division of labor: How computers are creating the next job market.* New York: Russell Sage Foundation.

Lipset, Seymour Martin, and Noah M. Meltz. 2004. *The paradox of American unionism.* Ithaca, NY: Cornell/ILR Press.

Malone, Thomas W. 2004. *The future of work: How the new order of business will shape your organization, your management style, and your life.* Boston: Harvard Business School Press.

Malone, Thomas W., Robert Laubacher, and Michael S. Scott Morton, eds. 2003. *Inventing the organizations of the 21st century.* Cambridge, MA: MIT Press.

McCall, Jr., M. W. 1998. *High flyers: Developing the next generation of leaders.* Boston: Harvard Business School Press.

McKinsey Global Institute. 2005. The emerging global market: Parts I – III. San Francisco: McKinsey & Company. http://www.mckinsey.com/mgi/publications/emerginggloballabormarket/index.asp.

Michaels, Ed, Helen Handfield-Jones, and Beth Axelrod. 2001. *The war for talent.* Boston: Harvard Business School Press.

Mishel, Lawrence, Jared Bernstein, and Sylvia Allegretto. 2005. *The state of working America 2004/2005: An Economic Policy Institute book.* Ithaca, N.Y.: ILR Press.

National Center on Education and the Economy. 1990. *America's choice: High skills or low wages!* Rochester, N.Y.

National Commission on Excellence in Education (NCEE). 1983. *A nation at risk.* Washington, D.C.: GPO.

O'Reilly, Charles A., III, and Jeffrey Pfeffer. 2000. *Hidden value: How great companies achieve extraordinary results with ordinary people.* Boston: Harvard Business School Press.

O'Toole, J., ed. 1974. *Work and the quality of life: Resource papers for* Work in America. Cambridge, Mass: MIT Press.

O'Toole, J. 1985. *Vanguard management: Redesigning the corporate future.* Garden City, NY: Doubleday.

O'Toole, James, Elisabeth Hansot, William Herman, Neal Herrick, Elliot Liebow, Bruce Lusignan, Harold Richman, Harold Sheppard, Ben Stephansky, and James Wright. 1973. *Work in America: Report of a special task force to the Secretary of Health, Education, and Welfare.* Cambridge, Massachusetts: MIT Press.

Osterman, Paul. 2000. Work reorganization in an era of restructuring: Trends in diffusion and effects on employee welfare. *Industrial and Labor Relations Review* 53 (2):179–196.

Pfeffer, J. 1998. *The human equation: Building profits by putting people first.* Boston: Harvard Business School Press.

Quinn, Robert P., Thomas W. Mangione, et al. 1973. *The 1969–1970 survey of working conditions: Chronicles of an unfinished enterprise.* Ann Arbor, MI: Institute for Social Research, University of Michigan.

Quinn, Robert P. and Graham L. Staines. 1979. *The 1977 quality of employment survey: Descriptive statistics with comparison data from the 1969–1970 survey of working conditions and the 1972–1973 quality of employment survey.* Ann Arbor, MI: Institute for Social Research, The University of Michigan.

Rosen, Corey, John Case, and Martin Staubus. 2005. *Equity: Why employee ownership is good for business.* Boston, MA.: Harvard Business School Press.

Rousseau, D. M. 1995. *Psychological contract in organizations: Understanding written and unwritten agreements.* Newbury Park, CA: Sage.

Schrank, Robert. 1978. *10,000 (Ten thousand) working days.* Cambridge, MA: MIT Press.

Teerlink, Rich, and Lee Ozley. 2000. More than a motorcycle. Boston: Harvard Business School Press.

Terkel, S. 1974. *Working.* New York: Random House.

Whyte, W. H. 1956. *The organization man.* New York: Simon and Schuster.

INDEX

Adobe Systems, 169
AES, 137, 166–67
Alcoa, 26, 179, 242
Amazon, 119
American Cast Iron Pipe
    Company (ACIPCO),
    179–80, 242
Amgen, 169, 188
Amoco, 19
Armstrong, Lance, 41
Arthur Andersen, 111
Asimov, Isaac, 40
AT&T, 19, 48, 62, 66, 83, 206
automation, 39, 40–46, 114,
    147

Bakke, Dennis, 166
Bardhan, Ashok, 31
Barley, Stephen, 89–90
Bayh-Dole Act, 188
benefits, 71–75. *See also*
    education benefits;
    employee stock
    ownership; family
    benefits; flexible plans;
    medical insurance;
    retirement
Berman, Ethan, 177
Bethune, Gordon, 164–65, 237
Bill and Melinda Gates
    Foundation, 190–91
Biogen, 188
biotechnology, 188–89
BJ's Wholesale Club, 160
Blasi, Joseph, 48
Boeing, 32, 54, 131, 239
Brown & Cole, 211

"canonical career path," 84–86
Capital One, 91
Cappelli, Peter, 140, 228
career, choosing a, 216–26
careers vs. jobs, 83
Cetus, 188
Chaplin, Charlie, 39
Chevron, 19
Churchill, Winston, 100
Cisco, 27, 69, 131, 169
Citibank, 29

Coca-Cola, 29
Cole, Craig, 211
college and university education,
    16, 83, 143, 194–201,
    208
"community," 135
compensation, 34, 57, 62, 64,
    65, 69–70, 81, 96,
    115–20, 140–43, 145,
    175–77, 210, 236
complex organizational
    structures, 35–36
Consolidated Omnibus Budget
    Reconciliation Act
    (COBRA), 208
Continental Airlines, 137, 164,
    165, 204, 237
contingent jobs, 68, 75–78
corporate ownership, 36
Costco, 137, 152, 156–63, 240,
    242
Craig, Elizabeth, 131
Crandall, Robert, 97
"creative destruction," 5, 203,
    235

Daimler Benz, 32
David, Daryl, 183
DaVita, 137
Dell, 26, 42, 131
Deloitte and Touche, 91
Delphi, 172, 239, 243
Delta Airlines, 164
Deming, W. Edwards, 51, 152
Dewey, John, 192
"Dilbert," 105, 226
Doerr, John, 198
downsizing, 4, 37, 53, 63, 127,
    170, 221, 239, 243
Drucker, Peter, 174, 181, 239
DuPont, 19, 59
Duran, Joseph M., 51

Eastman Kodak, 48
eBay, 206
education:
    benefits, 96, 175
    "career," 230
    choices in, 15, 189–201

college and university, 16,
    83, 143, 194–99, 208
community colleges,
    199–201
company training and, 128,
    130–31, 179
demand for higher levels of,
    28
gap, 28, 81
income and, 115–16
individual success and, 186,
    216, 218
K–12, 16, 185, 189–94
lifelong learning and, 86
social stratification and, 16
women and, 142
employee stock ownership, 13,
    20, 48–49, 69, 70,
    119–20, 122, 152, 162,
    169, 170, 240
employment needs, types of,
    8–9
Enron, 111, 166, 167, 229
Enthoven, Allen, 209
executive pay, 117–18, 140, 176
Exxon, 19, 206

factory jobs, 39, 40, 41–42, 43,
    53, 82, 102, 135, 225
family benefits, 74–75
"family-friendly" workplaces, 96
Family Medical Leave Act of
    1993, 95
Farber, Henry, 225
FedEx, 158
Fetzer Vineyards, 175
Finegold, David, 189
Fiorina, Carly, 141
Fisker, Henrik, 207
flexible plans, 72
Ford, 25, 65, 172, 206, 207,
    211
Ford, Henry, 43
Ford, William Clay, 211
Fortune 500 companies, 4, 11,
    26, 28, 113, 155, 176,
    206
Fortune 1000 companies, 22,
    27, 47, 50, 67, 69, 71,

72, 74, 77, 90, 95, 96, 152
Freeman, Richard, 48
free-trade policies, 5, 185, 200
Friedman, Milton, 156

gain sharing, 48, 69, 177
gender gap, 116
Genentech, 169, 182, 188
General Electric (GE), 19, 22, 27, 28, 52, 97, 98, 183, 201
General Foods, 19, 48, 122
General Motors, 19, 25, 26, 32, 65, 123, 172, 206
Global Competitor (GC) corporations, defined, 12–13
global economy, 5–7, 10, 12, 19, 22, 29, 35, 66, 104, 205, 212, 234, 237, 243, 244
globalization, 19, 21, 29, 30, 32, 33, 37, 38, 54, 64, 116, 123, 203, 204, 208, 234
global organizations, 29–34, 35
Gompers, Samuel, 241
"good jobs," 9–10, 15, 34, 38, 54, 47, 97, 202–209
Goodwin, Jim, 164
Google, 119, 206
Gore, 26, 57, 59–60, 137, 152, 166, 240, 242
Gore, Bill, 57, 59
Guggenhime, David, 192

Haase, Leif Wellington, 212
Hall, Douglas, 131
Hansen, Kirk, 183
Harley-Davidson, 26, 171–72, 242, 243
healthcare system, 17, 64, 74, 92. See also medical insurance
health insurance. See medical insurance
Heenan, David, 196, 197, 199
Herman Miller, 137, 166, 222
Hewlett-Packard (HP), 31–32, 42, 141, 152, 222
High-Involvement (HI) companies, defined, 13–14
Honda, 33, 51, 122
Honeywell, 48
human capital, 10, 12, 18, 34–35, 63, 70, 128, 147, 155, 167, 174, 191, 234, 238

Hutchins, Robert Maynard, 192

IBM, 19, 27–29, 62, 66, 83, 91, 120, 239
Icahn, Carl, 37
Independent Means, 208
Industrial Revolution, 94, 136, 201, 241
information technology (IT), 20, 27, 28, 32, 33, 40–46, 53, 55, 58, 60, 79, 188, 202, 205, 216–17
Intel, 131
Iverson, Ken, 154–55, 237

Japanese management, 51, 136–37
Jefferson, Thomas, 130
Jefferson Wells International, 181
job-related stress, 102–106
job satisfaction, 18, 48, 103, 107–109, 112, 142, 143, 171
Junior Achievement, 208

Kelleher, Herb, 175, 237
"knowledge capital," 173
Kochan, Thomas, 165
Kossek, Ellen, 99
Kozlof, Emme, 162
Kroger, 120
Krohe, Jim, 118
Kroll, Cynthia, 31
Kruse, Douglas, 48
Kunda, Gideon, 89–90

Laffer, Arthur, 241
Levenson, Alec, 76
Levi-Strauss, 183, 222
Lorenzo, Frank, 165
Low-Cost (LC) operators, defined, 11–12
"loyalty" career model, 86–87, 140

manufacturing, 3, 9–12, 15, 26–29, 32–34, 38, 39–43, 45, 47, 50, 52–53, 55, 102, 128, 171, 204–205
Maslow, Abraham, 241
Mattel, 29–30
McDonald's, 129
McGregor, Douglas, 241
McGuire, William, 140
McKinsey Global Institute, 30, 34
McWare, Inc., 180

Medicaid, 74, 212
medical insurance, 17, 65, 73–74, 77, 106, 124, 140, 156, 158, 208, 209–12, 224, 244
Medicare, 38, 74, 103, 212, 213
Medtronic, 137, 169
Men's Wearhouse, 137
Microsoft, 22, 37, 45, 169, 206
Millennium Pharmaceuticals, 131
Mittal, 236
Mobil Oil, 207
Modern Times, 40
Morgan, J. P., 177
Motorola, 52, 201

Nation at Risk, A, 189–90
new employment contract, 13, 17, 22, 66–69, 88, 130, 131, 224
Nissan, 33, 51, 122
Nixon, Richard, 101, 212
Northwest Airlines, 164
NRC Holdings, 129, 137
Nucor Steel, 59, 137, 154–55, 236, 237, 242

occupational safety and health, 101–106
Occupational Safety and Health Act (OSHA), 101
offshoring, 30–31, 33, 53–55, 113, 135, 144, 170, 211, 224, 235, 239
Okun, Arthur, 119
O'Neil, Paul, 179
onshoring, 33–34
"organization men," 4, 25, 84, 87
Osterman, Paul, 21, 37
overwork, 106, 111–13
Ovitz, Michael, 141

Paley, Grace, 93
part-time employment, 4, 5, 18, 75–77, 89, 90, 95, 159, 173, 174, 213, 222, 228, 243
Patagonia, 181–82
PepsiCo, 131
performance pressure, 111–14
personal computer (PC) business, 28, 32, 42, 44
Pfeffer, Jeffrey, 137, 163
Philip Morris Company, 40, 43
Pillsbury, 48
Polaroid, 19, 83, 222

Procter & Gamble, 26, 28, 29, 47, 48, 131
profit sharing, 18, 48–49, 69, 70, 170, 177, 240
Putnam, Robert, 134

quality circles, 51–52
quality of work life (QWL), 3, 43, 103, 122

RCA, 19
Renault, 32
research and development (R&D), 29, 41, 71, 186, 199, 201–202
retirement, 17, 64, 65, 72–73, 75, 85, 89, 110, 119, 120, 160, 213, 225, 226–29, 243
retirement age, 90, 213
Richardson, Elliot L., viii, ix, 3
RiskMetrics, 177
Rivlin, Gary, 42
Roelandts, Wim, 170
Rousseau, Jean-Jacques, 67
rules, 58–60

Sam's Club, 160–61
Sarbanes-Oxley legislation, 157, 181
SAS, 69, 137, 166
Scanlon, Joseph, 48
Schultz, Howard, 210
Schwinn, 41
self-employment, 4, 113, 134, 208, 219, 224–26
self-management, 45, 46–50, 52, 58, 71, 103, 158
senior executives, 118, 139–40, 141
September 11, 2001, 164–65, 186, 196
service jobs, exportation of, 30
shared capitalism, 48–49
Sharpnack, Rayona, 189
Shaw, Kathryn, 154, 155, 193
Silicon Valley, 4, 23, 29, 78, 89, 122, 183, 188, 196, 224
Sinegal, James, 160, 162, 163
Six-Sigma, 52
Sloan, Alfred, 25
small businesses, 10, 22–23, 87, 206, 208, 224

Smith, Adam, 241
Smith, Douglas, 157
Social Security, 38, 72, 146, 186, 201, 213
Solectron, 29–30
Sony, 37, 51
Southwest Airlines, 137, 165, 175, 237, 240, 242
SRC Holdings, 157, 166, 240, 242
Stack, Jack, 157
Standard Oil, 19
Starbucks, 4, 77, 137, 210, 226, 243
stock options, 48, 69, 70, 110, 118, 119, 141, 176, 177, 227, 243
stock ownership, 13, 20, 48–49, 69, 70, 119–20, 122, 152, 162, 169, 170, 240
Sun Microsystems, 27, 45
supervision, 9, 25, 36, 53, 57–58, 60, 121, 153, 168, 172, 180–81

Taylor, Frederick Winslow, 42, 52
Teerlink, Richard, 171
Terkel, Louis "Studs," ix, x
themes, major, 14–18
TIAA-CREF, 36
Timberland, 182
Tocqueville, Alexis de, 134–36, 159
total quality management (TQM), 39, 50–52, 53, 55, 57
Toyota, 32, 33, 51, 122, 205
Trade Adjustment Assistance Act, 200
traditional practices, ineffectiveness of, 64–66
Trek, 26, 41, 43, 207
Trex, 207
TRIPS agreement, 188

unions, 62, 65, 94, 107, 119, 121–25, 134, 179, 223–24, 237, 241
airlines and, 54, 164, 165
blue-collar workers and, 144
Costco and, 160

decline of, 143, 147
entertainment industry and, 78
Wal-Mart and, 160, 162, 174
See also United Auto Workers (UAW)
United Airlines, 120, 164
United Auto Workers (UAW), 41, 122, 124, 172, 239
United Health Group, 140
UPS, 31, 120, 137, 152, 158, 159, 242
U.S. Airways, 164, 165
U.S. Steel, 19, 236
UTC, 91

Vagelos, Roy, 182
Vogel, David, 182
Volvo, 47

Wal-Mart, 5, 26–27, 41, 74, 120, 147, 159–62, 174, 176, 183, 220–21, 228, 241, 243
Walton, Sam, 162, 176, 220
Washington Mutual, 183
Welch, Jack, 97–98, 141, 191
Weyco, 178
Whole Foods, 59, 137, 175
WL Gore Associates, 26, 57, 59–60, 70, 137, 152, 166, 240, 242
Work in America (report), viii, ix, x, 13, 18, 48, 84, 86, 103, 122, 129, 133, 146, 151, 155, 174, 195, 200, 215, 218
Work in America task force, 3, 7, 9, 127
Worker Self-Renewal Program, 127
World War II, 50, 83, 94, 136, 241

Xerox, 19, 27, 48, 152, 222
Xilinx, 69, 137, 170–71, 240, 242

Yahoo!, 119

Ziemer, James, 171